Emerging Issues and Trends in Education

Emerging Issues and Trends in Education

EDITED BY Theodore S. Ransaw AND Richard Majors

Michigan State University Press | East Lansing

Michigan State University Press
East Lansing, Michigan 48823-5245

Printed and bound in the United States of America.

26 25 24 23 22 21 20 19 18 17 1 2 3 4 5 6 7 8 9 10

LIBRARY OF CONGRESS CATALOGING-IN-PUBLICATION DATA
Names: Ransaw, Theodore S., editor.
Title: Emerging issues and trends in education / edited by Theodore S. Ransaw and Richard Majors.
Description: East Lansing, Michigan : Michigan State University Press, 2017. | Series: International race and education | Includes bibliographical references and index.
Identifiers: LCCN 2016049793| ISBN 9781611862607 (pbk. : alk. paper) | ISBN 9781609175429 (pdf) | ISBN 9781628953114 (epub) | ISBN 9781628963113 (kindle)
Subjects: LCSH: Discrimination in education. | Education—Social aspects. | Educational equalization.
Classification: LCC LC212 .E58 2017 | DDC 379.2/6—dc23 LC record available at https://lccn.loc.gov/2016049793

Book design by Charlie Sharp, Sharp Des!gns, East Lansing, Michigan
Cover design by Shaun Allshouse, www.shaunallshouse.com

Michigan State University Press is a member of the Green Press Initiative and is committed to developing and encouraging ecologically responsible publishing practices. For more information about the Green Press Initiative and the use of recycled paper in book publishing, please visit www.greenpressinitiative.org.

Visit Michigan State University Press at *www.msupress.org*

Contents

PART 2. Policy, Leadership, and Innovation

Foreword

William A. Howe

The world is becoming more interconnected. These are the first thoughts that come to my mind as I write about this new book edited by Theodore Ransaw and Richard Majors. There is an abundance of data about ethnic minority achievement gaps, underrepresentation of girls in STEM (science, technology, engineering, and math), and literacy issues related to both gender and education all across the globe. The United Nations Educational, Scientific, and Cultural Organization (UNESCO) has been collecting damning evidence that worldwide basic education is currently underfunded by $26 billion a year, and that fifty-seven million children across the globe are not in school. However, educational access is not the only issue. Teacher training, teacher diversity that is reflective of their students, poverty, and equitable policy implementation are all concerns that affect learning internationally.

To read yet another book about the complexity of race and education would be depressing. And that is what makes this book so meaningful and refreshing. It offers insight. It offers new perspectives. It offers value for lived experiences. Ransaw and Majors have brought together a team of highly qualified experts from varied disciplines to offer much-needed, helpful guidance on critical educational issues affecting all of us.

Educators, administrators, policymakers, and parents should immediately find the contents tantalizing. After being in education for more than forty years, I was still excited to read titles like "STEM SISTA Spaces: Creating Counterspaces for Black Girls and Women," "Female Education: Gender Discrimination in Northern Nigerian Secondary Schools," "Surviv-ing: An African American Man Reconstructing Masculinity through Literacy," "Understanding the Classroom Matrix of Race, Class, Gender, and Cultural Competency in Analyzing Same-Race Students and Teacher Arguments," "Defining High-Quality Education through the Eyes of Policymakers in American Indian Tribal Governments," "Distributed Leadership and Educator Attitudes: A Multilevel Analysis of TALIS 2013," "Mexican Dance Group: Breaking Barriers One Tap at a Time," and "The Future of Education: Nouveau 'Plus Ça Change . . .'" These chapters offer what experienced educators want—not just more deficit theory, but sound advice, effective skills, and credible solutions.

The topics chosen are clearly targeted toward up-to-date research on improving educational outcomes for students around the world. This text, therefore, is meaningful. As a teacher educator I am drawn toward research on students conducted by actual representatives from that group and individuals who have established a track record of experience and success. I am far more impressed by those researchers who write from a position of positivity, reality, and hopefulness. *Emerging Issues and Trends in Education* tackles some of the most critical issues I try to get across to preservice and in-service teachers. Culture and learning styles and the connection to teaching and learning alone would be a standout topic. Understanding race and gender identity could not be a more relevant and current topic. The phenomenon of using education to improve lives and transform communities remains a critical issue that teachers must understand. Informed and caring educators make a difference that positively influences the world every day. I am particularly excited to see instructional strategies like CRP (culturally relevant pedagogy) explained from a balanced perspective. These topics and more should be essential reading for anyone working with minority ethnic populations. Policymakers should take special note. This text promises progress and should not be ignored.

Editor's Note

Theodore S. Ransaw

Unless issues and trends in education are given a voice through print media, they sometimes go unnoticed, or at the very least ignored. Having a tangible object in one's hand, like a book that can be given to a chair, dean, or government official, and placed on a desk, can have a lasting impact that reverberates with permanence. Yes, concerns related to race and education exist all over the world, even if you are unaware of them. Somehow, sharing what is happening in different places around the globe and putting it into printed type makes it "real." Thoughts, ideas, and stories capture the imagination. A book evokes a permanence that cannot be easily brushed aside. Substance. That was the purpose of crafting *Emerging Issues and Trends in Education*. In it, you will find solid, evidence-based, researched, and informed thought offered in individual chapters that illuminate matters that are useful to study in relationship to others around the globe.

Emerging Issues and Trends in Education is divided into two parts: "Global Perspectives on Race and Gender in Education" and "Policy, Leadership, and Innovation." Part 1 highlights issues of STEM for Black girls, gender in Nigeria, African American male literacy development, and same-race student and teacher classrooms. Part 2 interrogates education policy regarding American Indian tribal governments, educational leadership and attitudes of forty-four countries, using Mexican dance to increase parental involvement, and emerging trends of education policy in the near future. Created by educators who specialize in the fields of gender education, STEM, literacy, achievement gaps, underrepresented minority groups, international and multicultural education, as well as education policy, *Emerging Issues and Trends in Education* was written to highlight what makes us individual and part of a whole in a way that makes the world a little smaller and much more human.

I would like to give a special thanks to, Judith Dunkerly-Bean, Old Dominion University; Samantha Baruah, Michigan State University; Brian Boggs, Michigan State University; Nathan Buroughs, Michigan State University; Kristen Guillory, University of North Texas at Dallas; Lorri Jenkins, Michigan State University; Cheryl McClean, Rutgers University; Leigh Patel, Boston College; Kristine E. Pytash, Kent State University; and Christopher B. Reimann, Michigan State University for their helpful review suggestions that pushed the volume forward.

Preface

Deborah Gabriel

The International Race and Education book series aims to provide a critical space for increasingly diverse and complex areas of interdisciplinary social science research that explores the relationship between race and education. This volume, *Emerging Issues and Trends in Education*, defines, shapes, and monitors new and evolving trends, advancing alternative ways of thinking and schools of thought, crossing geographical boundaries to create original approaches to education research. Its dual focus is to highlight the challenges of race and education while presenting innovative, culturally appropriate solutions.

Demographic changes across the globe, especially in Europe and North America, have resulted in more ethnically and culturally diverse classrooms, sensitizing governments and stakeholders to the important implications this diversity presents in terms of education policy and practice. Globalization has contributed to the internationalization of education since population diversity has financial implications in terms of student recruitment, resourcing, and educational outcomes. Understanding how best to meet the needs of increasingly diverse student populations with respect to issues of equity and justice, while ensuring the education sector produces skilled workforces that serve the needs of national and global economies, has acquired paramount significance in recent years. This book presents cross-cultural case studies from around the world that take an intersectional approach to extend understanding of the complex and dynamic nature of race in education in a global context. Part 1 examines issues around race and gender in educational experiences and outcomes, while Part 2 presents the latest research on policy, leadership, and innovation.

"STEM SISTA Spaces: Creating Counterspaces for Black Girls and Women" highlights the underrepresentation of Black women in STEM fields in the United States and advances innovative approaches to increase participation that depart from mainstream STEM intervention programs. The concept of a "SISTA" space within an educational context is characterized by shared raced and gendered experiences that foster collaboration and learning and strengthen community ties. The authors advance a framework for a STEM SISTA space model as places for providing positive and meaningful STEM learning experiences.

"Female Education: Gender Discrimination in Northern Nigerian Secondary Schools" highlights how gender inequality in Nigeria contributes to discrimination against females within the education system. Approached through theories of multiculturalism and critical pedagogy, the study identifies religion, sociocultural factors, poverty, and child marriage as the primary causes of gender discrimination in education. Recommendations to bring about social change include the provision of interactive learning spaces, the use of multiple perspectives in the classroom that emphasize diversity, and social awareness campaigns around gender equality at the community level.

"Surviv-ing: An African American Man Reconstructing Masculinity through Literacy" highlights how race intersects with perceptions of Black male identity in the United States, creating an inner conflict among young African American males whereby engaging with educational literacy is perceived as "acting white." This identity crisis has often been cited as a contributory factor to educational underachievement among Black males. The study examines how a thirty-six-year-old African American man negotiates Black male identity as a self-published writer. The findings challenge dominant discourses on how Black males enact masculinity, countering stereotypical views on the performativity of masculinity and fatherhood and providing new insights into the realities and cultural complexities of Black masculinity.

"Understanding the Classroom Matrix of Race, Class, Gender, and Cultural Competency in Analyzing Same-Race Students and Teacher Arguments" provides an analysis of literature that examines issues around same-race student and teacher interactions in classrooms in the United States, highlighting that in 2011, while White students attended schools that were less than 10 percent Black, Black students attended schools where almost 80 percent were Black, and there is a huge achievement gap between Black and White pupils. The analysis reveals that while some studies suggest Black students have higher educational achievement when taught by Black teachers, other studies suggest the opposite is true and point to teacher quality, socioeconomic status, and educational resources as intersecting contributory factors. The author asserts that culturally competent pedagogy can be combined with race, class, and gender to form a mix of good teaching regardless of student-teacher ethnicity.

"Defining High-Quality Education through the Eyes of Policymakers in American Indian Tribal Governments" highlights how definitions of the term "high-quality education" vary according to knowledge, expertise, and value system. It offers a descriptive case study of how the term is perceived by five educational policymakers representing three Native American tribal governments in California. The findings reveal that while equity was the main lens by which high-quality education was defined, the main focus of educational programs for Native youth was excellence. This is attributed to the importance tribal policymakers ascribe to human capital supporting larger economic and political endeavors, namely expanding business enterprise and protecting tribal sovereignty. The study demonstrates the importance of understanding the diversity that exists among educational policymakers and how they operate in and are governed by their own unique, social, political, and economic contexts.

"Distributed Leadership and Educator Attitudes: A Multilevel Analysis of TALIS 2013" highlights the important role that leadership plays in the success of a school in terms of shaping the environment in which learning and teaching take place. "Distributed" leadership involves teachers and other stakeholders in the management and operation of a school. The authors conducted a study to understand the relationship between stakeholder participation in school leadership and principal and teacher satisfaction, cohesion, and commitment. The findings suggest that distributed leadership in terms of shared decision-making among teachers, parents, and students has a significant, positive impact on principal and teacher attitudes and leads to stronger school cohesion, higher commitment, and greater satisfaction. The study highlights the important role contribution distributed leadership makes toward organizational cohesion in schools.

"Mexican Dance Group: Breaking Barriers One Tap at a Time" presents a case study of Rosa, a Mexican teacher in a school where 84 percent of the students are Hispanic, who leads the school assembly by inviting Hispanic parents and Anglo teachers to dance a traditional Mexican dance together. The study analyses Rosa's use of the dance to create a welcoming and respectful community-oriented environment for Mexican parents. The findings suggest that the dance had positive impacts in terms of improving interaction between parents and teachers at school events. In particular, it enhanced teachers' understanding of students' culture and helped them to develop intercultural communication skills. This chapter demonstrates that solidifying students' cultural identity can yield important benefits in terms of enhancing parent-teacher relationships in cross-cultural settings.

"The Future of Education: Nouveau 'Plus Ça Change . . .'" provides an informed commentary on the state of education policy in America in several key areas, including local versus state control and choice versus traditional public schools. The author provides an analysis utilizing critical political theory. He seeks to untangle the issues of power from the policy cycle and to illustrate deeply who came to shape policy and how. The result is a deeper understanding of how political acts, tactical rules, and praxis influence policy that directly influences interactions and power.

This book provides a wealth of new information, approaches, and perspectives drawn from the latest interdisciplinary research on race and education and should appeal to advanced students, educators, policymakers, and researchers seeking to engage with cutting-edge, international research on emerging issues and trends in education.

PART 1.

Global Perspectives on Race and Gender in Education

STEM SISTA Spaces

Creating Counterspaces for Black Girls and Women

Shetay N. Ashford, Jessica Alyce Wilson, Natalie S. King, and Tiffany M. Nyachae

Some of the most fun people I know are scientists.

—Mae C. Jemison

Historically, in the science, technology, engineering, and mathematics (STEM) fields, students of color and women, particularly Black women, have been underrepresented in the United States (National Science Foundation, 2015; White House Council on Women and Girls, 2014). As a result, an onslaught of K–20 STEM intervention programs have been implemented to retain these students in the STEM fields (Valla & Williams, 2012). However, the goal, to increase participation in the STEM fields among students of color and women, is embedded in maintaining U.S. global competitiveness and economic prosperity (Palmer & Wood, 2013; National Academy of Sciences, 2007), which carries a parochial, informed self-serving initiative rather than sincere moral concern or commitment to the well-being of these students (Martin, 2009). Further, the Census Bureau projects that by 2042, people of color will represent the majority population in the United States (Vincent & Velkoff, 2010), yet current trends in STEM education relative to achievement and persistence do not suggest that students of color will represent the majority population in the STEM fields (Fealing & Myers, 2012). The concern is that students of color endure a particular set of experiences in STEM fields as members of marginalized populations. Therefore, an evaluation of student STEM educational experiences, relative to their academic persistence and overall well-being, as contributors to the STEM fields, is significant in developing retention efforts that will influence students' interest in pursuing and persisting in STEM fields.

As a result, innovative solutions to broaden the participation of Black girls and women in the STEM fields must consider students' experiences, developing relevant interventions for members of marginalized racial and gender groups that challenge traditional power dynamics and seek to reclaim the voices of Black women and girls in STEM academic and institutional spaces.

Race and Gender

Martin (2009) highlights the need for future research in the field of mathematics education to understand race as a sociopolitical, historically contingent construct, since racism is endemic and embedded in the United States (p. 298). There is evidence of this approach in STEM educational research, since race is often listed as a factor when evaluating achievement and persistence; however, it is often used only to invoke simplistic categories (Martin, 2009). This often yields a deficit approach to understanding the experience of racial minority groups (Castro, 2014), because this research fails to link the meanings of the findings about race to larger societal structures in which racism is entrenched in the United States, adding another layer to how students of color experience education, particularly in STEM fields (Martin, 2009). As a result, we are left with research that does not address the everyday nature and experiences of racism, classism, and sexism that are embedded in students' STEM experiences.

Furthermore, gender is used to distinguish biological sex from performed identities of femininity and masculinity, which have been socially constructed (Cole, Manuh, & Miescher, 2007). African American girls and women have been socially constructed, depicted, and normalized as amoral, sexually promiscuous, exotic, presumptuously wild creatures (Stephens & Phillips, 2003). These descriptors are broadly accepted and socialized and shape ideologies about African American girls and women (hooks, 1992). Therefore, spaces are needed to address the everyday nature and experiences of Black women and girls as significant members and contributors to the STEM fields.

I Need My Space: STEM Counterspaces

A primary contributing factor to the lack of students enrolled in STEM disciplines is their diminished interest in science and mathematics while pursuing secondary education. This negatively affects students' interest in pursuing STEM majors upon entering college (NACME, 2008), which has been verified by the data presented by the National Science Foundation's evaluation of freshmen intentions in 2012. Of the Black women assessed by the National Science Foundation (2015), 35.4 percent intended to major in science and engineering fields, which was slightly lower than Black men (37.8 percent). The majority of these Black women entering are interested in the biological and agricultural sciences (15 percent) and social and behavioral sciences (14.3 percent), and these numbers drop significantly when looking at intentions to major in engineering (3.2 percent) or mathematics, statistics, or computer sciences (1.4 percent) (National Science Foundation, 2015). Furthermore, Black girls and women have reported feelings of isolation and a lack of support from teachers and peers in their secondary and postsecondary STEM schooling experiences (Ashford, 2016; Borum, 2012; Borum & Walker, 2012; Bush, 2013; da Rosa, 2013; Espinosa, 2011; Frillman, 2011; Gibson & Espino, 2016; McPherson, 2012; Robinson, 2012; Rodriguez, 2015; Somerville-Midgette, 2014; Smith-Evans & George, 2014), which may further dissuade them from pursuing and persisting in STEM disciplines upon entering college. STEM intervention programs, such as service-learning projects, summer bridge programs, undergraduate research programs, and summer enrichment programs, have traditionally been developed to meet the needs of majority students, as they offer effective programmatic components to improve targeted students' retention in STEM education (Geisinger & Raman, 2013; Veenstra, Padró, & Furst-Bowe, 2012). These are viable options to implement *STEM counterspaces* to support the distinct needs of marginalized students. Since these programs are most prevalent in postsecondary education, we find relatively few programs that expose girls and people of color, particularly Black girls, to STEM disciplines in secondary education and that operate from social justice and culturally relevant perspectives to help students of color succeed in the STEM fields (King et al., in press; Wilson, Gaines, & Cooper, 2015). Moss (2010) implements a SISTA (Sisters Informing Sisters about Topics on AIDS) space in the context of literacy, defined as a

> space where they come together as Black women to act as a group and on behalf of their community—for their own cultural enrichment, as a way to strengthen their shared community ties, as a way to teach each other, and to teach other women. (p. 5)

Moss describes the importance of a SISTA space that provides a viable framework for culturally relevant programs that target Black girls and women. As a result, this chapter builds on Moss's work to propose a STEM SISTA space, which is a model for providing meaningful and positive STEM learning experiences (e.g., mentoring and Black women as role models) that embraces the strengths of Black girls and women and encourages their participation in STEM.

According to Barton et al. (2003), "Spaces are defined by the individuals who come together for particular reasons . . . and are shaped by the rules and expectations for participating together" (p. 39). The capital that individuals bring to the space frames the patterns and assumptions that guide the social interactions within that space (Barton et al., 2003). Furthermore, administrators and educators have proposed counterspaces in social and academic settings to shield African American women (Howard-Hamilton, 2003) and African Americans in general (Solórzano, Ceja, & Yosso, 2000) from microaggressions and negative racial climates. In this chapter, we will propose a STEM counterspace for Black girls and women that is undergirded by our conceptual framework (i.e., critical race theory, intersectionality, critical race feminism, and culturally relevant pedagogy), and supported by a review of relevant literature. The theoretical underpinnings in our conceptual framework will serve as recurring themes as we connect existing bodies of knowledge to our proposed model.

Our Motivation

In STEM education, the push to increase the participation of students of color and women can fail to acknowledge the concerns that negatively influence their academic persistence and overall well-being as students in the STEM fields. Essentially, those of us who want to encourage girls and women of color in these fields must focus our efforts on understanding and supporting the needs of these historically underrepresented populations, particularly Black girls and women, if we seek social justice in STEM education. Furthermore, retention efforts must consider the experiences that present challenges to students every day by developing spaces that confront racism and sexism, critiquing power structures so as to empower the experiences of Black women and girls in STEM academic and institutional spaces (Martin, 2009). It is then that STEM intervention programs can provide a culturally relevant space for students. Therefore, through this research, we advocate for equitable opportunities to encourage and support Black girls and women to persist, endure, and thrive in the K–20 STEM education pipeline. Furthermore, as educators, program developers, and evaluators, we reference our practical experiences of implementing and evaluating culturally relevant programs for women and students of color to inform our research.

The purpose of this chapter is to propose a new STEM SISTA space that targets Black girls and women in K–16 (i.e., elementary, secondary, and postsecondary) STEM education. Our goal is to offer a model that is grounded in existing research and builds upon our experiences as program directors, evaluators, and scholars. As Black women scholars with significant relevant experiences, we provide a "unique angle of vision" that informs our proposed model. Three of us are STEM degree holders in computer science, mathematics, or applied physiology and kinesiology. We are Ph.D. holders or candidates in curriculum and instruction with emphases in career and workforce, mathematics education, science education, or reading education and science of learning. Collectively, we have taught STEM subjects at the secondary and postsecondary education levels, and we have past experiences with program design, development, implementation, and management of culturally relevant programs for girls and students of color. These experiences inform our research and motivation for this study. In this chapter, we first define the conceptual framework that undergirds our model, followed by a review of relevant literature. Next we describe our recommendation for a STEM SISTA space, and then close with discussion and implications.

Conceptual Framework

Critical Race Theory, Intersectionality, and Critical Race Feminism

In this section, we describe critical race theory (CRT) in education as our main framework, intersectionality as an outgrowth, and critical race feminism (CRF) as an extension, foregrounding the STEM SISTA space we propose. During the 1980s, legal scholars Derrick Bell, Richard Delgado, and Kimberlé Crenshaw responded to critical legal studies' absence of race with CRT (Tate, 1997). Building from their work, educational scholars Gloria Ladson-Billings and William Tate IV developed CRT in education in the 1990s (Ladson-Billings & Tate, 1995). CRT recognizes race as a social construction and racism as an ever-present aspect of life in the United States. CRT challenges color-blind beliefs and mainstream ideologies through activism and a social justice agenda (Ladson-Billings, 1998). As with counterspaces and our proposed STEM SISTA space, CRT centers the voices of racialized people (Ladson-Billings, 1998). Crenshaw (1989) introduced the concept of *intersectionality* in response to CRT's inability to address the unique locations of Black women, and in response to the women's rights and feminist movements' fight for women as a homogenous group of elite White women, erasing color and class. Intersectionality considers the nexus of race, gender, and class in how women of color experience the world based on structures, politics, and representation (Crenshaw, 1991, 1993).

Bell (1980), through his principle of interest convergence, argued that African Americans only experience social, political, and economic gains when their interests match the needs of the White elite. With this in mind, Evans-Winters and Esposito (2010) urged educators and developers of intervention programs for Black women and girls to consider the following:

> If a young Black woman's worth is measured through her aptitude for reproducing the next generation's labor (i.e. capital), what would be the interest of the privileged class in assisting in the development of her educational well-being through self-empowerment or social and financial support? Once more, where does the interest of the White middle class converge with the interest of young women of African descent? (p. 18)

SISTA spaces are interested in the interests of Black women and girls, and the intersectionalities that they experience (Evans-Winters & Esposito, 2010). As we consider counterspaces for Black women and girls in STEM, we must take care to center their needs and interests.

CRF explicates the relationship between CRT and intersectionality. CRF argues that the experiences of women of color are different from White women and Black men because they face multiple oppressions due to race, gender, and class (Evans-Winters & Esposito, 2010). In terms of critical consciousness, CRF does not essentialize consciousness, but instead acknowledges the multiplicity of consciousnesses and identities among Black women (Evans-Winters & Esposito, 2010). Similar to CRT, CRF calls for interdisciplinary approaches when working with Black girls and women; however, these approaches must take on gender, race, and class oppressions directly (Evans-Winters & Esposito, 2010).

Culturally Relevant Pedagogy

As an African American women researcher, Gloria Ladson-Billings (1995) advocates a culturally relevant pedagogy (CRP), using the work of Collins as a resource to validate the credibility of "individuals who have lived through the experiences about which they claim to be experts" as more believable than that of those who simply read and think about such experiences (Collins, 1991, p. 209). Additionally, Ladson-Billings (1995) links the tenets of Black feminist thought to the context and methodology of the study she conducted with successful teachers of African American students. The work of Collins and Ladson-Billings foregrounds the double oppression Black girls and women may encounter in educational settings. To promote the success of Black girls and women in STEM education, we referenced CRP's three primary tenets to describe culturally relevant practices that should be exhibited in counterspaces: (1) students must achieve academic success, (2) students must maintain their cultural competence, and (3) students must develop critical consciousness. Ladson-Billings also draws upon Freire's (1970) definition of critical consciousness and learners' power to transform their reality. In particular, we believe Black girls must develop critical consciousness early in their schooling experiences to establish a strong sense of belonging in STEM education.

To foreground our proposed STEM SISTA space, we have defined its theoretical underpinnings based on critical race theory, intersectionality, critical race feminism, and culturally relevant pedagogy. Our next task is to conduct a review of literature of existing STEM intervention models that specifically provide counterspaces for Black girls and women in elementary, secondary, and undergraduate (i.e., K–16) STEM education.

Review of Literature

The literature on existing K–16 STEM intervention programs that operate from a critical and culturally relevant perspective, developed for Black girls and women, is scarce. Moreover, existing programs that fit this description may not be documented in peer-reviewed literature, due to their infancy (Valla & Williams, 2012). In this integrative literature review (Torraco, 2005), we first conducted a broad search of peer-reviewed literature on K–16 STEM intervention programs that targeted Black girls and women and, in most cases, included culturally relevant and social justice practices (e.g., Lindsay-Dennis, Cummings, & McClendon, 2011; Patton, 2009; West, 2011). Because literature on K–16 STEM intervention programs for Black girls and women is limited, we borrowed literature from other non-STEM disciplines to identify effective programmatic and instructional practices. Next, we describe our literature search process.

Literature Search Process

To create a list of representative findings, we conducted searches of the Academic Search Complete, Education Source, ERIC, Google Scholar, PsycINFO, and SocIndex databases using search terms such as "Black girls or women," "African American girls or women," "after-school programs," "out-of-school-time programs," "informal learning programs," "STEM intervention programs," "STEM outreach programs," "STEM enrichment programs," "STEM education," and "science education." We used the following criteria to narrow our search: peer-reviewed journal articles published within a ten-year span (2006–16), programs or research that targeted girls or women, and programs or research that included effective program components, instructional practices, or research outcomes. Based on these criteria, we identified nine representative programs and strategies to inform our proposed STEM SISTA space, based on three categories: (1) effective K–16 STEM intervention programs for students of color, (2) K–16 STEM programs for Black girls and women, and (3) K–16 non-STEM programs for Black girls and women.

Effective K–16 STEM Intervention Programs for Students of Color

First, we describe effective K–16 STEM Intervention programs for students of color in the United States (table 1). In our review of literature, we found multiple references

TABLE 1. Effective K–16 STEM Intervention Programs for Students of Color

NAME	SETTING	DEMOGRAPHICS	GRADE	FEATURES	EVALUATION	STATE
Mathematics, Engineering, Science Achievement (MESA) (Campbell et al., 2012; Tsui, 2007)	In-school, out-of-school time	Latino/a, Asian	K–12	Career and college exploration, competitions, field trips, guest speakers, hands-on activities, parent leadership, study skills training	Survey of students	CA, AZ, CO, MD, NM, OR, UT, WA
Meyerhoff program at UMBC (Tsui, 2007)	On-campus	Black women and men	13–16	Academic advising, community building, counseling, faculty support, family support, mentoring, summer bridge, tutoring, study groups, summer research internships	Control group comparison of students, program observations, surveys	MD
Minority Engineering Program (Tsui, 2007)	On-campus	Black, Mexican Americans, Latino/a, Native American women and men	13–16	Academic advising, clustering, Community building, counseling, cooperative learning, faculty support, monitoring academic progress, precollege and community college outreach, summer bridge, study groups, study centers, tutoring	Comparison groups of students, retention rate data monitoring, degree attainment monitoring	Varies

to certain programs that were noted as exemplary models of STEM intervention and specifically target students of color. As long-standing programs, these models have been replicated and proven in several U.S. states. Although these programs may not exclusively target Black girls and women, they targeted diverse audiences that included Black girls and women. According to Tsui (2007), these exemplary STEM intervention programs follow an integrated approach to implement various intervention strategies, which help recruit, retain, and provide equitable STEM pathways for students of color, such as precollege summer bridge programs (i.e., transitional programs for low-income and students of color), mentoring (i.e., one-on-one support), tutoring (e.g., tutoring from peers or other students), career counseling (i.e., career exploration of STEM disciplines), learning or study centers (i.e., centralized study areas), academic advising, and financial support. Below we provide a summary of four representative programs.

Mathematics, Engineering, Science Achievement (MESA)

MESA is a K–12 STEM intervention program for students of color that first primarily targeted Latino/a students in the California public school system in the 1970s (Campbell et al., 2012). Since its inception, MESA has reached more than fourteen thousand students throughout the United States (Gibbons, 1992). Through MESA, students are engaged in programmatic activities such as career and college exploration, competitions, field trips, guest speakers, hands-on activities, and study skills training in school and in informal learning settings.

Campbell et al. (2012) collected survey responses from 169 students in grades 7–12, who were predominantly students of color (79 percent) in Utah MESA's Wind Energy Challenge to assess their perceived benefits of the program. The results showed that students perceived the MESA program as influencing their improvements in science, engineering, and mathematics. Additionally, they indicated their most enjoyable experiences in MESA were hands-on activities (45 percent), MESA competitions (21.3 percent), and career and college exploration field trips (17.2 percent). Overall, the results of this study supported the notion that informal learning programs foster the development of STEM identities and increase students' interest, particularly students of color, in STEM careers.

Meyerhoff Scholars Program

The Meyerhoff Scholars Program is a comprehensive STEM intervention that recruits first-year, high-achieving Black students in science, mathematics, and engineering disciplines (SME) at the University of Maryland, Baltimore County (UMBC) to ensure their successful undergraduate degree completion and attainment of advanced STEM degrees (Tsui, 2007). UMBC initiated it to mitigate four risk factors that impede Black students' progression in STEM education: (1) knowledge and skills, (2) motivation and support, (3) monitoring and advising, (4) and academic and social integration. Specifically, students engage in programmatic activities such as a summer bridge program, tutoring, study groups, and summer research internships. Students also receive substantial financial support in the form of scholarships, academic advising, personal counseling, mentoring, and faculty and family support to encourage a "family-like" community environment. Maton, Hrabowski, and Schmitt (2000) investigated the long-term impact (five years) of the Meyerhoff program on participants and the factors that influenced its effectiveness. To compare results, they used a control group consisting of SME students who declined the Meyerhoff scholarship and three cohorts of past Meyerhoff participants. In summary, the Meyerhoff program had significant lasting results on former participants. Former participants had higher degree attainments, higher GPAs, and pursued advanced SME degrees at higher rates than SME students who declined the scholarship. One student indicated the Meyerhoff program afforded an opportunity to be "surrounded by a large number of high-achieving Blacks who were striving toward the same goal of academic achievement" (Fries-Britt, 1998, p. 564).

Minority Engineering Program (MEP)

The Minority Engineering Program (MEP) was founded in 1973 by Ray Landis (engineering professor at California State University at Northbridge) as a university extension of the MESA program. It has been distinguished as a "well-established and widely replicated program" (Tsui, 2007, p. 570) that has been extended to more than one hundred universities in the United States (May & Chubin, 2003). With linkages to colleges of engineering, the MEP targets students of color, by way of precollege and community college outreach and programmatic activities such as cooperative learning, community building, study groups, clustering students together in courses, study centers, freshmen orientation courses, tutoring, and summer bridge activities. Additionally, students receive supplemental instruction in math and science, academic and personal counseling, and strong faculty support. Program staff also actively monitors students' academic progress to ensure their success. Although MEPs have historically improved STEM degree enrollments among students of color, more efforts are needed to decrease attrition (Morrison & Williams, 1993). Morrison and Williams (1993) report that the MEPs that are most successful at attracting and graduating students of color have strong recruitment and retainment efforts, ranging from high school outreach programs to specialized summer programming emphasizing critical thinking and study skills. Furthermore, the MEPs provide participants with tutors and study centers and have strong institutional support in terms of faculty and funding.

Summary

We identified three effective models of K–16 STEM intervention programs that targeted students of color in the United States. During our review of literature, we found multiple references to these programs and their integrative usage of STEM intervention strategies (i.e., summer bridge, mentoring, tutoring). Of these three programs, MESA targeted K–12 students (i.e., primarily in middle school and high school), while Meyerhoff and the MEP targeted college undergraduates. All three programs had documented evaluation results, but the Meyerhoff program had the most compelling effectiveness, while the MEP was the most widely used and proven model. Overall, these programs demonstrated an ongoing need for culturally responsive evaluation measures to sustain long-standing initiatives. The most salient features of these programs included academic advising, community building, counseling, faculty support, summer bridges, study groups, and tutoring, which informs our proposed STEM SISTA model.

K–16 STEM Intervention Strategies for Black Girls and Women

Second, we discuss existing K–16 STEM intervention strategies in formal and informal learning environments that may be useful to engage Black girls and women (table 2). In light of our conceptual framework, we sought to find existing STEM intervention strategies that were constructed with the appropriate lenses and frame of references to situate the experiences of Black girls and women. Specifically, we

TABLE 2. K–16 STEM Intervention Strategies for Black Girls and Women

NAME	SETTING	DEMOGRAPHICS	GRADE	FEATURES	EVALUATION	STATE
Biological Communities and Populations at Spelman College (Pai et al., 2010)	University classroom	Black women Spelman College for Black women	13	Biodiversity course, case study approach, rigorous academic curriculum	Class evaluations, course grades, pre- and posttests, surveys of students	GA
Learning Practices of Science (Buck et al., 2014)	Classroom	99% Black, 1% multiracial girls in an urban school district in a low-SES community	1	Experiential learning, hands-on learning, rigorous science curriculum, Black role models	Pre- and postsurveys using the Young Children's Views of Science (Lederman, 2009) instrument	Unknown
Science Enrichment Activities (Ferreira & Patterson, 2011)	Classroom	Black girls	9–12	Black women role models, learning cycle inquiry-based approach (Marek & Cavallo, 1997), hands-on application, classroom discussions, tutoring	Preexperimental design approach with single group, pre- and posttests	GA

identified three relevant studies that investigated an existing program model or an instructional practice in formal or informal STEM education environments.

Biological Communities and Populations

The purpose of Pai et al.'s (2010) study was to evaluate students' reactions to the implementation of a case study approach in an introductory biology intervention course entitled Biological Communities and Populations (BCP) at Spelman College, which is a historically Black college and university (HBCU). Since the late 1990s, HBCUs have significantly contributed (40%) to the production of Black STEM degree holders in the United States (Owens et al., 2012; Perna et al., 2009). As a HBCU for Black women, Spelman has a long-standing history of excellence and student achievement, particularly in STEM disciplines (Jackson & Winfield, 2014; Owens et al., 2012). For example, since 2001 Spelman is one of the top three private HBCUs for producing graduates in mathematics, physical, and biomedical sciences. As such, Spelman has distinguished its undergraduate science program as an exemplary model for STEM education. Jackson and Winfield (2014) shared several of Spelman College's instructional practices that promoted a holistic approach to student success. These practices, which were informed by the Spelman Model for Empowerment, included embracing identity through the recognition of uniqueness, the promotion of sisterhood, and cultivating success through mentorship by Black female scholars, all of which influenced the design of the BCP course.

Pai et al. (2010) investigated the BCP's effect on academic content knowledge and students' perceptions of their learning. The instructional components consisted of case study work (i.e., groups of two or three), assignments (i.e., one or more articles), small-group discussions, and end-of-module quizzes, and students received updates on their grades individually and as a group. Pai et al. (2010) found the case study-based approach was most effective in engaging students in science education, which proved to successfully engage Black female freshmen students. In light of Spelman's exemplary undergraduate science program, these practices should be considered for broad application in other STEM-related programs. Furthermore, Spelman provides an excellent model to prepare Black women for STEM doctoral degrees and the STEM workforce. The instructional approaches were infused with culturally relevant pedagogy, which is foundational to constructing programs for Black women, along with rigorous academic coursework. Moreover, the Spelman empowerment model provides another practical example to inform our proposed model.

Learning Practices of Science

Buck et al. (2014) conducted a participatory action research project to explore effective instructional practices that best influenced twenty-three Black girls to learn science practices in elementary school in a low SES (socioeconomic status) community that is located in a large urban school district. They explored first graders' comprehension of observation, inference, and evidence using the Young Children's Views of Science (Lederman, 2009) interview protocol, which was administered at pre-, mid- (ten days), and post- (ten days) program intervals to measure how these comprehensions changed based on instruction. The programmatic components introduced the science of practice and incorporated some aspects of culturally relevant pedagogy by introducing first-grade African American girls to historical lived experiences of other African Americans, such as George Washington Carver and Barbara McClintock, which promoted these students' early development of critical consciousness and a sense of belonging in STEM. The instructional practices, performed in a classroom-based setting, were scientific in nature, but they were useful to encourage the girls to develop a critical awareness about science practices. During the study, one of the girls shared her observations and inferences about an object in a handwritten journal. She wrote, "I think it is something that looks like a circle and it is hard too. And it feels pretty hard. When you pull [the string], it goes in. When you start at the bottom it goes back in again." Another girl named Keira replied, "It think it's a ball because it sounds like a ball and rolls like a ball." Overall, 62 percent of the girls demonstrated an informed level of understanding after the intervention. Additionally, the girls' responses provided qualitative support of their positive experiences. Overall, this study connected to the concept of scientific literacy and the development of critical consciousness (i.e., critical science literacy) at an early age (Basu, Barton, & Tan, 2011). Developing critical science literacy allows students to engage in agency and reflect on their own development of awareness. Exercising their voice and acting on issues that matter to them was a viable intervention strategy to create opportunities for African American girls to gain early access to STEM education.

Science Enrichment Activities

Ferreira and Patterson (2011) investigated the influence of science enrichment activities on the achievements and attitudes related to science of seventeen African

American girls who were enrolled in an after-school program at an urban public high school in the Southeast. The after-school programmatic components, which targeted ninth and tenth graders, included role models (i.e., weekly lessons about African American female scientists), inquiry-based activities (i.e., hands-on laboratory and class projects), one-on-one tutoring, and in-class small-group discussions. Moreover, their inquiry-based activities followed Marek and Cavallo's (1997) learning cycle approach, which started with introductory hands-on activities, followed by classroom-wide discussions and practical applications of the related concept. Over a six-week period, pre- and posttests were implemented to measure attitudinal changes, and test scores from a Biology class were tracked to measure student achievement. Ferreira and Patterson used a preexperimental design approach, which included a single group and administration of pre- and posttests to evaluate the effectiveness of the study. The findings indicated science enrichment activities positively influenced African American girls' attitudes toward science, and their achievement in a Biology course, which directly supported Miles and Matkins's (2004) notion that African American students' achievements in science education are positively influenced by activities such as tutoring, mentoring, informal learning, and hands-on application. This study offers effective programmatic components to consider when constructing a STEM SISTA space.

Summary

In this section, we reviewed three STEM intervention strategies that examined the influence of science instructional practices on the engagement and learning outcomes of African American girls at the elementary school (Buck et al., 2014), high school (Ferreira & Patterson, 2011), and college (Pai et al., 2010). In these studies, we discovered the need to target girls and women of color from low socioeconomic statuses. Furthermore, Jackson and Winfield (2014) presented best practices from Spelman College's exemplary undergraduate science program, which highlighted the use of Black women professionals as role models to engage more Black girls and women in STEM disciplines. Overall, we identified intervention strategies (e.g., rigorous curriculum, hands-on learning, Black women role models) that inform our model. In particular, these studies verified the need for culturally relevant pedagogy through the introduction of critical consciousness and role models.

K–16 Non-STEM Programs for Black Girls and Women

In this section, we borrow from other disciplines (e.g., social work and clinical psychology) to glean from non-STEM programs (table 3) that targeted Black girls and women. Although these programs operated in a different context, their conceptual models and programmatic structures provide additional insight for our proposed model. Overall, we identified three relevant studies that targeted Black and Latina girls and women in middle school and college.

Claiming Your Connections

To assess the effectiveness of the intervention, Jones and Warner (2011) recorded outcome scores for CYC participants in comparison to a control group.

Jones and Warner (2011) examined the effectiveness of the Claiming Your Connections (CYC) intervention program, which helped undergraduate Black women access coping skills to overcome depression and maintain their overall physical and emotional health. CYC is a ten-week program that integrates culturally relevant approaches with a clinical therapeutic intervention model. Specifically, the programmatic constructs include psychosocial competence (i.e., promotes coping and adaptive practices) and group work such as coping skills, role modeling, and information sharing. After intervention, CYC participants' depressive symptoms decreased significantly, while control group participants had no significant change, which indicates the effectiveness of the CYC intervention. This non-STEM program example was selected because of its target audience and focus on intervention. Although the context was clinical in nature, the programmatic constructs may be applied in nonclinical settings. Culturally relevant practices (i.e., role modeling, critical consciousness) are foundational for programs that target people of color, including Black women. Additionally, coping mechanisms may be useful skills for Black girls and women in light of daily microaggressions and campus racial climates. Overall, the programmatic components of this model positively informed our framework.

Project Sister Circle

Williams, Karlin, and Wallace (2012) provided details on Project Sister Circle (PSC), which is a school-based intervention program that targets Black and Latina middle

TABLE 3. K–16 Non-STEM Programs for Black Girls and Women

NAME	SETTING	DEMOGRAPHICS	GRADE	FEATURES	EVALUATION	STATE
Claiming Your Connections (Jones & Warner, 2011)	Community-based	Black women	13–16	Afrocentric paradigm, psychosocial competence, Role-modeling, Information sharing	Experimental design, intervention, wait-list control group comparison, pre- and posttests	Unknown
Project Sister Circle (Williams & Wallace, 2012	In-school	Black and Latina girls in urban schools	6–8	Activity-based: centering, circle closing, cultural norms, gratitude, group discussion, group facilitators, group rules and, physical space, project work, holistic approach, spiritual	Concurrent cross-sectional, pre- and post-tests, provides formative and summative evaluation	Unknown
The SISTA Project (Collins, Whiters, & Braithwaite, 2007)	Community-based	Black women	Adults	Behavioral skills, discussions, group lectures, practical application, role-playing, videos, social cognitive theory take-home activities, theory of gender and power	Anonymous evaluation forms	Varies

school girls to prevent sexual risk vulnerability. Specifically, it offers a physical "safe space" in a structured (i.e., with group rules), but supportive and welcoming, environment. It also incorporates culturally relevant practices such as cultural norms and group facilitators who are women of color, and a holistic curriculum including activities such as centering, group discussion, project work, and circle closing. PSC administrators enforce effectiveness through trained counselors, parent involvement, targeted recruitment efforts, consideration of environmental factors, and program evaluation. Although PSC is a non-STEM program, it incorporates a culturally relevant approach, which is foundational for engaging Black girls and women. Moreover, it offers a "safe space" for Black women to reveal their struggles and fears without rejection or dismissal. Black women in the circle were in a protective space with trusted facilitators who were also women of color and had similar experiences. These programmatic components provide effective approaches to engage Black girls in the context of STEM education.

The SISTA Project

Sisters Informing Sisters about Topics on AIDS (SISTA) (Collins, Whiters, & Braithwaite, 2007) is a peer-led intervention program that targets the prevention of HIV infection among African American women. SISTA is a national program recognized by the Centers for Disease Control and Prevention as an effective behavioral intervention. SISTA is delivered in a community-based setting and consists of five sessions that follows culturally relevant pedagogical and gender approaches. The programmatic components included an infusion of behavioral skills, practical application, group discussions, lectures, role-playing, videos, and take-home activities. Skilled women facilitators lead the small-group sessions. The intervention model uses social cognitive theory and the theory of gender and power. The SISTA model also serves as a "safe space" for African American women in a non-STEM context. As a proven and nationally recognized model, its processes are well developed. Although it follows culturally relevant pedagogy, it also borrows from feminist theory. Overall, it provides a useful example of a SISTA space in a non-STEM context.

Summary

These studies represent non-STEM intervention programs for Black (and Latina) girls and women. Although these programs represented non-STEM disciplines (e.g., social work and clinical therapeutic interventions), they provide pertinent details about frameworks and theory to consider in our STEM SISTA space. Additionally, they provide more support for culturally relevant practices and the development of critical consciousness. Although we discovered the SISTA project after we had conducted our first literature search, it served as a nationally recognized and proven model. In table 3, we summarize our findings. Next, we will develop our suggested STEM SISTA space, which is based on a conceptual framework that consists of critical race feminism, critical consciousness, and culturally relevant pedagogy and extends our review of literature.

Recommendation: The STEM SISTA Space

The STEM SISTA space is a synthesis of best practices for Black girls and women compiled from current literature and our own experiences as program directors and evaluators of programs to broaden STEM participation. We have identified five major tenets for this SISTA space that fosters a social justice agenda to ensure Black girls and women receive equitable access to high-quality STEM experiences and careers and are aware of the systems and structures that prevent their access. Based on our experiences in intervention and community-based programs, we acknowledge the critical need to utilize culturally responsive evaluation approaches to ensure the effectiveness of STEM initiatives that target individuals who are underrepresented in STEM disciplines, including Black girls and women (Rodríguez-Campos & Ashford, 2015).

Our model for a STEM SISTA space is timely, as Bernal (1998) recommends a more critical approach to examine science education that moves away from deficit models to models that are epistemologically consistent with youth living in high-poverty urban areas. Furthermore, Barton (2003) calls for a reconceptualized model that reflects a more holistic understanding of youth's lives that challenges deficit thinking as it relates to science participation and achievement. This reconceptualized model challenges traditionally held beliefs about the achievement, resources, and educative opportunities for urban youth, keeping in mind their contexts outside of school (Barton, 2003). The STEM SISTA space is a reconceptualized model that provides a framework for providing meaningful and positive STEM learning experiences that embrace the strengths of Black girls and women and encourage their participation in STEM.

Strengthen Creative Thinking and Critical Consciousness of Black Girls and Women in STEM through Learning Communities and Dialogic Spaces

Gloria Ladson-Billings (1995) highlights basic tenets of culturally relevant pedagogy and states that students must achieve academic success, maintain their cultural competence, and develop critical consciousness. In developing critical consciousness, African American girls need opportunities to think critically and engage in conversations that are meaningful to them. This first component of the STEM SISTA space highlights the importance of providing opportunities for Black girls and women to be creative in how they communicate their ideas and their understanding of scientific concepts. In examining the demographics of the STEM workforce, our current traditional approaches to teaching science and mathematics have been ineffective in diversifying the STEM workforce and do not promote an inclusive environment for all populations of students (Hanson, 2009; McNeil & Blad, 2014). A recent report released by McNeil and Blad (2014) reveals that 25 percent of high schools with the highest percentages of Black and Latino students do not offer Algebra 2, and 33 percent of those schools do not offer chemistry, both of which are essential courses in preparing students for success in college STEM coursework (McNeil & Blad, 2014). Furthermore, Brickhouse, Lowery, and Schultz (2000) report that girls are alienated by science because it is viewed as masculine, competitive, and impersonal.

The disparities in the quality of education that exists in schools with predominantly ethnically minority populations compounded with the gender disparities that exist within science and mathematics courses undermine the participation of Black girls and women entering and persisting in STEM fields. Basu, Barton, and Tan (2011) state that scientific literacy is a process of developing critical consciousness which they term *critical science literacy*. Freire (1970) posits that critical consciousness is a way for learners to exercise their power to transform reality. Developing critical science literacy allows students to engage in agency and reflect on their own development of awareness—exercising their voice and acting on issues that matter to them. As part of one of the STEM intervention programs that we directed, Black middle school girls were introduced to ecojustice, investigating ecological and social issues locally and their implications on a more global scale. Participants learned about waste management systems, water reclamation systems, and recycling programs in their local communities, the locations of the plants and landfills, and the direct impact of the location on their neighborhoods. Students discussed issues that mattered to them and shared their knowledge with their parents and peers by creating public service announcements, music videos, and even poems. These types of activities provided spaces for dialogue to take place and opportunities for students to respond in their own communities.

Incorporate Lived Experiences, Strengths, and Cultures of Black Girls and Women in the STEM Curriculum and Learning Environment

Wolowiec, Rutledge, and Cellitioci (2012) propose that investment and innovation begin at an early age and therefore encourage teachers to adapt the science curriculum to respond to students' interests and strengths so that all students are actively engaged in scientific phenomena early on. Too often, teachers are mandated to enact curriculum that ignores the cultures and lived experiences of underrepresented groups in STEM disciplines. Furthermore, many teachers are underprepared to teach in today's multicultural classroom and, consequently, struggle to engage in teaching practices that are culturally relevant and responsive (Aikenhead & Jegede, 1999; Barton, Tan, & Rivet, 2008). Culturally responsive approaches to teaching integrate the cultural identities and experiences of diverse students to enhance the quality of their learning environments and maintain students' cultural competence (Banks et al., 2005; Ladson-Billings, 1995; Villegas & Lucas, 2002). Teachers must acknowledge and value the funds of knowledge students bring with them to the classroom in order to make learning meaningful. Funds of knowledge refer to the "historically accumulated and culturally developed bodies of knowledge and skills essential for household or individual functioning and well-being" (Moll et al., 1992, p. 133). Appendix D of the Next Generation Science Standards (NGSS) acknowledges that nondominant groups have been underserved by the educational system and highlights the importance of making science accessible to all groups of students (NGSS, 2013). Even though current reform efforts in science seek to encourage effective instruction, the needs of underrepresented populations, especially African American girls, are still not being met (Pringle et al., 2012). Therefore, Black women are severely underrepresented in the STEM disciplines. Incorporating the strengths, cultures, and lived experiences of African American girls and women will foster a sense of belonging in the STEM disciplines.

Sustained Mentoring from Black Women Who Serve as Role Models and Mentors to Black Girls

Providing Black women role models and mentors who have succeeded in STEM fields is an effective method in encouraging Black girls and women to persist in fields where they have historically been underrepresented. Black women role models can inspire girls and women to project themselves in that image. Mentors serve many roles, from providing guidance and support, to exposing mentees to new perspectives and ideas, to challenging them to reach new levels of achievement (Hawkey, 1997). In Eisenhardt and Finkel's *Women's Science: Learning and Succeeding from the Margin* (1998), the authors argue that a strong network and mentoring system are both positive reinforcers for women and girls in science as well as indicators of success in the sciences. The need for mentoring Black girls and women is further substantiated because of the sparsity of Black women pursuing and persisting in STEM disciplines (Smith-Evans et al., 2014). Ferreira and Patterson's (2011) study describes in the literature review a science enrichment after-school program that was facilitated by a Black woman teacher who was a biochemist prior to teaching high school science. This curriculum was designed to provide inquiry-based science activities for African American girls, complemented with tutoring and mentoring. The participants also learned about the contributions of Black women scientists such as Dr. Mae Jemison, and the study revealed the participants' science achievement and attitudes toward science became more favorable, such that they could project themselves into that image. In our STEM programs, we partnered with student organizations such as the National Society of Black Engineers (NSBE) and successful Black women in academia and industry who served as mentors to the participants. Not only did they engage students in activities within their fields, but also provided sustained mentoring throughout the year, serving as a resource for students. Ferreira and Patterson's (2011) study (described in the literature review) brought in role models each week for African American high school girls to see Black female scientists as contributors to science.

Train Providers of STEM Intervention Programs to Facilitate Early and Sustained Access to STEM Disciplines and Careers for Black Girls

African American girls and women often have difficulty navigating the bureaucracy in schools and STEM careers because of the discrimination that occurs as a result of race and gender. The barriers to pursuing the STEM trajectory are compounded if the Black girls and women experience poverty in their home lives (King et al., in press). However, early and sustained involvement in STEM enrichment programs has positively impacted girls and women of color by providing authentic experiences in STEM careers and a safe space that validates their identities as scientists, mathematicians, and engineers (Ong, 2005; Ong et al., 2011). Some students have suggested that middle school is an ideal time to introduce African American girls and other students of color to rigorous mathematics and science courses (Ashford et al., 2016). However, other studies have found African American girls may quickly become disengaged in STEM as they transition into high school and college, because they had negative learning experiences in science and mathematics in middle school (Gallagher, 1994; King et al., in press; Tai et al., 2006). Therefore, providing early access to STEM disciplines and careers in positive "safe spaces" is crucial to broadening the reach of African American girls before they develop negative attitudes toward STEM fields and a disinterest in these disciplines. An example of an activity enacted in one of our intervention programs is a Medical Career Outreach Day. This program is in partnership with the university hospital; health professionals ranging from emergency medical technicians to anesthesiologists come on the program site to immerse participants in their professions. Groups such as the Black Nurses Association, Student National Medical Association, and Student National Dental Association not only discuss the pathways to getting into the career, but also the specializations options. This tenet reemphasizes the previous notion about the importance of Black women role models who serve as a face to what the girls can become in the future, if they only persist! Allowing African American girls to project themselves into that image of a scientist, mathematician, or engineer at an early age and providing them with access to equitable high-quality STEM programming and experiences can broaden their participation in STEM careers.

Assess the Effectiveness of STEM Intervention Programs or Black Girls through Culturally Responsive Evaluation

STEM SISTA spaces are designed to provide opportunities and experiences that validate the strengths, experiences, and unique abilities that African American girls and women bring to the science classroom and STEM workplace. Learning communities promote fruitful discussions and exchange of ideas. One important aspect of learning communities is the safe space to learn with and from one another. Allowing Black girls and women to form learning communities and counterspaces to discuss issues that are of importance and share insights from one SISTA to another is powerful. The impacts of the programs, curriculum, and environment should always be assessed to ensure the objectives and outcomes are being met.

Evaluators follow culturally responsive evaluation strategies to assess a program's effectiveness based on the cultures of its participants, rejecting the notion that evaluations should be devoid of culture (Frierson, Hood, & Hughes, 2002). In the context of STEM SISTA spaces, we describe culture as the shared experiences of Black girls and women, which includes their "languages, values, customs, beliefs, worldviews, ways of knowing, and ways of communicating" (American Evaluation Association, 2011, para 9).

> Hence, assessing the effectiveness of STEM intervention programs through culturally responsive evaluation is increasingly important for Black girls and women. Our recommendation is that Black girls and women are not only provided with curricula that incorporate their lived experiences and cultures, but also evaluators who are culturally competent and evaluations that are culturally responsive.

As such, evaluators must exhibit a strong level of cultural competence (i.e., understanding of factors such as race, ethnicity, religion, social class, or language) to evaluate culturally responsive programs that target Black girls and women (American Evaluation Association, 2011). Moreover, evaluators should incorporate their lived experiences and cultures (see the second tenet) to assess the effectiveness of culturally responsive program curricula and frameworks in order to meet the unique and individual needs of Black girls and women. Based on these strategies, we suggest that culturally responsive evaluation approaches include (1) Black women evaluation team members with shared lived experiences, (2) evaluators that engage critical stakeholders, (3) multiethnic evaluation teams that magnify the voices of historically underrepresented audiences, (4) evaluation teams that consider experiential findings as concrete truth, and (5) evaluators that maintain openness to new approaches (Frierson, Hood, & Hughes, 2002).

Summary

In summary, our proposed model for a STEM SISTA space provides a formative proposal to increase the engagement of Black girls and women to foster their sustained interest and participation in STEM fields. Because our purpose was to propose a new STEM SISTA space that targets Black girls and women in K–16 STEM education, we developed our approach based on proven STEM intervention strategies and programmatic components. Additionally, we supplemented our model with additional research to address existing gaps in the literature. It is our hope that program developers and researchers will use our model in their respective disciplines to strengthen is validity and to extend its reach. As we conclude this chapter, we offer the following implications and final conclusions.

Implications and Conclusions

Due to the country's changing demographics and America losing its global competitiveness, policymakers have initiated a national push to broaden the STEM pipeline and prepare and engage historically underrepresented populations in the STEM disciplines. Accordingly, our motivation for this STEM SISTA space is undergirded with a social justice agenda to provide equitable access for Black girls and women to gain access to STEM fields. If we provide Black girls and women awareness of, and equitable access to, systems and structures in STEM fields, this population will begin to associate positive experiences and perceptions with STEM disciplines and careers. Ultimately, their participation in the STEM workforce will diversify not only the STEM workplace, but also new ideas and innovations, which will emerge from their sustained participation and interest. Furthermore, we believe this proposed counterspace for Black girls and women may also foster the development of STEM counterspaces for Black males and their Latino/a counterparts, as the model becomes more mature. The STEM SISTA space was designed based on current research on intervention and outreach programs and our practical experiences with designing and evaluating outreach programs. We proposed this model because there was a void in the literature on effective STEM programs for African American girls and women with a critical stance. Directions for future research are to study the implementation of the proposed STEM SISTA space in practice through qualitative studies and longitudinal studies following the girls' participation over time, in comparison to a control group who do not benefit from this model. This information will provide evidence regarding the effectiveness of the proposed conceptual framework and provide insight in how we can strengthen the model to foster the participation of African American girls and women in STEM disciplines.

REFERENCES

Aikenhead, G. S., & Jegede, O. J. (1999). Cross-cultural science education: A cognitive explanation of a cultural phenomenon. *Journal of Research in Science Teaching 36*(3), 269–87.

American Evaluation Association (2011). Public statement on cultural competence in evaluation. Fairhaven, MA. Retrieved from www.eval.org.

Ashford, S. N. (2016). Our counter-life herstories: The experiences of African American women faculty in U.S. computing education. Ph.D diss., University of South Florida.

Ashford, S. N., Lanehart, R. E., Kersaint, G. K., Lee, R. S., & Kromrey, J. D. (2016). STEM pathways: Examining persistence in rigorous math and science course taking. *Journal of Science Education and Technology 25*(6), 961–75.

Banks, J., Cochran-Smith, M., Moll, L., Richert, A., Zeichner, K., LePage, P., Darling, Hammond, L., et al. (2005). Teaching diverse learners. In L. Darling-Hammond & J. Bransford (eds.), *Preparing teachers for a changing world: What teachers should learn and be able to do.* San Francisco: Jossey-Bass.

Barton, A. C. (2003). *Teaching science for social justice.* New York: Teachers College Press.

Barton, A. C., Ermer, J. L., Burkett, T. A. and Osborne, M. D. (2003). *Teaching science for social justice.* New York: Teachers College Press.

Barton, A. C., Tan E. & Rivet A. (2008). Creating hybrid spaces for engaging school science among urban middle school girls. *American Education Research Journal 45*, 68–103.

Basu, S. J., Barton, A. C., & Tan, E. (eds.) (2011). *Democratic science teaching: Building the expertise to empower low-income minority youth in science*, vol. 3. Springer Science & Business Media.

Bell, D. (1980). *Brown* and the interest-convergence dilemma. In D. Bell (ed.), *Shades of brown:*

New perspectives on school desegregation. New York: Teachers College Press.

Bernal, D. D. (1998). Using a Chicana feminist epistemology in educational research. *Harvard Educational Review 68*(4), 555–83.

Borum, V. (2012). Promoting equity: Examining a model of success for African American women in mathematics. *Journal of Mathematics Education at Teachers College 3*(2), 85–89.

Borum, V., & Walker, E. (2012). What makes the difference? Black women's undergraduate and graduate experiences in mathematics. *Journal of Negro Education 81*(4), 366–78.

Brickhouse, N. W., Lowery, P., & Schultz, K. (2000). What kind of a girl does science? The construction of school science identities. *Journal of research in science teaching 37*(5), 441–58.

Buck, G. A., Akerson, V. L., Quigley, C. F., & Weiland, I. S. (2014). Exploring the potential of using explicit reflective instruction through contextualized and decontextualized approaches to teach first-grade African American girls the practices of science. *Electronic Journal of Science Education 18*(6), 1–21.

Bush, J. L. (2013). The persistence of Black women in engineering: A phenomenological study. Ed.D. diss., Wilkes University.

Campbell, T., Lee, H., Kwon, H., & Kyungsuk, P. (2012). Student motivation and interests as proxies for forming STEM identities. *Journal of the Korean Association for Science Education 32*(3), 532–40.

Castro, E. L. (2014). "Underprepared" and "at-risk": Disrupting deficit discourses in undergraduate STEM recruitment and retention programming. *Journal of Student Affairs Research and Practice 51*(4), 407–19.

Cole, C. M., Manuh, T., & Miescher, S. F. (2007). *Africa after gender?* Indiana University Press.

Collins, C. E., Whiters, B. D. L., & Braithwaite, R. (2007). The saved SISTA project: A faith-based HIV prevention program for Black women in addiction recovery. *American Journal of Health Studies 22*(2), 76–82.

Collins, P. H. (1991). *Black feminist thought.* New York: Routledge, 1991.

Committee on Underrepresented Groups and the Expansion of the Science and Engineering Workforce (US), Committee on Science, Engineering, and Public Policy (US), & National Research Council (US) (2010). *Expanding underrepresented minority participation: America's science and technology talent at the crossroads.* Washington, DC: National Academies Press.

Crenshaw, K. (1989). Demarginalizing the intersection of race and sex: A Black feminist critique of antidiscrimination doctrine, feminist theory and antiracist politics. *University of Chicago Legal Forum,* 139–67.

Crenshaw, K. (1991). Mapping the margins: Intersectionality, identity politics, and violence against women of color. *Stanford Law Review 43*(6), 1241–99.

da Rosa, K. D. (2013). Gender, ethnicity, and physics education: Understanding how black women build their identities as scientists. Ph.D. diss., Columbia University.

Eisenhardt, M. A., & Finkel, E. (1998). *Women's science: Learning and succeeding from the margin*. Chicago: University of Chicago Press.

Espinosa, L. (2011). Pipelines and pathways: Women of color in undergraduate STEM majors and the college experiences that contribute to persistence. *Harvard Educational Review 81*(2), 209–41.

Evans-Winters, V. E., & Esposito, J. (2010). Other people's daughters: Critical race feminism and Black girls' education. *Journal of Educational Foundations 24*(1–2), 11–24.

Fealing, K. H. & Myers, S. L., Jr. (2012). Pathways v. pipelines to broadening participation in the STEM workforce. *Journal of Women and Minorities in Science and Engineering 21*(4), 271–93. doi:10.1615/JWomenMinorScienEng.2015004760.

Ferreira, M. M., & Patterson, C. M. (2011). Improving equity through a science enrichment program. *Advancing Women in Leadership 31*(1), 119–24.

Freire, P. (1970). *Pedagogy of the oppressed*. Trans. M. B. Ramos. New York: Continuum.

Frierson, H., Hood, S., & Hughes, G. (2002). Strategies that address culturally responsive evaluation. In J. Frechtling (ed.), *The 2002 user-friendly handbook for project evaluation*. Arlington, VA: National Science Foundation.

Fries-Britt, S. (1998). Moving beyond Black achiever isolation: Experiences of gifted Black collegians. *Journal of Higher Education 6*(9), 556–76.

Frillman, S. A. (2011). A hermeneutic phenomenological study of the experiences of female African American undergraduate engineering students at a predominantly White and an historically Black institution. Ph.D. diss., Purdue University.

Gallagher, S. A. (1994). Middle school classroom predictors of science persistence. *Journal of Research in Science Teaching 31*(7), 721–34.

Geisinger, B. N., & Raman, D. R. (2013). Why they leave: Understanding student attrition from engineering majors. *International Journal of Engineering Education 29*(4), 914–25.

Gibbons, A. (1992). Minority programs that get high marks. *Science 258*(5085), 1190–96.

Gibson, S. L., & Espino, M. M. (2016). Uncovering Black womanhood in engineering. *NASPA Journal About Women in Higher Education 9*(1), 56–73.

Hanson S. (2009). *Swimming against the tide: African American girls and science education*. Philadelphia, PA: Temple University Press.

Hawkey, K. (1997). Roles, responsibilities, and relationships in mentoring: A literature review and agenda for research. *Journal of Teacher Education 48*(5), 325–36.

Hill, C., Corbett, C., & St. Rose, A. (2010). *Why so few? Women in science, technology, engineering, and mathematics*. Washington, DC: AAUW.

hooks, b. (1992). *Black looks: Race and representation*. Toronto, ON: Between the Lines Press.

Howard-Hamilton, M. F. (2003). Theoretical frameworks for African American women. *New directions for student services* (104), 19–27.

Jackson, K. M., & Winfield, L. L. (2014). Realigning the crooked room: Spelman claims a space for African American women in STEM. *Peer Review 16*(2), 9–12.

Jones, L. V., & Warner, L. A. (2011). Evaluating culturally responsive group work with black women. *Research on Social Work Practice 21*(6), 737–46.

King, N., Pringle, R. M., Cordero M. L., & Ridgewell, N. (2016). African American middle school girls in an informal community-based program: Mining rare gems to pursue STEM. In *Girls and women of color in STEM: Navigating the double bind*, eds B. Polnick, B. Irby, & J. Ballenger. Charlotte, NC: Information Age.

Ladson-Billings, G. (1995). Toward a theory of culturally relevant pedagogy. *American Educational Research Journal 32*(3), 465–91.

Ladson-Billings, G. (1998). Just what is critical race theory and what's it doing in a nice field like education? *International Journal of Qualitative Studies in Education 11*(1), 7–24. doi:10.1080/095183998236863.

Ladson-Billings, G., & Tate, W. F. (1995). Toward a critical race theory of education. *Teachers College Record 97*(1), 47–68.

Lederman, J. S. (2009). Development of a valid and reliable protocol for the assessment of early childhood students' conceptions of nature of science and scientific inquiry. Ph.D. diss., Curtin University of Technology.

Lindsay-Dennis, L., Cummings, L., & McClendon, S. C. (2011). Mentors' reflections on developing a culturally responsive mentoring initiative for urban African American girls. *Black Women, Gender & Families 5*(2), 66–92.

Marek, E. A., & Cavallo, A. M. (1997). *The learning cycle: Elementary school science and beyond*. Rev. ed. Portsmouth, NH: Heinemann.

Martin, D. B. (2009). Researching race in mathematics education. *Teachers College Record 111*(2), 295–338.

Maton, K. I., Hrabowski, F. A., & Schmitt, C. L. (2000). African American college students excelling in the sciences: College and postcollege outcomes in the Meyerhoff Scholars Program. *Journal of Research in Science Teaching, 37*(7), 629–54.

May, G. S., & Chubin, D. E. (2003). A retrospective on undergraduate engineering success for underrepresented minority students. *Journal of Engineering Education 92*(1), 27–39.

McNeil, M., & Blad, E. (2014). Nation falls far short on educational equity, data show disparities seen from pre-K to high school. *Education Week 33*(26), 8.

McPherson, E. (2012). Undergraduate African American women's narratives on persistence in science majors at a PWI. Ph.D. diss., University of Illinois, Urbana-Champaign.

Moll, L. C., Amanti, C., Neff, D., & Gonzalez, N. (1992). Funds of knowledge for teaching: Using a qualitative approach to connect homes and classrooms. *Theory into Practice 31*(2), 132–41.

Miles, R., & Matkins, J. J. (2004). Science enrichment for African-American students. *The Science Teacher 71*(2), 36–41.

Morrison, C., & Williams, L. E. (1993). Minority engineering programs: A case for institutional support. *NACME Research Newsletter 4*(1), 1–11.

Moss, B. (2010). "Phenomenal women," collaborative literacies, and community texts in alternative "Sista" space. *Community Literacy Journal 5*(1), 1–24.

National Academy of Sciences. (2007). Rising above the gathering storm: Energizing and employing America for a brighter economic future. Retrieved from https://www.nsf.gov/attachments/105652/public/NAS-Gathering-Storm-11463.pdf.

National Action Council for Minorities in Engineering (NACME). (2008). Synergies: 2008 annual report. Retrieved from http://www.nacme.org/publications/annual_reports/2008NACME_AnnualReport.pdf.

National Science Foundation, Louis Stokes Alliances for Minority Participation (n.d.). NSF STEM Classification of Instructional Programs Crosswalk. Retrieved from https://www.lsamp.org/help/help_stem_cip_2010.cfm.

National Science Foundation, National Center for Science and Engineering Statistics (2015). *Women, minorities, and persons with disabilities in science and engineering: 2015*. Special Report NSF 15-311. Retrieved from http://www.nsf.gov/statistics/2015/nsf15311.

NGSS Lead States. (2013). *Next generation science standards: For states, by states*. Washington, DC: The National Academies Press.

Ong, M. (2005). Body projects of young women of color in physics: Intersections of gender, race, and science. *Social Problems 52*(4), 593–617.

Ong, M., Wright, C., Espinosa, L. L., & Orfield, G. (2011). Inside the double bind: A synthesis of empirical research on undergraduate and graduate women of color in science, technology, engineering, and mathematics. *Harvard Educational Review 81*(2), 172–209.

Owens, E. W., Shelton, A. J., Bloom, C. M., & Cavil, J. K. (2012). The significance of HBCUs to the production of STEM graduates: Answering the call. *Educational Foundations 26*, 33–47.

Pai, A., Benning, T., Woods, N., McGinnis, G., Chu, J., Netherton, J., & Bauerle, C. (2010). The effectiveness of a case study-based first-year biology class at a Black women's college. *Journal of College Science Teaching 40*(2), 32–39.

Palmer, R. T., & Wood, J. L. (2013). *Community colleges and STEM: Examining underrepresented racial and ethnic minorities*. Hoboken, NJ: Taylor and Francis.

Patton, L. D. (2009). My sister's keeper: A qualitative examination of mentoring experiences among African American women in graduate and professional schools. *Journal of Higher Education 80*(5), 510–37.

Perna, L., Lundy-Wagner, V., Drezner, N. D., Gasman, M., Yoon, S., Bose, E., & Gary, S. (2009). The contribution of HBCUs to the preparation of African American women for STEM careers: A case study. *Research in Higher Education 50*(1), 1–23.

Pringle, R. M., Brkich, K. M., Adams, T., West-Olatunji, C., & Archer-Banks, D. A. M. (2012). Factors influencing elementary teachers' positioning of African American girls as science and mathematics learners. *School Science & Mathematics 112*(4), 217–29.

Robinson, C. (2012). The characteristics and experiences of successful undergraduate Latina students who persist in engineering. Ed.D. diss., Arizona State University.

Rodriguez, S. L. (2015). *Las mujeres* in the STEM pipeline: How Latina college students who persist in STEM majors develop and sustain their science identities. Ph.D. diss., University of Texas, Austin.

Rodríguez-Campos, L. & Ashford, S. (2015). Metaevaluation of a technology literacy program in underserved communities. *International Journal of Interdisciplinary Studies in Communication 10*(4), 1–8.

Smith-Evans, L., & George, L. (2014). *Unlocking opportunity for African American girls: A call to action for educational equity*. New York: NAACP Legal Defense and Educational Fund.

Smith-Evans, L., George, J., Graves, F. G., Kaufmann, L. S., & Frohlich, L. (2014). *Unlocking opportunity for African American girls: A call to action for educational equity*. National Women's Law Center, Washington, DC.

Solórzano, D., Ceja, M., & Yosso, T. (2000). Critical race theory, racial microaggressions, and campus racial climate: The experiences of African American college students. *Journal of Negro Education 69*(1–2), 60–73.

Somerville-Midgette, K. (2014). An engineering journey: A transcendental phenomenological study of African-American female engineers' persistence. Ed.D., Liberty University.

Stephens, D. P., & Phillips, L. D. (2003). Freaks, gold diggers, divas, and dykes: The sociohistorical development of adolescent African American women's sexual scripts. *Sexuality and Culture 7*(1), 3–49.

Tai, R., Liu, C., Maltese, A., & Fan, X. (2006). Planning early for careers in science. *Science 312*(5777), 1143–44.

Tate, W. F. (1997). Critical race theory and education: History, theory, and implications. *Review of Educational Research* 22, 195–247.

Torraco, R. J. (2005). Writing integrative literature reviews: Guidelines and examples. *Human Resource Development Review* 4(3), 356–67.

Tsui, L. (2007). Effective strategies to increase diversity in STEM fields: A review of the research literature. *Journal of Negro Education* 76(4), 555–81.

Valla, J. M., & Williams, W. M. (2012). Increasing achievement and higher-education representation of under-represented groups in science, technology, engineering, and mathematics fields: A review of current K–12 intervention programs. *Journal of Women and Minorities in Science and Engineering* 18(1), 21–53.

Veenstra, C. P., Padró, F. F., & Furst-Bowe, J. A. (eds.) (2012). *Advancing the STEM Agenda: Quality Improvement Supports STEM. Selected Papers from the 2011 Advancing the STEM Agenda in Education, the Workplace, and Society Conference at the University of Wisconsin-Stout, July 2011.* Milwaukee: ASQ Quality Press.

Villegas, A. M., & Lucas, T. (2002). *Educating culturally responsive teachers: A coherent approach.* Albany: State University of New York Press.

Vincent, G. K., & Velkoff, V. A. (2010). *The next four decades: The older population in the United States, 2010 to 2050* (No. 1138). US Department of Commerce, Economics and Statistics Administration, US Census Bureau.

West, N. M. (2011). The African American women's summit: A case study of a professional development program developed by and for African American women student affairs professionals. Ph.D. diss., University of South Florida.

White House Council on Women and Girls (2014, November). *Women and girls of color: Addressing challenges and expanding opportunity.* Retrieved from https://www.whitehouse.gov/sites/default/files/docs/cwg_women_and_girls_of_color_report_112014.pdf.

Williams, W., Karlin, T., & Wallace, D. (2012). Project Sister Circle: Risk, intersectionality, and intervening in urban schools. *Journal of School Counseling* 10(17). Retrieved from http://jsc.montana.edu/articles/v10n17.pdf.

Wilson, J. A., Gaines, J. E. & Cooper, D. (2015). Bulls-EYE mentoring: Developing a program intervention in the college of engineering. Proceedings of the 2015 American Society for Engineering Education Annual Conference Exposition. Retrieved from https://peer.asee.org/bulls-eye-mentoring-developing-a-program-intervention-in-the-college-of-engineering pdf.

Wolowiec, M., Rutledge, A. & Cellitioci, J. (2012). Designed to invent: Camp invention, a 21st century program, 7–18. In *Exemplary science for building interest in STEM careers*, ed. R. E. Yager. NSTA Press.

Handout: Background of the STEM SISTA Space Model

DIRECTIONS: This handout provides background information on the underlying concepts that were referenced in the STEM SISTA space model.

STEM SISTA Space Model

S	Strengthen creative thinking and critical consciousness of Black girls and women in STEM through learning communities and dialogic spaces
I	Incorporate lived experiences, strengths, and cultures of Black girls and women in the STEM curriculum and learning environment
S	Sustain mentoring from Black women who serve as role models and mentors to Black girls
T	Train providers of STEM intervention programs to facilitate early and sustained access to STEM disciplines and careers for Black girls
A	Assess the effectiveness of STEM intervention programs for Black girls through culturally responsive evaluation

Strengthen Creative Thinking and Critical Consciousness of Black Girls and Women in STEM through Learning Communities and Dialogic Spaces

- Culturally relevant pedagogy (Gloria Ladson-Billings, 1995)
- Must achieve academic success and maintain their cultural competence
- Develop critical consciousness
- Critical science literacy (Basu, Barton, & Tan, 2011): Process of developing critical consciousness
- Critical consciousness (Freire, 1970): A way for a learner to exercise his/her power to transform reality

Incorporate Lived Experiences, Strengths, and Cultures of Black Girls and Women in the STEM Curriculum and Learning Environment

- Culturally relevant and responsive teaching practices (Aikenhead & Jegede, 1999; Barton, Tan, & Rivet, 2008)
- Integrates cultural identities and experiences of diverse students
- Enhances quality of learning environments

- Maintains students' cultural competence (Banks et al., 2005; Ladson-Billings, 1995; Villegas & Lucas, 2002)

Sustained Mentoring from Black Women Who Serve as Role Models and Mentors to Black Girls

- Mentorship roles (Hawkey, 1997)
- Strong network and mentoring system are positive reinforcers for women and girls in Science (Eisenhardt & Finkel, 1999)
- Mentoring for Black girls and women (Smith-Evans et al., 2014)

Train Providers of STEM Intervention Programs to Facilitate Early and Sustained Access to STEM Disciplines and Careers for Black Girls

- Barriers to pursuing the STEM trajectory are compounded if the Black girls and women experience poverty in their home lives (King et al., in press).
- Early and sustained involvement in STEM enrichment programs has positively impacted girls and women of color by providing authentic experiences in STEM careers and a safe space that validates their identities as scientists, mathematicians, and engineers (Ong, 2005; Ong et al., 2011).
- Moreover, middle school is an ideal time frame to introduce historically underrepresented students, particularly African American girls, to rigorous mathematics and science course-taking (Ashford et al., 2016)
- By the time African American girls have reached middle school many have had negative learning experiences in science and mathematics and quickly become disengaged in STEM as they transition into high school and college (Gallagher, 1994; King et al., in press; Tai et al., 2006).

Asess the Effectiveness of STEM Intervention Programs for Black Girls through Culturally Responsive Evaluation

- Science achievement and interest in the sciences are not only shaped by gender and race, but also the environment (Hill, Corbett, & St. Rose, 2010)

Female Education

Gender Discrimination in Northern Nigerian Secondary Schools

Felix Peter Umeana

In Nigeria, along with its West African neighbor Ghana, women are now starting businesses in greater numbers than men.

—Gayle Tzemach Lemmon

Female illiteracy is a serious problem throughout the developing world. According to UNICEF (2002), girls form the majority of the 120 million children who never go to school in the developing world, and the Nigerian national literacy rate for women is only 56 percent, as compared to 72 percent for males. Among the developing countries of West Africa, Nigeria has a very large population of girls who do not attend school. The *Gender in Nigeria Report* of 2012 ranked the country 118th out of 134 countries on the Gender Equality Index. In some states of Nigeria, for example Sokoto, the female literacy enrollment and achievement rates are especially low. Girls' net enrollment in Sokoto is 15 percent, while that of boys is 59 percent (UNICEF, 2002). This low literacy rate affects the achievement rate of women, and it has no doubt led to the low economic status of women in Nigeria.

In order to understand better this issue, the study presented in this chapter addresses the issue of girls' education from gender and sociocultural perspectives. I argue that the root causes of the low enrollment of Nigerian girls in secondary schools, as compared with boys of the same age group, are gender inequality and discrimination against women in the Nigerian education system. This study considers four main factors that contribute to this problem: (1) gender and religion; (2) sociocultural factors; (3) gender and poverty; and (4) gender and early marriage.

Theoretical Framework

The conceptual framework of this chapter consists of theories of multiculturalism and critical pedagogy. Each of these theories addresses factors that are imperative to achieving educational access, equity, and excellence in a culturally pluralistic society such as Northern Nigeria. Both theories complementarily elucidate inequities in the sense that students from diverse cultural backgrounds can experience educational equality. Multiculturalism and critical pedagogy provide the building blocks for a transformative multicultural pedagogy and praxis for individuals interested in addressing the problem of discrimination in our public school system. These theories explicate the hidden inequities of schools in which cultural attitudes, curricular access, and after-school activities serve as sorting apparatuses that propel students on trajectories of either success or failure. They aid in bringing a focus on a cultural approach grounded in critical pedagogy. I used multiculturalism and critical pedagogy as two theories because many of their concerns and perspectives are relevant to issues of educational access, equity, and excellence in a culturally pluralistic society such as that of Northern Nigeria. I opted for these two theories as the best lenses through which to view the pertinent issues because, when used effectively in classrooms, they help individual students to reach their highest level of competence; both theories make teaching relevant to the students' learning experiences and cultural background; finally, the theories support teaching strategies that incorporate more student engagement.

Multiculturalism and critical pedagogy must be seen as tools that can be used to develop a solution to the gendered problem in Northern Nigerian secondary schools because of the advantages of both theories. In light of this assertion, I have identified three objectives that are essential to creating change and bringing about progress:

1. Provision of interactive learning spaces where all children can engage with each other.
2. Use of a variety of multiple perspectives in lessons that emphasize diversity.

3. Social awareness campaigns that can foster change in the minds of individual men and women, groups, and members of the communities as a whole.

Strategies to achieve higher enrollment in girls' education need to become more integrated in terms of building productive and progressive programs and curriculum. The use of multiple lenses is a basic necessary criterion for providing a comprehensive evaluation of the issues that young girls face in Nigeria's education system, and the theories of multiculturalism and critical pedagogy provide a comprehensive overview in understanding this education system. In order to demonstrate the utility of these two theories, the following sections highlight the background history of Nigerian educational policy, factors responsible for the low enrollment of females in schools, theories of multiculturalism and critical pedagogy, and possible solutions, recommendations, and conclusions.

Historical Background on Educational Policies in Nigeria

Historically, formal education in Nigeria started with the advent of foreign missionaries and the various colonial governments that occupied the region. Nigeria's first colonial policy on education was introduced in 1952, with the aim of providing primary, secondary, and adult education to citizens. Before then, a number of different educational policy reforms had been introduced at different times in the country, in 1935, 1940, and 1945 (Aladekomo, 2004). However, most of these educational reforms were not implemented effectively and efficiently, due to sociocultural reasons such as rapid population growth, lack of political will, and poor management of scarce resources. The formal Nigerian educational system is only one of six components included in basic education in the implementation guidelines of the federal government. Data from the Federal Ministry of Education (1996) show that Nigeria's literacy rate was 52 percent in 1998. Only 40 percent of all heads of households had any education: 21 percent had only primary education, 14 percent had up to secondary education, while only 5 percent had postsecondary education. In 1999, the government formally launched a new Universal Basic Education (UBE) policy, to provide free and compulsory education for all Nigerian children, from primary school up to the junior secondary school level.

Universal Basic Education (UBE) is a broader system than Universal Primary Education, which focuses only on providing educational opportunities for primary school children. UBE stresses the inclusion of girls and women and a number of underserved groups: the poor, street and working children, nomads, minorities, refugees, and the disabled. Former Nigerian president Olusegun Obasanjo launched UBE on September 30, 1999, and he signed the UBE bill into law on May 26, 2004, following its passage by the National Assembly. The UBE act of 2004 makes provision for basic education comprising primary and junior secondary education. The UBE program is Nigeria's strategy for the achievement of education for all.

According to UNICEF (2001), the Nigerian Ministry of Education adopted the African Girls' Education Initiative (AGEI) program to do the following: (1) raise national awareness of girls' education through public campaigns, rallies, and seminars; (2) help develop girl-friendly school environments; and (3) assist communities in sustaining girls' education by reviewing existing curricula and teaching materials for gender-inclusive education. The AGEI was grounded in the premise that by targeting girls, the program would reach a major proportion of the population of children that have been denied access to education. The AGEI initiative was essentially based on a gender-equity approach, which aimed at reducing gender discrimination and promoting increased access to basic education and training for girls. Thus, it is obvious that the AGEI played a useful role in raising the prominence of girls' education as a gender equity issue. According to the evaluation report *Changing Lives of Girls: Evaluation of the African Girls' Education Initiative* (Evaluation Office, 2004), the AGEI contributed to a sustained discussion about the importance of girls' education, and about the best ways to encourage greater female school access. The AGEI has been the centerpiece of UNICEF's effort to promote girls' education. Started in 1994 with funding from the Canadian International Development Agency, it was continued in 1996 with funding from Norway. The initiative was grounded in the premise that by targeting girls, the program would reach a major proportion of the population of children who have been denied access to education.

Over the course of the program, the Norwegian government has provided finances to support AGEI activities in a total of thirty-four countries. With regards to its approach to equity, gender is viewed as a sociocultural construct that supports institutions through which women are systematically discriminated against and maintained in subordinate positions. The AGEI focuses on structural transformations in society to end discriminatory practices.

A wide variety of relatively discreet activities to promote girls' education have been undertaken under the AGEI, ranging from small-scale models (e.g., girls' clubs) to community action and policy development. Other activities include the establishment of satellite schools, girls' hostels, school feeding programs, girl-to-girl tutoring, and teacher training. Some degree of community participation has also been sought for the promotion of girls' enrollment. The 2004 evaluation report shows that the AGEI has been a significant force in making a widespread and meaningful contribution to improving girls' education.

Factors

The above paragraphs highlight the contribution of the AGEI in increasing the enrollment of girls in school. However, in Nigeria, girls' access to basic education, especially in northern states, has remained low. The number of children out of school is particularly high, and few women in the northwest and northeast of the country have attended school. Several factors have been identified for the low enrollment of females in schools. The root causes, based on literature review, include the following: (1) gender and religion; (2) sociocultural factors, which are rooted in patriarchy; (3) gender and poverty; and (4) gender and early marriage.

Gender and Religion

Religion is one major factor affecting girls' education. In the far north, the level of girls' education is the most appalling. This is partly because, apart from the cultural and traditional norms that encourage early marriages, and the purdah system, there is also a deep-seated religious misconception about Western education. Obasi (2003) reports that formal Western-style education was brought by missionaries and was strongly resisted because it was treated with suspicion by Nigerians parents as something alien and threatening to their religion and culture. This negative attitude of parents has contributed to the low number of females enrolled in Northern Nigerian schools. Obasi's (2003) study also reveals the strict observance of the Islamic custom of purdah. Purdah refers to the seclusion of women from the sight of men and from interaction with strangers, both inside and outside the home. However, the Islamic injunction that a girl may be married off once she attains puberty has been misconstrued. Being married does not have to mean that the girl must stop going to school. It is no wonder that Uduigwomen (2004) observes that there is progress in women's education with the exception of Northern Nigeria. With the practice of purdah in Northern Nigeria, where we have the exhibition of the fanatical attitudes of some Muslims that have led to the destruction of lives and churches, Western-style education has almost become an impossible practice to achieve.

The Federation of Nigeria was granted full independence on October 1, 1960. At the Nigerian independence ceremonies, Jaja Wachuku, the first Nigerian speaker of the House of Representatives, received Nigeria's Freedom Charter. The federal government was given exclusive powers in defense, foreign relations, and commercial and fiscal policy. Political parties tended to reflect the makeup of the three main ethnic groups. The Nigerian People's Congress represented the conservative, Muslim, and largely Hausa people who dominated the northern region. The northern region consisted of three-quarters of the land area and more than half the population of Nigeria. The National Council of Nigerian Citizens represented the interests of the Igbo and Christian-dominated people of the Eastern Region of Nigeria, and the Action Group represented the interests of the Yoruba people in the west.

Despite rapid changes in the sphere of education in independent Nigeria and the attempt to create a unified system of education, there is a lingering fear, especially among the illiterate, that education exposes their children to alien Christian influences. Parents feel that Western-style education is contrary to their faith and way of life (Sulaiman, 1978). It is believed among the Muslims that women, who are the embodiment of Islamic values and the custodians of Islamic morality, should be guarded against the corruption of unsuitable schooling (Sulaiman, 1978).

An analysis of the implications of fear exhibited by Muslim parents regarding the influence of Western education yields many constrains on female access to education in Northern Nigeria. These constrains could be a result of the "non-conscious ideology" that Muslim parents hold, which Bem (1993) discusses in his book *The Lenses of Gender: Transforming the Debate ōn Sexual Inequality.* He defines the concept of nonconscious ideology to describe how implicit beliefs and attitudes are used to maintain the status quo in terms of gender inequality. These constraints include (1) family values and beliefs that do not value education for girls; (2) economic constraints; and (3) the views of some parents that educating a girl is counterproductive to arranging a good marriage for her (Bem, 1993).

Sociocultural Factors

Gender inequality marginalizes women. Oppression is a large factor in the subordination and status of women. This subordination originates in the family and in society. Sensoy and DiAngelo's (2011) studies indicate that women are offered less educational opportunity than men in the Northern Nigeria, which stems from its patriarchal structure, and many parents in the north would prefer not to enroll their daughters in schools due to their misconception of the influence of Western education.

This discrimination against women is also a form of oppression, which Sensoy and DiAngelo (2011) argue is embedded in all dimensions of culture. It is a multidimensional imbalance of social, political, and institutional power that builds up over time and then becomes normalized and acceptable to most people in the society. Oppression is a process of assigning pervasive and political relationships of unequal power among members of social groups. Aladekomo (2004) asserts that because Northern Nigerian society, tradition, and religion support male authority and superiority, privilege is embedded in being a member of the dominant group (which in this case allows men to be given priority when it comes to education) that occupies the positions of power.

According to Aladekomo's (2004) findings, a major deterrent to female education is a near-universal, fundamental, cultural bias in favor of males' power and privilege. There is the widespread patriarchal system of social organization, as well as a generally lower regard for the value of female life. In Africa, Nigeria included, the male child is preferred to the female. When a male is born, both father and mother believe that an heir is born. A woman who has only female children feels highly insecure in the eyes of her husband's family. The result is that a high premium is placed on the male child. This preference is also shown in terms of giving education to children. If a family must train only one child because of lack of funds, the child to be trained is usually the male child, since it is believed that the girl will leave the home one day for another man's home. So, in order not to "waste" funds on her, it is better to train the male, who will stay at home and thus be able to contribute to the family economically. This practice has had a tremendous effect on the enrollment of females in schools.

Gender and Poverty

Poverty has remained another major factor militating against the education of girls. According to Gordon et al. (2003) and Chapa and Valencia (1993), poverty is the main correlate of limited educational achievement, since it leads to lack of access to education, which is a denial of choices and opportunities. It contributes to social discrimination and to the exclusion of individuals and communities. In Nigeria, women and girls have been most affected by the negative effects of structural adjustment programs, due to the rapid decrease in the economic capacity of parents and guardians to meet the school needs of their children. A structural adjustment program was introduced in 1986 by General Ibrahim Babangida. Its emphasis was on reducing government expenditures and on the privatization of government-owned enterprises. The failure to achieve the goals of this reform program has led to an increased level of poverty. Obasi (2003) notes that economic hardships mean that about 70 percent of the Nigerian population lives below the poverty line, and most often girls are withdrawn from school to generate income by selling in markets. Nigerian women experience poverty economically through deprivation, politically through marginalization, and socially through discrimination.

Despite the fact that Western education was long ago introduced in Nigeria, the country has yet to attain 100 percent success in educating its citizens. The main problem, to a very large extent, is poverty. As Igbuzor points out (2006), many Nigerians are living below the poverty level. Indications of this poverty can be seen in welfare costs, health and housing problems, loss of tax income, and lack of jobs, just to mention a few examples. Duncan and Brooks-Gunn (2001) assert that poverty, especially family poverty, affects the education of schoolchildren. Family poverty and the socioeconomic status of the family significantly impact children's cognitive and educational outcomes in schools. A good percentage of children and youth in Nigeria leave primary and secondary schools before completing their legally required number of years of education. The inability to complete their studies may be due to lack of funds, a poor background in academics (which is manifested in poor writing and reading), and poor family status.

Another consequence of poverty for educational outcomes, according to Duncan and Brooks-Gunn (2001), is that these poor students are generally less equipped to undertake a school program. Parents are not in the position to provide most of their children's needs, such as textbooks and good uniforms, nor do they have the ability to pay their children's fees. Poverty has pushed many families allow their girls to be used in child trafficking, which is more dangerous than engaging a child as a domestic servant. Child trafficking involves taking the girl outside her location, at times also outside the country, and forcing her into prostitution, sexual exploitation, or forced labor.

Gender and Early Child's Marriage

Early marriage has really affected the education of women in Nigeria. Nigerian girls are usually given in marriage as early as eleven or twelve years of age. Since the culture of the northern Hausa people in Nigeria defines the woman's role as primarily that of housewife, education seems to have little relevance for the roles women are expected to play. According to Adesina (1982), in some countries marriage is not thought to be compatible with continued schooling. Parents express the fear that going to school will make girls lose their interest in their role as a housewife. It has been discovered that women who marry very early, with little or no education, tend to remain in the lower economic classes all of their lives, as indicated in Adesina's (1982) research. The case of truncating school for married life may not be limited to Nigeria alone; it also occurs in some other African countries, such as Tanzania, Malawi, and Central African Republic. Many people in Tanzania believe that educating girls is like watering another man's garden. In Nigeria, parents in coastal areas prefer marrying off their daughters once they reach eighteen years of age. To these parents, if a girl gets a good husband, the parents need not worry about educating her.

Access to quality education is another factor that girl education has to contend with, even when the family has some funds for school fees. This is because quality education puts the girls on a good pedestal in terms of job opportunities and being able to express themselves in public. As a result of limited access, the girl has to be content with the quality of education within her vicinity. Some Nigerian parents even believe that it is not right for girls to be as well educated as the boys. These same parents, especially those in rural areas, do not know the difference between getting an education and getting a quality education.

Discussion

Although critical pedagogy began to appear in educational scholarship a decade or so after the initiation of multicultural education, they are mirror images of each other. Both theories represent variations on the imperative of achieving educational equity, access, excellence, and social equity for culturally diverse groups. Both are at once a philosophy and a methodology. As philosophies, they constitute a set of beliefs that value educational processes that celebrate individual diversity, autonomy, and empowerment. As methodologies, they are approaches to education that are driven by critical analysis, multiple perspectives, cultural pluralism, sociocultural contextualism in instructional processes, and expected learning outcomes (Giroux, 1992).

In fact, the term "multiculturalism" is commonly used to refer to collective movements that demand inclusion, respect for differences, and equal rights for the values and worldviews of many economically disadvantaged and culturally marginalized groups (Rogler et al., 1987). Multiculturalism is a social-intellectual movement that promotes the value of diversity as a core principle and insists that all cultural groups be treated with respect and as equals. Multiculturalism advocates for the recognition of the rights of all people and equal dignity for the entire citizenry.

Sue and Sue beautifully express that multiculturalism

> extols the right of different groups to follow their unique path to development, free from the imposition of other groups' norms and standards, since all people must be allowed to unfold toward their unique destinies, which requires resisting external pressure and other inducements of another culture. Many multiculturalists have argued that the challenge of true multiculturalism is in working toward a cohesive society while understanding, respecting, and protecting cultural differences. (1990, p. 105)

Wink (2011) defines critical pedagogy as learning, relearning, and unlearning that transforms us and our world for the better. Critical pedagogy gives us the courage to say what we have lived, and it challenges us to question our long-held assumptions. It calls us to critical reflection and complete reexamination of our beliefs (pp. 12–35). For Wink, learning, which is very challenging, always leads to relearning, and relearning often involves a shift in methodology. Relearning takes place when students teach teachers all those things they did not learn in teacher education. Unlearning involves a shift in beliefs and assumptions.

Critical pedagogy asks us to reflect deeply and to take action on our new and emerging ideas. It moves us from passivity to the level of knowing that we know, meaning that we have voice and the courage to question ourselves and the roles we are playing in maintaining our educational processes. Critical pedagogy, according to Wink (2011), is about finding the power of our own voice, our own knowledge, our own experiences, coming to know that we know. Critical pedagogy is like a lens that enables us to see more clearly, more critically, and more keenly.

The foundational principles of critical pedagogy and multicultural education emphasize economic, political, and ethical analyses of how schools routinely perpetuate inequalities among marginalized ethnic, social-class, and cultural groups, and how they violate their rights. Inherent in these analyses is a concerted effort to link schooling with liberation. Critical pedagogues see schools as "agencies of social and cultural reproduction, exercising power through the underlying interests embodied in the overt and hidden curricula" (Aronowitz and Giroux 1985, p. 143).

The ideological relationship between critical pedagogy and multicultural education is parallel and complementary. Their terrains are closely juxtaposed and overlap. The underlying philosophy of multicultural education is, in essence, a form of pedagogy (Giroux, 1992), and its content and strategies can be perceived as a set of methodological tools for translating and contextualizing general principles of critical pedagogy with respect to the specific educational needs of socially, culturally, and ethnically different students who have been marginalized and oppressed by schools. Both have transformative and revolutionary potential for reforming education because of their inherent conviction that school practices can be transformed in order to better embrace and emulate the cultural, racial, social, and ethnic pluralism that characterizes society. Both provide a transformative multicultural pedagogy and praxis to individuals interested in resolving the problems of discrimination in public schools.

Both multicultural education and critical pedagogy refocus the role of schools as agents of socialization and cultural transmission. Schools must become places where everyone learns how their destinies are inextricably linked, where inequities and injustices are examined critically, and where a commitment to collective struggle to improve the quality of life is cultivated. Students from all social backgrounds and cultural groups must be allowed to find their own voices, develop a sense of individual and collective identity, and learn how to act upon their commitments to personal and social well-being (Giroux, 1981). Both theories situate the debate over the primary purpose of education in broader contexts, rather than restricting it to the narrow domain of preparation for economic purposes.

Solutions

For responsible practices and possible creative solutions to the problem of gender discrimination against female education in Northern Nigerian secondary schools, I elaborate in this section on the following points: provision of learning space for all children to interact with each other; multiple perspectives that emphasize diversity;

and building awareness and changing the mind-set of individual men and women, groups, and members of the communities as a whole.

Provision of Learning Space for All Children to Interact with Each Other

I identify oppression as part of gender discrimination in female education in Northern Nigerian secondary schools. Kumashiro (2000) defines oppression as a situation in which certain people (in this context men) are privileged in society, while others (women) are marginalized. To address oppression and build equity in the school system, Kumashiro (2000) argues, schools need to provide learning space for *all* children to interact with each other. He further maintains that educators need to acknowledge and embrace diversity among their students, and to teach in ways that are equitable, so as to connect their teaching personally with their students. Evidence of this diversity among students' population is obvious from the results of my personal interviews with principals, teachers, students, parents, and guardians, during my Fulbright-Hays Doctoral Dissertation Research Abroad field data collection program in Nigeria. For example, students from several schools in Ibadan (T. L. Oyesina Model Secondary School Monatan; Monatan High School; The International School, University of Ibadan; and Marverick College, Samonda, Ibadan) were from families with different cultural and linguistic backgrounds. Their differences of language reflect the multiethnicity of Nigerian culture.

Multiple Perspectives

Morrish (2009) identifies the following factors that constrain girls' participation in schooling: (a) family values and beliefs that do not value education for girls; (b) economic constraints on the family, often centering on the need for girls' labor in the home; and (c) the view of some parents that educating a girl is counterproductive to arranging a good marriage for her. This study supports the approach employed by the AGEI in experimenting with a wide variety of activities to promote girls' education. It highlights the importance of using multiple perspectives to study multiple cultures. The AGEI approach is generally viewed as a positive feature, because many interventions are tested, and the most effective are identified for possible use.

The approaches used to study multiple perspectives on issues and school events should be equally diverse so as to be interdisciplinary. All of these approaches are combined to teach students that when any school event is experienced by many different people, it generates multiple realities. In the quest for knowledge, truth, and human understanding, these different realities are worthy of careful analysis. In the language of critical pedagogy, broadening the boundaries of knowledge provides students with opportunities to reexamine their presumptions about cultural preference, and to learn about cultural systems other than their own. Banks (1990) explains that when broader pedagogy contextualizes learning in different cultural perspectives and experiences, it facilitates students becoming border crossers as they explore different cultural realms of meaning, social relations, and bodies of knowledge.

Attitude Change

Another solution to the low enrollment of female students in Northern Nigerian secondary schools is both the government and private agencies undertaking social awareness campaigns that can foster change in the minds of individual men and women, groups, and community members in general. Female enrollment in the rural regions of Northern Nigeria is likely to continue to be restricted unless attitudes can be changed. Deeply engrained ideas are not likely to change unless education comes to be viewed as an economic and social necessity. The first strategy involves complete change of the mind-set of both women and men regarding the importance of female education. Byrne and Baron's (1997) studies have demonstrated the extensive relationship between attitudes and behavior change, and it is likely that an effective campaign on attitude change can contribute to the elimination of gender bias and discrimination. Access to education is very important, but it is not sufficient to increase women's effective participation in the region. An integrated approach to both education and training is required for success, and this integrated approach involves changes in the negative personal and collective attitudes of individuals, groups, and communities.

Recommendations and Conclusion

An emphasis on girls' access to basic education is not sufficient in the Nigerian context. Large-scale girls' education initiatives need to balance improving gender equity in school access with promoting equality in female participation in leadership in society. I contend that the strategies to achieve higher enrollment in girls' education need to be intersectoral. That is, the approach should be inclusive of men and boys and consider them as partners, as opposed to viewing them as part of the problems faced by girls and women.

Schools should encourage enrollment of girls through using *multicultural language diversity* in the school curriculum. This means that schools should broaden their enrollment to include students from different cultural and language backgrounds. Schools should also be more conscientious of working with families from diverse cultural and linguistic backgrounds. When this happens, schools become more flexible, responsive, child centered, culturally sensitive, community linked, and family connected, according to Haynes, Gebreyesus, and Comer (1993, p. 165). Students need to be multicultural in their cultural orientation so that they can interact in a "pluralistic, multiethnic environment" (Falicov, 1998, p. 74) where they will have freedom to invent themselves as they create unique blends of cultural identity, and where they will be guided by the stable social controls of group norms.

Universalism is one of the components of multicultural language diversity. A universalist position maintains that families are more alike than different; this position emphasizes similarities rather than differences in interpersonal processes. This is the antithesis of the particularist position, which states that families are more different than they are alike, recognizing and respecting the uniqueness of each family (Falicov, 1998, pp. 271–75). The goal of universalism is the ability to see the universal human similarities that unite us beyond color, class, ethnicity, and gender, while simultaneously recognizing and respecting culture-specific differences that do exist due to color, class, ethnicity, and gender (Falicov, 1998, p. 275). With this goal in mind, people would be participating in what Hardwood (1994) called "global culture" (quoted in Falicov, 1998, p. 71), which promotes coexistence of cultural meanings and behaviors. Global culture encourages a cultural and personal dialogue that takes into account all meanings of intercultural relations. The American Psychological Association's *Guidelines for Providers of Psychological Services to Ethnic, Linguistic, and Culturally Diverse Populations* (1990) outlines two practical approaches to encourage intercultural dialogue:

1. Respecting the unique character of all cultural groups: Multiculturalists and psychologists are called on to celebrate the variety of cultural groups encountered and recognize them as unique and equal contributions to humanity since there are profound differences in moral perspectives across

cultures. The Guidelines encourage us to work "within the cultural setting . . . if there is a conflict between cultural values and human rights" (p. 4).

2. Cultural equality as a universal standard: Central to multiculturalism is the equal value of all cultures; and this equality seems to require a radical relativism in which each culture can only be understood and evaluated on its own terms (American Psychological Association, 1990).

The guidelines represent general principles that are designed to provide suggestions in working with ethnic, linguistic, and culturally diverse populations. The guidelines acknowledge that understanding of ethnicity and culture impacts behavior, enhancing the ability to address the needs of particular ethnic group more appropriately and effectively. With regard to recognizing cultural diversity, it admits the role that culture plays in the economic development of ethnic and culturally diverse populations. The guidelines understand the interaction of culture, gender, and sexual orientation on behavior and needs. This study has reiterated that girls' access to basic education is not enough without arriving at an equilibrium between gender equity and schooling. This study has made the case that the strategies to achieve higher enrollment of girls in school should entail an inclusive approach.

Conclusion

Discrimination against women in the Nigerian educational system has been a topic of interest to educators. Factors examined in this chapter that are responsible for the low enrollment of females in schools are gender and religion, sociocultural factors, gender and poverty, and gender and early marriage. Multiculturalism and critical pedagogy frameworks address the factors that are imperative to achieving educational access, equity, and excellence in a culturally pluralistic society such as Northern Nigeria. For creative solutions to the problem of gender discrimination against female education in Northern Nigerian secondary schools, the following three points were presented: (1) provision of learning space for all children to interact with each other; (2) multiple perspectives that emphasize diversity; and (3) building awareness and changing the mind-set of individual men and women, groups, and community members. I recommend further that strategies to achieve higher enrollment in girls' education be intersectoral, and that schools adopt "multicultural language diversity" in their curriculum.

REFERENCES

Adesina, S. (1982). *Planning and educational development in Nigeria*. Lagos: Board Publications.

Aladekomo, O. F. (2004). Nigeria education policy and entrepreneurship. *Journal of Social Science 9*(2), 75–83.

American Psychological Association (1990). Guidelines for providers of psychological services to ethnic, linguistic, and culturally diverse populations. Washington, DC. Retrieved from http://www.apa.org/pi/oema/resources/policy/provider-guidelines.aspx.

Aronowitz, S., & Giroux, H. A. (1985). *Education under siege: The conservative, liberal, and radical debate over schooling*. South Hadley, MA: Bergin and Garvey.

Banks, J. A. (1990). Citizenship education for a pluralistic democratic society. *Social Studies 81*(2), 210–12.

Bem, S. L. (1993). *The lenses of gender: Transforming the debate on sexual inequality*. New Haven: Yale University Press.

Byrne, D., & Baron, R. A. (1997). *Social psychology.* 8th ed. Boston: Allyn & Bacon.

Chapa, J., & Valencia, R. R. (1993). Latino population growth, demographic characteristics, and educational stagnation: An examination of recent trends. *Hispanic Journal of Behavioral Sciences 15*(2), 165–87.

Duncan, G. J., & Brooks-Gunn, J. (2001). Poverty, welfare, and children's achievement. In B. J. Biddle (ed.), *Social class, poverty, and education: Policy and practice*. New York: Routledge.

Evaluation Office, UNICEF (2004). Changing lives of girls: Evaluation of the African Girls' Education Initiative. Retrieved from http://www.unicef.org/evaldatabase/index_25900.html.

Falicov, C. J. (1998). *Latino families in therapy: A guide to multicultural practice*. New York: Guilford Press.

Federal Ministry of Education. 1996. *The development of education, 1994–1996*. National Report of Nigerian Education Statistics. International Conference on Education, 45th Session, Geneva, 1996.

Giroux, H. A. (1981). *Ideology, culture and the process of schooling*. Philadelphia: Temple University Press.

Giroux, H. A. (1992). Educational leadership and the crisis of democratic government. *Educational Researcher 21*(4), 4–11.

Gordon, D., Nandy, S., Pantazis, C., Pemberton, S., & Townsend, P. (2003). *Child poverty in the developing world.* Bristol: Policy Press.

Hardwood, A. (1994). Acculturation in the postmodern world: Implications for mental health research. In R. G. Malgady & O. Rodriguez (eds.), *Theoretical and Conceptual Issues in Hispanic Mental Health.* Malabar, FL: Krieger.

Haynes, N. M., Gebreyesus, S., & Comer, J. P. (1993). *Selected case studies of national implementation of the school development program.* New Haven: Yale Child Study Center.

Igbuzor, O. (2006). Review of Nigeria millennium development goals 2005 report. A review presented at the MDG/GCAP Nigeria planning meeting held in Abuja, Nigeria, March 9, 2006.

Kumashiro, K. (2000). Toward a theory of anti-oppressive education. *Review of Educational Research 70*(1), 25–53.

Morrish, A. (2009). *Marriage and family life*. Lagos: Zoe Publishing and Printing Company. 105–15.

Obasi, E. (2003). Structural adjustment and gender access to education in Nigeria. *Gender and Education 9*(2), 161–65.

Rogler, L. H., Malgady, R. G., Constantino, G., & Blumenthal, R. (1987). What does culturally sensitive mental health services mean? The case of Hispanics. *American Psychologist 47*, 565–70.

Sensoy, O., & DiAngelo, R. (2011). *Is everyone really equal? An introduction to key concepts in social justice education.* New York: Teacher College Press.

Sue, D. W., & Sue, S. (1990). *Counseling the culturally different: Theory and practice*. New York: Wiley.

Sulaiman, I. (1978). Development of Islamic education in Nigeria. Keynote address at opening session of the International Islamic seminar, Bayero University, Kano, Nigeria.

Uduigwomen, A. F. (2004). A philosophy of education for Nigerian women: Problems and prospects. *African Symposium 4*(1). Retrieved from http://www2.ncsu.edu/necs/aern/udomen.html.

United Nations International Children's Emergency Fund (UNICEF) (2001). *Children's and women's rights in Nigeria: A wake-up call, situation assessment and analysis*. Lagos: UNICEF.

United Nations International Children's Emergency Fund (UNICEF) (2002). *The state of the world's children*. New York: UNICEF.

Wink, J. (2011). *Critical pedagogy: Notes from the real world.* 4th ed. Upper Saddle River, NJ: Pearson Educational.

Surviv-ing

An African American Man Reconstructing Masculinity through Literacy

Barbara Guzzetti and Mellinee Lesley

Hold fast to dreams
For if dreams die
Life is a broken-winged bird
That cannot fly

—Langston Hughes

Contemporary researchers have called for studies of cultural notions about masculinity and their relationship to men's everyday lives, including men's engagement in literacy practices (Gottzen, 2011; Kehler, 2013). All too often, from their early years boys have received a literacy education in school that "reinscribes normative masculinity and limitations stemming from strategies that perpetuate and legitimize a 'boys will be boys' position" where little is expected of their academic performance (Kehler, 2013, p. 121). Teachers' perceptions of masculinity have typically equated enactment of masculinity with physical prowess (Haase, 2010) and aggression (Neal, 2003). Boys themselves often consider hard work in school to be incompatible with enacting "cool" masculinities (Bean & Ransaw, 2013; Jackson & Dempster, 2009). Further, several researchers have noted that engaging in literacy practices, such as reading a book or writing a letter, has been described as acting White for Black boys (Buck, 2010) and socially self-ostracizing (Bean & Ransaw, 2013).

Yet young men's lack of engagement in literacy, particularly for African American males, is an issue that is more complex than simple opposition to academic achievers and requires nuanced understandings of cultural and relational contexts (Bean & Ransaw, 2013; hooks, 2004a, 2004b; Tatum, 2005a). Although there is a distinct literary tradition of African American men creating an intellectual legacy for other African American men (e.g., Gaines, 1993), few studies or public sharings of men's literacy practices have highlighted Black men's writing, either for each other or for a wider audience (e.g., Smith et al., 2013). As a result, more needs to be known about how African American men represent and enact masculinity through their literacy practices.

This issue of contemporary masculinity performance is timely and important to pursue, as the educational outlook for boys and young men is stark (Bristol, 2015). Boys are more likely to underachieve and drop out of school than girls, and they lag behind girls in both reading and mathematics (UNESCO, 2012). Boys of color and those from poor or working-class families are more likely than their White or middle-class peers to exhibit detrimental in-school and out-of-school outcomes and tend to be academic underachievers compared to their female peers (UNESCO, 2012, 2014). President Barack Obama has declared that boys and young men of color face some of the most severe challenges of the twenty-first century (Goldfarb & Wilson, 2014).

Descriptive statistics illustrate these challenges and indicate racial disparities in performance and achievement in education. African American males are two to three times more likely to be suspended from school than are White students, and African American boys perform below their While male and African American female peers (Aratani, Wight, & Cooper, 2011). Data from 2003 to 2009 indicate that by fourth grade, African American boys score lower in reading than White boys, and this gap has remains at eighth grade. Research sponsored by the Schott Foundation for Public Education (2015) predicted a 59 percent high school graduation rate for African American males, compared to 80 percent for White males, for 2012–2013. Further, research has indicated that the time parents can give to supporting and reinforcing their children's learning contributes to these racial gaps in achievement (National Education Association, 2012–15). Research from the National Center for Children in Poverty indicates that 61 percent of African American children live in low-income families, as compared to 28 percent of White children (Jiang, Ekono,

& Skinner, 2015). African American homes are more likely to have fathers who have no full-time, year-round job (51 percent), compared to 27 percent of White children (Barton & Coley, 2007). One in every 15 African American men is incarcerated, in comparison to 1 in every 106 White men (Kerby, 2012). African American children are twice as likely as other children to live in single-parent homes (Kids Count, 2014).

Despite these data, there is little extant research on fathers' participation in their children's education or how men become involved as active parenting partners (Gottzen, 2011). Prominent discourses around motherhood have perpetuated gendered divisions of labor where mothers are seen as primary caregivers and fathers as breadwinners (Griffith & Smith, 2005). Minority fathers who are not present in children's lives tend to distance themselves from their children by believing that raising a child is a mother's responsibility (Ivery, 2014). Cultural notions of fatherhood and discourses around parental practices represent discursive struggles on how to understand culturally acceptable fatherhood (Forsberg, 2007). Recent research has indicated the need for, and significance of, studying how cultural notions of masculinity relate to men's everyday practices, such as men's parenting and literacy practices (Gottzen, 2011).

Yet there is a paucity of current research on the parental relationship between African American men and their children (Smith et al., 2005). Typically, African American men have not been associated with active parenting or involvement in their children's education either formally or informally (Ransaw, 2014). Media portrayals of Black men perpetuate stereotypes of African American men as absentee fathers—both physically and emotionally—who are financially irresponsible, hypermasculine, and uninvolved (Smith et al., 2005; Smith, 2013).

Although inactive parenting can contribute to racial disparities in achievement, classroom environments that are not culturally relevant and sensitive also perpetuate African American boys distancing themselves from academics (Bristol, 2015; Tatum, 2006). These students often have to deal with negative stereotypes in schools. As Archer and Yamashita (2003) note, "Working-class, inner city and certain minority ethnic young men have been positioned as high profile problems within current social and educational policy discourses" (p. 115). Even the texts African American youth encounter in classrooms typically ignore their cultural contexts and their desires for self-definition and identity development, further distancing them from relevant and appealing literacy instruction (Tatum, 2006).

Although classroom environments like these can lead to boys' disengagement (UNESCO, 2012), schools are still considered one of the last remaining social institutions able to address social inequities (Bristol, 2015). Schools can be sites of social critique and deconstruction of hegemonic models of what it means to be male (Bean & Ransaw, 2013). In addition, culturally relevant texts can serve as "soft" role models in the absence of physical role models and help boys and young men develop their self-concepts and identities (Tatum, 2006).

Therefore, studies of how and why men choose to write beyond their schooling years and how they represent inclusive performances of masculinity in doing so can provide important implications for supporting and motivating young men to engage in transformative literate practices. Recent research has indicated the need for and significance of studying how cultural notions of masculinity relate to men's everyday practices, such as their literacy and parenting practices (Gottzen, 2011). Identifying models of how African American males write against the stereotypical notions of masculinity performance can supply alternative portrayals of what it means to be a man. Such texts can serve as archetypes for the deconstruction of narrow views of masculine identity in schools and offer new constructions of masculine performance.

Our Purpose

This case study (Stake, 1995) focuses on investigating the triangulated role of being an African American, male, a father, and an author writing against hegemonic structures through self-publications called "zines." Zines incorporate aspects of print literacy as well as new digital literacies, as zines often have an online presence through e-zines or are extended and advertised through the zinester's social media. They have been referred to as new media or new literacies by literacy researchers (e.g., Knobel & Lankshear, 2012). We focused this study around the question, *How does Jonas Cannon* [our subject participant] *construct notions of masculinities as an African American man through the zines he publishes?* More specifically, we wondered about the ways Jonas Cannon problematized masculinity through his writing. In examining this question, we explored the intersections of multiple subjectivities—race, social class, and gender—in describing how notions of masculinity are performed and represented in one adult male zinester's writing.

We intended to contribute to the literature that presents alternative representations, counternarratives, and discourses around the enactment of masculinity through literacy. We also anticipated offering a model for overcoming the perpetuation of hegemonic pedagogy in literacy instruction for African American adolescents. We hoped to identify "complex identities and inequities across race, ethnicity, gender and class" and provide an alternative model of masculinity that would allow for more inclusive performances of gender roles and representations that would have implications for writing instruction for young men (Archer & Yamashita, 2003, p. 115).

The Researchers

Barbara, the first author, became interested in gendered expectations for African American boys' participation and achievement in literacy in the late 1960s following the surge of the civil rights movement. As an undergraduate doing an internship in Chicago's School District 8 at an upper-grade center and high school that had predominantly African American student populations, she observed boys' low to nonexistent expectations for their own academic achievement. A contributing factor may have been that their teachers tended to emphasize discipline over academics; the old adage "Don't smile until Christmas" was common advice among faculty primarily concerned with establishing and maintaining control in their classrooms.

When Barbara became a fifth-grade classroom teacher for five years at the first half of the 1970s, she chose to teach at a target school where the student population was 98 percent African American and the faculty was 75 percent African American. The school was recognized by the Florida State Board of Education as having one of the most innovative programs in the nation for addressing students' reading achievement and raising expectations for students' success. Yet the African American boys in Barbara's classroom continued to demonstrate low levels of engagement in literacy and academics outside of school; they voiced concerns about avoiding the gang-related activity their relatives and friends were involved in at the time; and they spoke of their futures as limited to blue-collar jobs or careers in sports. Barbara's home visits revealed that most of their homes were matriarchal, lacking role models of educated and successful African American men. Since students are the best predictors of their own success (Hattie, 2012), it is important that African American boys have role models of men of their own race who can help them envision academics as a way to a future with limitless possibilities.

Flashing forward to the present day, once a week, Mellinee, the second author, works as a writing coach at an urban high school with a predominantly low-income, African American and Hispanic student population. This volunteer work is important to Mellinee because she believes that a philosophy of writing pedagogy reminiscent of Tatum and Gue's (2010, p. 91) "raw writing" and "writing to live" is critical for creating academic opportunities for this population of learners, especially for African American male adolescents. The students Mellinee works with have many stories to tell that do not always fit within the structures of schooling and the twenty-six-line essay high school students must compose for their mandated state assessment. Restricting writing instruction to the perimeters of state-mandated, on-demand writing tests limits the possibilities of discovery and a sense of purpose for writing that is important for adolescents to acquire. This is particularly true for historically disenfranchised adolescents.

As educators and literacy researchers, we brought these lenses to the present study of a thirty-six-year-old African American zinester, Jonas, who came from a working-class, inner-city background, to examine his sense-making of masculinities and impetus for writing zines. We wanted to understand his trajectory for writing from adolescence to adulthood. We wanted to understand his identity as an adult male writer and the ways race and gender shaped his perspectives.

Theoretical Framework

This study was informed by contemporary perspectives on masculinity and a theory that views gender as socially constructed through personal interactions, relationships, education, and reminders of appropriateness produced and reproduced through individuals' social actions (Alexander, 2006; Kimmel, 2002; Kimmel & Messner, 2007). Men are taught gender performance through their social interactions. Further, men's social relations may both constrain and enable the development and enactment of gender (Lusher, 2011; Connell, 2005).

In gender studies, the concept of manhood is distinctive from masculinity. Manhood is seen as the ideas and ideals about what it means to be a man that men construct for themselves. These constructs are formed through social interactions although there is room for multiple definitions of manhood (Hunter & Davis, 1992). In essence, manhood pertains to how men see themselves as men. Masculinity is generally defined as the socially constructed and influenced behaviors, demonstrations, or performances of men that emerge from constructions of manhood

(Dancy, 2011). Masculinity concerns the behaviors and performances that result from manhood constructions (Dancy, 2011). In essence, masculinity constitutes the ways men enact notions of manhood. In this manner, masculinity theory posits that masculinity is identity performance or a social construction that is subject to change and critique with the hope of transforming stereotypical social scripts and their enactments (Bean & Harper, 2007). Masculinities are constantly under construction; evolving versions of the performance of masculinity are discursively constructed and positioned and subject to being reworked (Archer & Yamashita, 2003).

Connell & Messerschmidt (2005) also note that there are internal contradictions within masculinities and a multiplicity of ways masculinities are enacted. Connell (1996) argues not all masculinities have equal power. This is particularly the case for ethnic minority masculinities where there is a hierarchy of hegemony in which one masculinity is culturally dominant. Connell (2005) explains, "Hegemonic masculinity is hegemonic not just in relation to other masculinities, but in relation to the gender order as a whole" (p. 17). Thus, not all masculinities are dominant or even visible in mainstream society.

For African American men, the performance of masculinity is typically portrayed by the media as acting cold, distant, and hypermasculine (Kirkland, 2013b). These stereotypical representations of gender affirm masculinity by avoiding behaviors that are considered to be feminine (Bean & Ransaw, 2013) and outside the construction of masculinity, such as engaging in traditional literacy practices (Archer & Yamahita, 2003). Resistance to academic interests may for some African American males stem from the notion that engaging in academics is not acting "cool" (Bean & Ransaw, 2013).

Yet the performance of masculinity is complex, influenced by ideologies and interpersonal relationships that may present competing views of gender performance (McKenry et al., 1989). What counts as literacy practice for young Black men may differ from traditional notions of academic literacy. African American males may find more relevance in their literacy practices in out-of-school contexts where youth are stimulated to tell their stories and author their lives in alternative forms and formats (Kirkland, 2013a; 2013b). Therefore, the performance of masculinity needs to be understood within the nuanced and relational contexts of lived experience where Black men have agency to overcome hegemonic views of masculinity (Bean & Ransaw, 2013; Noguera, 2003) and challenge dominant notions of masculinity and literacy performance (Kehler, 2008; Kirkland, 2013b).

Our Participant

For this study, we focused on one thirty-six-year-old African American male zinester, Jonas Cannon. Jonas grew up on the South Side of the segregated city of Chicago, which is mostly populated by African Americans, but after college he migrated to the city's north-side community of Andersonville, an area mostly populated by Whites, to be geographically closer to his job and his friends. Jonas has a bachelor's degree in English and works at a commercial company as a self-described "office lackey," but he dreams of taking up the teaching profession. Jonas is currently married with an infant son.

Jonas identified himself as a member of the middle class despite his upbringing in a working-class family. His mother worked as a professional psychic, and his father was employed in a series of blue-collar jobs as a postal worker, grocery bagger, school janitor, trucker, and construction worker. Jonas's father was also twice arrested during his youth—once for fighting and once for impersonating a police officer. Jonas recalled wearing cheap and "ratty" second-hand clothes to high school, being ridiculed, and beaten up several times for his appearance (resulting in a suspension from school), his father filing for bankruptcy three times, and eating breakfast for dinner when his family's money was sparse.

Jonas described college as a "revelation" and a "breakthrough" where everything changed for him. He reported that doors that were closed to him in high school suddenly opened up in college. He met a variety of people, including vegans, straight-edge kids or those who eschew drugs and premarital sex, stoners, anarchists, and socialists who lived together within the same college community in a small town, in striking contrast to the big city, where dividing lines between these groups were clearly set.

Jonas related to punk culture throughout high school and college by listening to punk music, attending punk shows, wearing punk clothes, and having friends who represented that alternative lifestyle. He still considers himself to be a member of the punk community, assimilating more of the culture of punk than the music. He embraces the punk ethic that scrutinizes and rejects the culture of consumerism and capitalism. The do-it-yourself (DIY) ethos of punk inspired his production of zines as alternative or indie media when he first began zining in high school. To disseminate his current zines, Jonas has annually attended the largest zine fests in the nation held in Chicago, Los Angeles, and Portland, Oregon.

The Zines

Jonas has authored six issues of a zine, *Cheer the Eff Up*, a collection of personal narratives, or perzines. In these issues, Jonas writes to his infant son (for him to read when he gets older); to other zinesters; and to those experiencing a quarter-life crisis. Each issue had a theme, commencing with the first issue on reconciling the past, from its troublesome adolescence, to a restless but complacent present. The second issue centered on trauma and how people define themselves in light of a traumatic experience; the third issue focused on activism; the fourth issue related tales of depression and coping; the fifth issue addressed identity; and his sixth zine focused on the nature of friendship, change, and overcoming loss.

Much of Jonas's writing consisted of stories that contain the common theme of conflict. For example, Jonas reported his experiences with personal conflict in attempting to reconcile the lifestyle he is passionate about as an activist and anarchist with the lifestyle that pays his bills. Each one of Jonas's zines was created in black and white with handprinted or typed text strategically placed in cut-and-paste style on their pages. Minimal graphics consisted of photographs and hand-drawn illustrations. Each issue of his zine grew longer, ranging from twenty pages in the first issue to fifty-five pages in issue 6.

In addition to this zine, Jonas edited two issues of another zine, *Srviv.* In this zine, he and his contributors, each well known in the zine community, responded to Jonas' query "What gets you out of bed in the morning?" This zine was characterized by a cut-and-paste format with paragraphs of typed text pasted onto a black background with comic-strip style illustrations of about fifty pages each.

Jonas also contributed to a zine titled *What Matters*. This zine was constructed by seven zinesters who all addressed the topic of what they value in life and explored the concept of matter as instances in their lives and tangible objects. Jonas's contribution to this zine was a piece titled "Broken Matter" where he discusses the importance of connecting with other people.

Data Collection and Analysis

The first author met Jonas at the 2013 Portland Zine Symposium, a two-day event in which more than one hundred zinesters and one thousand of their readers gathered together to exchange, sell, and acquire zines and attend workshops centered on aspects of zining. Jonas was observed distributing and discussing his zines; photos were taken of Jonas, and the third issue of his zine, *Cheer the Eff Up*, was collected. The other five issues of this zine and the two issues of his other zine, *Srviv*, were ordered online (at www.pioneerspress.com). The data for this study were mostly drawn from *Cheer the Eff Up*, particularly from the first issue and the last three issues.

In addition to these data, Jonas verbally responded to a ten-item open-ended questionnaire that addressed his demographic information and the purpose and audience for his zines. These data were triangulated by a semistructured, audio-recorded, and transcribed telephone interview in which Jonas elaborated on his history and trajectory for zining. Finally, a series of informal interviews were conducted by electronic mail in which Jonas elaborated on his background, his writing, his intentions, his writing process, his audience, and their feedback.

These data were analyzed by thematic analysis (Patton, 1990). Data were read, reread, annotated, and coded. Codes were grouped into categories and categories were compared across data sources and types. Reoccurring categories resulted in themes or assertions. Member checks were conducted by returning interview transcripts and reports to Jonas for his modifications, reactions, and additions by using Track Changes in Word or by sending modifications to us by electronic mail as a measure of trustworthiness (Lincoln & Guba, 1985). These comments were typically minor corrections of spelling or requests for privacy, such as Jonas's request that we not identify the type of company where he was employed or not relay a story he told us in the interview about a friend.

Findings

Three main themes evident in Jonas's zines provide counter narratives to mainstream beliefs and dominant discourses surrounding African American males' enactment of masculinity: (1) Jonas's *reconstructions of fatherhood through literacy*, (2) Jonas's *reflections on multivoiced masculinity*, and (3) Jonas's *re-representations of masculinity in literacy construction* as a writer. Both the structure and substance of Jonas's writing offer alternative textual representations that promote an inclusive view and counter rigid stereotypes of how masculinity and fatherhood are to be performed, particularly by African American males. Jonas's personal narratives that construct his titles disrupt restrictive enactments of gender, counter stereotypical and limiting views of men's roles, and provide insight into the realities and cultural complexities of the performance of masculinity.

Reconstructions of Fatherhood through Literacy

Writing as a Safe Haven for (Re)constructing Fatherhood

Jonas's writing presents an alternative to the image of African American men as uninvolved fathers. His missives defied traditional enactments of masculinity expressed by an emotionally distant father. Jonas's messages to his son illustrate alternative performances of masculinity in parenting that are framed and influenced by the events of Jonas's past, particularly Jonas's experiences interacting with his now deceased father and his personal reflections on and deconstructions of those occasions.

Jonas's writings often reflect reconstructions of his experiences, with the enactment of fatherhood stemming from his emotionally distant and noncommunicative father. In writing in this vein, Jonas engages in memoir as he reflects on his father's parenting. For example, Jonas recalls his father in issue 5 as "a master at warding off questions" (p. 18) who possessed "the ability to end a conversation in two seconds" (p. 18) if Jonas asked a question his father did not want to answer or if there was a topic he did not want to discuss. Jonas's father was not often physically present due to working overtime and double shifts, and he was not prone to verbal communications when he was at home.

In writing to his child in his zines, Jonas shares his personal experiences, like these with his own father. In doing so, Jonas challenges his father's enactment of fatherhood from his unique position as his father's child. For example, in issue 5, Jonas writes:

> My father didn't teach me an awful lot. He worked most of the time, & when he wasn't working he was in the living room on his recliner watching television or out at a bar. He was also a man of few words & those words often weren't very kind. His main method of parenting could be summed up as, "Look, I don't want any bullshit today." (p. 16)

Although Jonas stated that he did not intend to use his zine as a teaching tool, but rather tended to write in a peer-to-peer way, this excerpt implies that Jonas believes that one of a father's role responsibilities should be to teach his children life lessons. In so suggesting, Jonas rebels against the notion of the absentee African American father who is physically and emotionally distant from his children. Rather, Jonas stakes a claim for active involvement in his son's upbringing and a parenting style of communication and instruction.

Having lacked a strong role model to demonstrate how fathers convey emotionality and parental guidance to their children through verbal communication, Jonas engaged in written communication as an alternative. Because Jonas "cannot imagine establishing a rapport" with his own son, Jonas explains in issue 6 that he uses zines as a "safe space" or a "buffer zone" (p. 2). This safe space found in the written word allows Jonas the emotional freedom and intellectual safety to explore and share himself, his views, and his experiences with his son. In writing and reading lines of print, communication between father and son may be timelier and more meaningful than oral communication by being accessed at his son's own will at times when he may need to hear his father's voice, but in a less direct way.

Jonas imagines his son in the future—perhaps as a teenager—picking up his zines and stealthily reading them in the privacy of his bedroom just as Jonas had once retreated to the safe space of his bedroom after school to read zines. Should his son become the type of adolescent who does not directly communicate with his parents, he will have Jonas's zines. Reading his father's writings will enable Jonas's son to interact with his father by engaging in the type of silent communication that occurs between reader and author.

For Jonas, writing serves as an option for conveying emotion that is less confrontational than conversation and emulates the model of communication that his father provided for him. For example, Jonas relates discovering notebooks filled with words, sentences, and messages in different font sizes and types scrawled in pen and pencil, including one notebook containing pages of just Jonas's name written in his father's handwriting. Jonas also shares in issue 5 that after his mother's death, he discovered a written message of comfort that Jonas initially thought had been authored by his mother, but later realized was actually penned by his father, who disguised its origin by forging her handwriting. Jonas observed of his father: "I think he reached a point in life where he could only express how much he cared by pretending to be someone else" (p. 18). By forging Jonas's mother's handwriting, his father was able to express his feelings of care though subterfuge. Disguising his writing as a woman's writing enabled Jonas's father to explore his own nontraditional notions of fatherhood and masculinity.

The lessons Jonas's father taught him by example about enacting masculinity were restrictive ones designed to constrain or suppress the performance of gender outside of hegemonic normative structures. In issue 4 of *Cheer the Eff Up*, Jonas describes gender as "more of a limitation than a set of characteristics" (p. 12), recalling that his father taught him that men should not show emotions or affection and should not share their feelings. For a man who believed that expressing emotionality was enacting femininity, as hegemonic masculinity is centered around opposition to feminine roles (Weaver-Hightower, 2003), writing disguised as a woman's would permit a man like Jonas's father, who held stereotypical notions of enacting masculinity, to act in a feminine way, but from a safe and distanced space, and behind the mask of gender duplicity.

Although Jonas's father used the device of gender disguise in his writing and Jonas did not, both Jonas' father and Jonas shared the commonality of using writing to convey emotion. For example, Jonas reflects on his father's actions following Jonas's mother's death: "I think he wanted to comfort me after she died, but he didn't know how to reach out to me. . . . Maybe it's not that much different from these zines" (p. 18). Jonas's observation alludes to how, like his father, Jonas used writing as a vehicle for conveying caring from a distanced space. One example of how Jonas did so was found in Jonas's writing to his son about his fears and his hopes about parenting:

> You are going to get older & have a whole world of thoughts & emotions & you might not want to share them with me. . . . Maybe you will keep to yourself & lay in bed wishing that someone understood you, that someone could relate to you so that you wouldn't feel so alone. Meanwhile, I'll be in the other room, not knowing how to approach you, wondering if you've made it to "that age" so that I could swoop in & be everything that my father wasn't for me, wishing you'd reach out to me & knowing you won't. I don't know if I'm more worried about you turning out to be just like me or not like me at all. (Issue 5, p. 4)

This message alludes to issues of separation and distancing between father and son. These kinds of approach-avoidance behaviors are coping mechanisms that preadolescents and adolescents typically display (Kahlbaugh & Haviland, 1994). Jonas's writing explores how he will deal with these avoidant behaviors that teenagers manifest. Since adolescence is usually a time of parental separation as teens experience attachment conflict (Bloom, 1980), Jonas expresses his parental anxiety regarding how he will respond in ways that will vary from his experiences with his own father.

These examples also illustrate how both his father's written communications in his notebooks about his son and Jonas's writing to his son share a common element. Each conveys emotionality and care from the safe distance of the printed word and allows both men to step outside the constraints of stereotypical enactments of gender. Writing in notebooks allowed Jonas's father that same safe haven to reconstruct gender roles and performances that Jonas found by creating his zines. The written word allowed both men to express emotions and care in a comfortable way without the immediate worry of how those feelings and thoughts would be received.

Writing for Intergenerational Communication

Zines also represent a space for Jonas to share his beliefs and his identities and, as he does so, offer advice to his child. Jonas writes of myriad personal topics, ranging from his involvement with the Occupy Chicago movement to his interpersonal relationships and friendships. Through his writing, his son may come to know Jonas as a person with multiple identities—as an activist, a father, a former child and adolescent, a friend, a husband, a feminist, and an anarchist.

Yet Jonas warns his son on the danger of adopting these labels in forming and representing identities, citing perspectives from bell hooks:

> There's an idea that I read in a book by bell hooks . . . it basically explains the value of saying, "I advocate feminism" over "I'm a feminist" because it puts the focus on ideals & not identity. It says what you stand for without trapping you into a corner that says, "This is all that I am." It's the believe [*sic*] in anarchism without identifying as an anarchist. You can focus on what you believe in & give up worrying about which box you fall into. (Issue 5, p. 28)

Here, in a direct way, Jonas advocates against narrow constructions of identity and limiting categorizations of individuals. In doing so, Jonas encourages his son to engage in metareflection and critical thinking about the notions of identities and the perspectives they convey. Since identities are fluid and sometimes competing (Gee, 2003), Jonas advocates for deconstructing their underlying ideas and ideologies.

Jonas also uses the pages of his zine to share his hopes and dreams for and with his child and to offer his advice or life lessons. In issue 1, Jonas writes:

> There is so much out there that I want to expose you to. So much you need to know. You need to know about the whole gay, lesbian, bisexual, queer and transgender community out there. And you need to not grow up feeling weird about it. You need to be exposed to people of different cultures and races and you need to feel like that are all your people and not like they are weird others that you have to tiptoe around. You need to be strong and not scared and not fall into those bullshit gender roles and rules that people around here fall into. Pink for girls, blue for guys. No way. Pick whatever color you want. (p. 25)

Jonas writes here of inclusivity, acceptance of difference, and rejection of narrow gender roles and relations. In doing so, he transmits his values and beliefs from father to child. Jonas writes from his lived experiences, which contradict the stereotypes he grew up with. He met "gay guys that were not experts in fashion" and learned "that being a lesbian had nothing to do with women hating men and everything to do with women loving women" (p. 6). Jonas shares life lessons he learned from experiences like these and conveys ideals and ideas that he hopes his son will adopt.

Writing for Reconstructing Masculine Performance

Like his father Jonas also found that writing could be a vehicle for reconstructing masculine performance. For example, Jonas shares his fears about fatherhood and about his father's influence on him as a man enacting masculinity in parenting:

> When I think to myself, "I'm a Dad, I'm someone's father," it feels like slipping into shoes that are 3 sizes too big. I can't shake the idea that being a father means becoming my father. I can read about radical parenting & call myself a rad dad. I can make a list of all the things my old man did & said that I don't want to do, then make a list of all the things I definitely want to say & do. I can point toward all the negative stereotypes of fathers that the media feeds us. I can embrace all the feminist ideas I've learned. I can surround myself with awesome radical female friends, I can tell myself that being a father only means I am a male identified parent

of a child. Still, I think of the word father & my mind conjures up a man's manly man that I don't want to be. (Issue 1, p. 25)

Jonas's writing conveys the desire for freedom from narrow gender roles and expectations surrounding parenting. His writings express emotion as a vehicle for change and resistance against repressive notions of masculinity. His text conveys a model of fatherhood that extends beyond fathers as breadwinners and eschews an essentialist model of fatherhood that reproduces men's power relations with women, children, and other men (Lupton & Barclay, 1997). Jonas's reconstructions of fatherhood illustrate rebellion against intergenerational models of restrictive gender performance as "a man's manly man" that were transmitted to him, express his fear of reproducing these constrained role relations, and offer promise for the re-creation of men's roles as active parents.

Reflections on Masculinity as Multivoiced

Much of Jonas's construction of masculinity in his *Cheer the Eff Up* series of zines consist of his coming to terms with an internal struggle of growing into an adult African American male. Through this journey, he periodically inserts voices that interject multiple views of masculinity into his thoughts. These voices served as mooring posts that he was both haunted and comforted by during his everyday life. For example, in *Cheer the Eff Up*, issue 6, Jonas quotes his father's advice on marriage and fatherhood: "I shit you not, kid, being a family man is like taking the ass whooping you always had coming to you" (p. 3). This quote summarizes the deeper conflict behind his response of "meh" to his wife when she asked if he wanted to start a family. "Meh" represents a hybrid of ideals between his father's perspectives that being a family man is akin to a beating with Jonas's enacted identity that makes him feel increasingly like a White, middle-class family man. Jonas explains, "My apprehension came from viewing family as the heart-shaped cage for straight, middle-class White America" (p. 4). Jonas portrays the process of getting married, working at a nondescript office job in a cubicle, and becoming a father as a progression of slowly giving in to a middle-class, White American view of masculinity.

Jonas juxtaposes his father's punitive definition of being a family man against the realization that he is "happy with marriage and parenthood" when he "finally step[s] back to think about that" (p. 6). Ultimately, Jonas reaches the conclusion that part of his struggle is the fact he swallowed other voices about what it means to be a family man. Further, these voices that told him being a middle-class family man means sacrifice, responsibility, and burden were deeply entrenched. Jonas reflects:

> What I had a problem with was the way those things had been defined for me. Marriage meant domestication & emotional disconnect. Parenthood meant responsibility. Responsibility meant burden. Stay in yr lane & accept it all & that's the path to happiness. (p. 6)

In this passage, Jonas writes about the ways family life was defined for him as an emasculating experience. Jonas also examines what it means to be happy as a man slipping into a conventional, White, masculine role against the advice of his father and his anarchist friends who disappeared from his life during his route to fatherhood.

In the first issue of *Cheer the Eff Up*, Jonas foreshadows this process of realization that he could be happy as a family man through reflecting on two notes from his mother. In the first note, his mother wrote, "Everything's going to be just fine sweetie. You'll see. I love you. Mom" (p. 37). This note appears twice in the zine. The note is first included in a section of the zine where he introduces his mother to his son and explains her "special" psychic gift. At the end of the zine, the note is reprinted in its original, handwritten form and serves as a revoiced sentiment from Jonas to the reader, whom he identifies primarily as his infant son. Thus, the reappearance of this note is meant to reassure his son by passing on fatherly advice his own father could not give him, representing counsel that his mother shared with him.

In this same zine, Jonas includes another note from his mother that she wrote toward the end of her life while his wife was in the early stages of a pregnancy with a child who was conceived prior to his son. The note reads, "Cheer up Jonas it's a girl" (p. 37). Ironically, the pregnancy ended in a miscarriage, which pushed Jonas into depression. His mother's view of parenthood as a positive experience, however, settled him in the midst of the turmoil Jonas felt about his misgivings over becoming a middle-class family man.

In a piece titled "Broken Matter" published in the zine entitled *What Matters*, Jonas explores the idea that his identity is tied to an imagined twin, a sister born "at the same time, on the same day" (p. 4). This sister looked nothing like Jonas. He imagines they had "different heights and different shades," but she met up with him in dreams and they "fixed" each other. Alone, they were "broken robots," but together they "knew how to fix one another just fine." Although this childhood belief in a secret twin faded at some point as a young adult, Jonas still thinks of his twin when he composes. He stated that part of him was always writing to his twin to both seek her approval and speak for her. This imagined relationship shaped his identity.

Re-representations of Masculinity in Literacy Construction

In authoring his zines, Jonas modeled identity expression and alternative enactments of masculinity through literacy, and, in doing so, he encouraged his son's involvement in literate practices. For example, in Issue 5, Jonas writes to his son:

> I hope you learn how wonderful it is to have pen pals. I'm sure that it's something I'll encourage you to do once you're old enough . . . there's nothing more intimate than letters. Handwritten or typed, folded into an envelope & stamped . . . [one] of the many great parts of having a pen pal is that you know for a fact that you are important to them. There are so many easier more convenient forms of communication available to us. But when you're writing a letter, it's not about convenience. Everything involved in mailing a letter tells the other person: you're worth my time. You're worth this effort. I value you more than I value convenience. (p. 36)

In this missive, Jonas not only transmits his values regarding writing as intimacy and personal expressions of caring, he also models for his son a man's engagement in literacy practices, a model that was transmitted to him by his own father. In issue 5, Jonas recalls that his father was partially responsible for teaching him to read by requiring him to read aloud from the *TV Guide* and the movie reviews in the newspaper. Although his father chastised Jonas for reading comic books, he encouraged Jonas to read other everyday texts.

In turn, Jonas models literacy engagement for his own son through his zining practices. He expresses enthusiasm for zines as a means of social connection by writing in issue 5: "When you make zines & spread them around it's amazing how quickly you'll feel the magnetic pull to other zinesters" (p. 14). In these words, Jonas conveys to his son that writing is interpersonal communication that has the power to facilitate connectivity and foster community. Jonas stated that he saw his zine as "a means to connect with people" and "a means to reach out to others that have similar thoughts or are experiencing the same trials" who might find it "warm, familiar, and comforting." When asked what function zining serves in his life, Jonas replied:

> Making zines is a creative outlet first and foremost. A lot of times it is a wonderful way to process more of the painful things that are on my mind. It's kind of like the final process. I think about something and think about something and I cannot deal with these huge issues and then when I write about it, it is the final steps of processing it, of really learning from an experience and processing it. It helps me understand myself and how I felt about the things that take up space in my mind.

Jonas freely wrote personal narratives like this that conveyed how writing has served as a catharsis for him in processing his emotions. In doing so, Jonas shared the function that writing has served in his life as a mechanism for sorting out troubling issues. Jonas modeled for his son how creating a written text can be therapeutic by serving as a way to engage in serious introspection and a way to make sense of difficult events of the past.

In writing about his feelings, Jonas engaged in a genre of writing that is atypical for men (Ball, 2003; Shamir & Travis, 2002). Traditional assertions of masculinity call for men to be in control of their emotions. Enacting masculinity is typically characterized by the emotional inexpressively and emotional isolation inherent in the common expression "Boys don't cry" (Shamir & Travis, 2002). Hence, men are not known for writing about sentiment and emotionality or for sorting out their interpersonal relationships through writing, yet Jonas commonly engaged in creating texts for this purpose. For example, Jonas expresses sentimentality and feelings of depression in issue 3 of *Cheer the Eff Up*: "When terrible things happen, I don't feel sad. I feel empty. It's much worse" (p. 2).

In writings like this, Jonas's missives represent a counternarrative to the public and personal discourses of how a man, particularly an African American man, should be and act. His writing about emotionality provides new archetypes for his son that offer possibilities for disrupting gendered notions of how men can and cannot be engaged in literacy. Jonas's zines serve as a model that illustrates the functions of communication, catharsis, comfort, and connection that writing can serve for a man.

Significance/Implications

Findings from this investigation offer new understandings of and models for African American males' enactment of masculinity and manhood. Jonas's writings provide evidence that men can overcome hegemonic elements of masculinity that are perpetuated and reinforced through the generations and portrayed in the media (Ivery, 2014). Findings from this investigation contribute to the growing body of literature providing evidence counter to the presupposition that African American men are uninvolved and irresponsible fathers (e.g., Culp-Ressler, 2014; Ransaw, 2012). This study also contributes to contemporary research (e.g., Kirkland, 2013a, 2013b; Kirkland & Jackson, 2009) that showcases disruption of the dominant discourse of the Black male as hypermasculine, distant, and cold (Kirkland, 2013b).

This case study presents an alternative to the limiting ways boys are taught to be engaged in literacy practices that reify traditional notions of masculinity (Kehler, 2013) by offering alternative constructions and models for men's writing, in both substance and style. This study contributes to the extant literature about the real-life literacy practices of African American men, such as Black male poets (Kirkland, 2013b), by expanding the focus on adolescents to the literacy practices of an adult man of color. Jonas's case illustrates the stories and circumstances (Rhym, 2014) that motivate Black men to write. Studies like these allow for variance in developing young Black men as readers and writers and provide current models for expanding notions of gender performance by demonstrating the functions that literacy can serve in a Black man's everyday life. Findings from this study offer educators alternative textual representations of masculine performance in literacy teaching and learning and advance the agenda of improving academic achievement for African American males.

Scholars promoting this agenda have advocated for student-centered literacy learning and instruction for African Americans that is both race based and gender based and is culturally responsive (e.g., Bean & Ransaw, 2013; Tatum, 2012). Providing African American boys with everyday texts like zines written by African American males who are not professional writers, but rather engage in writing for identity representation, can demonstrate how literacy can play an important part in men's lives. Supplementing historical and canonical literature authored by African American men and young adult literature that is culturally and gender enabling (Tatum, 2008) with these ordinary texts of zines can assist in providing a wide range of textual forms that have cultural relevance in contemporary society and offer contextual relevancy to young men's lives. There has been a call for educators to "come to know and learn to value adolescent boys' interests and literate practices beyond the school walls." (Brozo, 2013, p. 3). Honoring zines and the creation and consumption of other new media texts as legitimate literacies that boys already engage in outside of school is a way to address this directive.

Reading zines written by African American males that offer counternarratives to stereotypical notions of masculinity could become a powerful "textual lineage" for African American adolescent males and push the "pendulum" between hope and defeat in a positive direction (Tatum, 2005a, p. 81). Textual lineages are "literary and nonliterary texts that are significant in one's development" (Tatum, 2005a, p. 81). African American male adolescents have an increased need for quality literacy instruction in the United States due primarily to the high poverty rates of their families and lack of engaging literacy instruction some encounter in school (Tatum, 2008). Thus, creating textual lineages are critical for this population of learners.

> A pendulum swings both ways for African American males. On one side are hopes and dreams, where the potential leads to promise. On the other side is defeat, where hopes unfulfilled become a record of human tragedy. (Tatum, 2008, p. 81)

African American boys need to encounter "text in school to help them critique and understand their experiences outside of school" (Tatum, 2005a, p. 84). The interior landscape of personal zines like the ones composed by Jonas can give African American boys models that both problematize stereotypes about manhood and cultivate men's literacy practices. Accordingly, this case study offers promise for advancing the agenda of providing new hope to youth for countering limiting and stereotypical models of masculinity through alternative portrayals of masculinity in literacy performance.

Like other researchers (Archer & Yamashita, 2003; Kirkland, 2013a, 2013b), we found that African American males may author alternative texts, such as poetry, music, or diaries in out-of-school settings that are more personally and culturally relevant than traditional writing assignments in schools. By describing Jonas's zining practices, this study identified another textual form that allowed an African American man to engage in alternative performances and representations of masculinity. It has been noted that the curriculum typically lacks specific texts and textual characteristics that engage and are relevant to African American males (Tatum, 2006, 2008). Positioning these alternative texts as legitimate literacy practices may raise educators' awareness of the literate lives of youth outside of school and assist in countering a deficit view of African American boys who may underperform in academic literacy yet are proficient in their production and consumption of "hidden" or "underground" literacy practices. Recognition of these kinds of texts may help boys to deconstruct dominant narratives and provide inclusive and affirmative texts that offer diverse youth opportunities for engagement with culturally relevant literacy practices (Morrell, 2002).

Conclusion

In imaging directions for future research, this case study raises questions regarding the interplay of multiple subjectivities, culture, and interpersonal relationships in facilitating African American men's literacy engagement. Our focal participant was fluid in his social class mobility, having obtained a college education that enabled him to transition from working class to middle class. Rather than "leaving behind" (Archer & Yamahita, 2003) his identity as a zinester during this transition, the do-it-yourself ethos inherent in zining engrained within Jonas's punk community supported his out-of-school writing in adolescence and sustained this literacy practice into his adulthood. Punk has been considered to be more than just a genre of music with subgenres, but also a belief system, a lifestyle, and a culture (Azerrad, 2001; Guzzetti & Yang, 2005). In addition, Jonas has a specific audience to which he writes in his zines, including his child and members of his punk community; he has a specific purpose for writing—to share himself and his views—that sustains his writing as a personally and culturally relevant literacy practice. Jonas's zining illustrates the enactment of alternative representations of masculinity for an African American man influenced by the kinds of cultural practices and interpersonal relationships posited by gender theorists (Kehler, 2008; McKenry et al., 1989). New media like Jonas's zine can serve as safe spaces for youth to interrogate dominant constructions of masculinity and those views within schools that "maintain, perpetuate, and reinforce" (Kehler, 2013, p. 127) constricting and stereotypical gender performances.

This case study provides an impetus for continuing lines of inquiry that further explore complex and competing views of masculinity and the intersections of race, culture, social class, and gender that influence literacy development and practice for African American males. The extant research that focuses on the literate lives of diverse men, particularly young African American men, is relatively sparse compared to other research agendas. A decade ago, this omission was noted by other scholars (Lindo, 2006; Tatum, 2008), but it still characterizes the professional literature. Yet it is important to ground efforts to assist Black male youth by knowing and understanding the cultural forms they produce (Noguera, 2002). Further ethnographic studies are needed that identify these forms and describe complex constructions of masculinity and performances of culturally relevant literacy practices that can provide alternative models for diverse youth.

REFERENCES

Alexander, B. K. (2006). *Performing black masculinity: Race, culture and queer identity.* Lanham, MD: Alta Mira.

Aratani, Y., Wight, V. R., & Cooper, J. L. (2011, April). *Racial gaps in early childhood: Socio-emotional health, developmental and educational outcomes among African-American boys.* New York: National Center for Children in Poverty, Columbia University.

Archer, L., & Yamashita, H. (2003). Theorizing inner city masculinities: "Race," class, gender and education. *Gender and Education 15*(2), 115–32.

Azerrad, M. (2001). *Our band could be your life: Scenes from the American rock underground, 1981–1991.* Boston: Little, Brown.

Ball, P. (2003, July 18). Computer program detects author gender. *Nature* 18. Retrieved from http://www.nature.com/news/2003/030714/full/news030714-13.html.

Barton, P. E., & Coley, R. J. (2007). *America's smallest school: The family.* Princeton, NJ: Educational Testing Service.

Bean, T. W., & Harper, H. (2007). Reading men differently: Alternative portrayals of masculinity in contemporary young adult fiction. *Reading Psychology 28*(2), 11–30.

Bean, T. W., & Ransaw, T. (2013). Masculinity and portrayal of African American boys in young adult literature: A critical deconstruction and reconstruction of this genre. In B. J. Guzzetti & T. W. Bean (eds.), *Adolescent literacies and the gendered self: (Re) constructing identities through multimodal literacy practices.* New York: Routledge.

Bloom, M. V. (1980). *Adolescent parental separation.* New York: Gardner Press.

Bristol, T. J. (2015). Teaching boys: Towards a theory of gender-relevant pedagogy. *Gender and Education 27*(1), 53–68.

Brozo, W. G. (2013). Outside interests and literate practices as contexts for increasing engagement and critical reading for adolescent boys. In B. J. Guzzetti & T. W. Bean (eds.), *Adolescent literacies and the gendered self: (Re) constructing identities through multimodal literacy practices*. New York: Routledge.

Buck, S. (2010). *Acting white: The ironic legacy of desegregation*. New Haven, CT: Yale University Press.

Connell, R. W. (1996). Teaching the boys: New research on masculinity, and gender strategies for schools. *Teachers College Record 98*(2), 206–35.

Connell, R. W. (1998). Masculinities and globalization. *Men and Masculinities 1*(1), 3–23.

Connell, R. W. (2005). *Masculinities*. 2nd ed. Berkeley: University of California Press.

Connell, R.W., & Messerschmidt, J.W. (2005). Hegemonic masculinity: Rethinking the concept. *Gender and Society 19*(6), 829–859.

Culp-Ressler, T. (2014, January 16). The myth of the absent Black father. *Think Progress*. Retrieved from http://thinkprogress.org/health/2014/01/16/3175831/myth-absent-black-father/.

Dancy, T. E. (2011). Colleges in the making of manhood and masculinity: Gendered perspectives on African-American males. *Gender and Education 23*(4), 477–95.

Forsberg, L. (2007). Negotiating involved fatherhood: Household work, childcare and spending time with children. *NORMA: Nordic Journal for Masculinity Studies 2*, 109–26.

Gaines, E. (1993). *A lesson before dying*. New York: Knopf.

Gee, J. P. (2003). *What video games have to teach us about learning and literacy*. New York: Palgrave Macmillan.

Goldfarb, Z. A., & Wilson, S. (2014, February 27). Obama sees focus on young black and Hispanic men post presidency. *Washington Post*. Retrieved from https://www.washingtonpost.com/politics/obama-sees-focus-on-young-black-and-hispanic-men-in-post-presidency/2014/02/27/259fc212-9f6e-11e3-9ba6-800d1192d08b_story.html.

Gottzen, L. (2011). Involved fatherhood? Exploring the educational work of middle class men. *Gender and Education 23*(5), 619–34.

Griffith, A., & Smith, D. (2005). *Mothering for schooling*. New York: Routledge.

Guzzetti, B. J., & Yang, Y. 2005). Punk rock fandom: Construction and production of lyrical texts. In B. Maloch, J. V. Hoffman, D. L. Schallert, C. M. Fairbanks & J. Worthy (eds.), *54th Yearbook of the National Reading Conference*, Oak Creek, WI: National Reading Conference.

Haase, M. (2010). Fearfully powerful: Male teachers, social power and the primary school pedagogy. *Culture and Society 18*(2), 173–90.

Hattie, J. (2012). *Visible learning for teachers: Maximizing impact on learning*. New York: Routledge.

hooks, b. (2004a). *The will to change: Men, masculinity and love*. New York: Atria Books.

hooks, b. (2004b). *We real cool: Black men and masculinity*. New York: Routledge.

Hunter, A. G., & Davis, J.E. (1992). Constructing gender: An exploration of Afro-American men's conceptualizations of manhood. *Gender & Society* 6(3), 464–479.

Ivery, C. (2014). *Black fatherhood: Reclaiming our legacy*. New York: Beaufort Books.

Jackson, C., & Dempster, S. (2009). "I sat back on my computer . . . with a bottle of whiskey next to me": Constructing "cool" masculinity through effortless achievement secondary and higher education. *Journal of Gender Studies 18*(4), 341–56.

Jiang, Y., Ekono, M., & Skinner, C. (2015). *Basic facts about low income children*. National Center for Children in Poverty, Columbia University. Retrieved from http://www.nccp.org/publications/pub_1099.html.

Jones, J. & Mosher, W. D. (2013). Fathers' involvement with their children, United States, 2006–2010. *National Health Statistics Reports 71*, 1–21.

Kahlbaugh, P. E., & Haviland, J. M. (1994). Nonverbal communication between parents and adolescents. *Journal of Nonverbal Behavior 18*, 91–113.

Kehler, M. (2008). Masculinities and critical social literacies practices: The read and misread bodies of high school young men. In R. F. Hammet & K. Sanford (eds.), *Boys, girls and the myths of literacies and learning*. Toronto, CN: Canadian Scholars Press.

Kehler, M. (2013). Who will "save the boys"? (Re)examining a panic for underachieving boys. In *Adolescent literacies and the gendered self: (Re) constructing identities through multimodal literacy practices*. New York: Routledge.

Kerby, S. (2012, March 17). One in three Black men go to prison? The top 10 most disturbing facts about racial inequality in the U.S. criminal justice system. *American Prospect*. Retrieved from http://www.alternet.org/story/154587/1_in_3_black_men_go_to_prison_the_10_most_disturbing_facts_about_racial_inequality_in_the__u.s._criminal_justice_system

Kids Count (2014). *Kids Count data book: An annual report on how children are faring in the United States*. 25th ed. Baltimore: Annie E. Casey Foundation. Retrieved from http://www.aecf.org/resources/the-2014-kids-count-data-book/.

Kimmel, M. (2002). Global masculinities: Restoration and resistance. In B. Pease & K. Pringle (eds.) *A man's world? Changing men's practices in a globalized world*, vol. 4. London: Zed Books.

Kimmel, M., & Messner, M. (eds.) (2007). *Men's lives*. 7th ed. New York: HarperCollins.

Kirkland, D. E. (2013a). *A search past silence: The literacy of young Black men*. New York: Teachers College Press.

Kirkland, D. E. (2013b). Inventing masculinity: Young Black males, literacy and tears. In B. J. Guzzetti & T. W. Bean (eds.), *Adolescent literacies and the gendered self: (Re) constructing identities through multimodal literacy practices*. New York: Routledge.

Kirkland, D. E., & Jackson, A. (2009). "We real cool": Toward a theory of Black masculine literacies. *Reading Research Quarterly 44*(3), 278–97.

Knobel, M., & Lankshear, C. (2012). Cut, paste, publish: The production and consumption of zines. In D. E. Alvermann (ed.), *Adolescents and literacies in a digital world.* New York: Peter Lang.

Lincoln, Y. E., & Guba, I. V. (1985). *Naturalistic inquiry.* Newbury Park, CA: Sage.

Lindo, E. (2006). The African American presence in reading intervention experiments. *Remedial and Special Education 27*(3), 148–153.

Lupton, D., & Barclay, L. (1997). *Constructing fatherhood: Discourses and experiences.* London: Sage.

Lusher, D. (2011). Masculinity, educational achievement and social status: A social network analysis. *Gender and Education 23*(6), 655–675.

McKenry, P., Everett, J., Rameur, H., & Carter, C. (1989). Research on Black adolescents: A legacy of cultural bias. *Journal of Adolescent Research 4,* 254–64.

Morrell, E. (2002). Toward a critical pedagogy of popular culture: Literacy development among urban youth. *Journal of Adolescent and Adult Literacy 46*(1), 72–77.

National Education Association (2012–15). *Identifying factors that contribute to achievement gaps.* Gaithersburg, MD: National Education Association. Retrieved from http://www.nea.org/home/17413.htm.

Neal, M. A. (2003). *New Black man.* New York: Routledge.

Noguera, P. (2003). The trouble with Black boys: The role and influence of environmental and cultural actors on the academic performance of African American males. *Urban Education 38*(4), 431–59.

Patton, M. (1990). *Qualitative evaluation and research methods.* 2nd ed. Newbury Park, CA: Sage.

Ransaw, T. (2012). A father's hands: African American fathering involvement and the educational outcomes of their children. Ed.D. diss., University of Nevada. Retrieved from http://digitalscholarship.unlv.edu/cgi/viewcontent.cgi?article=2613&context=thesesdissertations.

Ransaw, T. (2014). The good father: African American fathers who positively influence the educational outcomes of their children. *Spectrum: A Journal on Black Men 2*(2), 1–25.

Rhym, D. (2014). Review of *A Search Past Silence: The Literacy of Young Black Men. Journal of Language and Literacy Education 10*(1), 221–27.

Schott Foundation for Public Education (2015). *Schott 50 state report on public education and Black males.* Cambridge, MA: The Schott Foundation for Public Education. Retrieved from http://blackboysreport.org/national-summary.

Shamir, M., & Travis, J. (eds.) (2002). *Boys don't cry? Rethinking narratives of masculinities and emotion in the U.S.* New York: Columbia University Press.

Smith, C. A., Krohn, M. D., Chu, R., & Best, O. (2005). African American fathers: Myths and realities about their involvement with their first born children. *Journal of Family Issues 26*, 971–1001.

Smith, D. T. (2013, March 14). Images of Black males in popular media. *Huffington Post.* Retrieved from http://www.huffingtonpost.com/darron-t-smith-phd/black-men-media_b_2844990.html.

Smith, M. D., Moore, D. L., Laymon, K., & Green, K. M. (2013). *Black men writing to live: Brothers' letters.* Retrieved from http://www.thefeministwire.com/2013/black-men-writing-to-live-brothers-letters/.

Stake, R. (1995). *The art of case study research.* Thousand Oaks, CA: Sage.

Tatum, A. W. (2005a). Building the textual lineages of African American male adolescents. In K. Beers, R. Probst, & L. Reif (eds.), *Adolescent literacy: Turning promise into practice.* Portsmouth, NH: Heinemann.

Tatum, A. W. (2005b). *Teaching reading to Black adolescent males: Closing the achievement gap.* Portland, ME: Stenhouse Publishers.

Tatum, A. W. (2006). Engaging African American males in reading. *Educational Leadership 63*(5), 44–49.

Tatum, A. W. (2008). Toward a more anatomically complete model of literacy instruction: A focus on African-American males and texts. *Harvard Educational Review 78*(1), 155–80.

Tatum, A. W. (2012, March). *Literacy practices for African American male adolescents.* Boston: Jobs for the Future. Retrieved from http://www.studentsatthecenter.org/sites/scl.dl-dev.com/files/Literacy%20Practices.pdf.

Tatum, A. W., & Gue, V. (2010). Raw writing: A critical support for adolescents. *English Journal 99*(4), 90–93.

UNESCO. (2012). *Youth and skills: Putting education to work.* Paris: UNESCO.

UNESCO (2014). *Teaching and learning: Achieving quality for all.* Paris: UNESCO.

Weaver-Hightower, M. (2003). The "boy turn" in research on gender and education. *Review of Educational Research 73*(4), 471–98.

Understanding the Classroom Matrix of Race, Class, Gender, and Cultural Competency in Analyzing Same-Race Students and Teacher Arguments

Theodore S. Ransaw

> We are all tied together in a single garment of destiny . . . an inescapable network of mutuality.
>
> —Rev. Dr. Martin Luther King Jr.

Race and inequitable education has been a long-standing topic of debate in American education. Much of the recent controversy over race and education in America is reflective of the *Brown v. Board of Education* ruling of 1954 that allowed Black students to attend schools with White students. Then, as now, conversation about what is best for Black students largely focuses on same-race student and teacher classrooms (Anderson, 2015; Boggs & Dunbar, 2015; Coleman, 2007; Cottman, 2015; Driessen, 2015; Dweck, 2013; Hyland, 2005; Ladson-Billings, 1995). However, despite the best intentions of those who tried to desegregate schools, classroom composition is still not racially balanced in the United States. In 2011, White students attended schools that were 9 percent Black, while Black students attended schools that were 78 percent Black (NAEP, 2015). Many of the Black students who attended predominantly Black schools lived in the South (NAEP, 2015). Regardless of location, educational outcomes for Black and White students are not the same. Black students are not performing as well as White students. The discrepancies between White and minority students' educational outcomes are so severe that Johnson and Kritsonis (2006) consider achievement gaps between Black and White students a national dilemma.

At the outset, it must be pointed out that the purpose of this chapter is not to present an exhaustive summary but to provide an overview of background information and research as a foundation for a much-needed discussion of same-race student and teacher classrooms.

Overview

Despite the fact that achievement gaps in the United States still persist, there have been some positive gains. For example, based on the National Assessment of Educational Progress (NAEP), Black and White student achievement gaps in both mathematics and reading have been steadily closing (Vanneman et al., 2009). Additionally, as of 2011, 80 percent of African Americans over the age of twenty-five have high school diplomas (Blackdemographics.com, 2015). Black, Latino, and American Indian student graduation rates are increasing more so than ever before (Krogstad, 2016), and between 2003 and 2015, public higher education institutions have improved graduation rates for minority students (Camera, 2015). It is also important to note that the average number of African Americans with at least a bachelor's degree has *increased* two percentage points to 19 percent since the year 2000 (Blackdemographics.com, 2015). However, according to Bohrnstedt et al. (2015), there is a 31 percent achievement gap between Black and White students in America. When it comes to gender and schooling overall in America, White male students still outperform Black male students in high school graduation: 59 percent for Black males, 65 percent for Latino males, and 80 percent for White non-Latino males (Sanzone et al., 2014). White students are also more likely to be offered more rigorous curriculum than Black students (Vanneman et al., 2009). Consequently, Black and White student educational outcomes are not equal. Achievement gaps between Black and minority students seem more alarming when you consider that, while 17 percent of public school students are Black, Black teachers make up just 8 percent of educators (Dee, 2004), leaving some researchers to argue that lack of diversity and lack of cultural competency of White teachers in the classrooms are crucial factors contributing to the achievement gap of minority students (Ladson-Billings, 1995; Desimone & Long, 2010; Fairlie, Hoffmann, & Oreopoulos, 2014).

Underachievement of Black students being taught by a predominantly White teaching force has set the stage for heated arguments about what is better for improving educational outcomes for Black students: reintroducing same-race student and teacher classrooms, or implementing cultural sensitivity practices in teacher training. While there are many discussions about how best to improve schooling for Black students, same-race student and teacher classrooms *and* cultural competency are the overarching themes in arguments why increasing the amount of minority teachers may help solve educational problems of minority students. A growing number of people are advocating for Black teachers to teach Black students (Martin, 2012; Anderson, 2014; Cottman, 2015) or, at the very least, for a diverse teaching force to teach an increasingly diverse American student population (Villegas & Irvine, 2010) as a way to close achievement gaps. Others, like Hunt (2012), assert that in some instances schools with a predominance of Black teachers can have negative effects for students, while Mickelson (2003) and Tavernis (2012) both say there are mitigating reasons that go beyond the classroom that impact both Black and White teachers of children of color. Gay (2000) feels that race is no guarantee of teacher effectiveness or cultural competency.

This chapter begins with the argument of same-race students and teachers versus cultural competency training since they are the overarching arguments on which other arguments are based, such as race and socioeconomic status (SES). According to National Center for Education Statistics (2012), SES can be defined broadly as one's access to financial, social, cultural, and human capital resources (p. 4). Since SES intersects with so many areas, including gender and the type of neighborhood students live in, it may help the reader to have a little background about the history of how race and education in America influence educational outcomes to provide context for deeper discussion.

Theoretical Framework

This chapter employs the theoretical framework of critical race theory (CRT). CRT emerged from post-civil rights legal issues led by activists in the field of law. Currently, CRT is also employed by educators as a framework to apply issues related to both the educational system and the juvenile justice system. CRT is an analytical framework that focuses on history, economics, equity, constitutional law, and, of course, racism (Delgado & Stefancic, 2001). For Bell (2003), "We live in a system that espouses merit, equality, and a level playing field, but exalts ties with wealth, power, and celebrity gained" (p. 8). Originally conceived by Derrick Bell, CRT challenges the idea that race is not an issue with regard to education and acknowledges that barriers such as school policies are often obstacles to opportunity for people of color. CRT shifts away from perspectives that suggest communities of color are culturally deficient (Yosso, 2005) and operates under the premise that Black students do not need to be rescued but do need to be empowered. CRT has led the way for other critical fields such as critical race feminism theory, queer critical theory, Latino/a critical race theory, Asian critical race theory, tribal critical race theory, and critical White studies.

Critical race feminism theory interrogates questions about race and gender in the twenty-first century (Razack, Smith, & Thobani, 2010). Queer critical theory explores the interplay of between sexual norms and attitudes, and race of queer, gay, lesbian, and transgender populations (Delgado & Stefancic, 2001). Latino/a critical race theory examines social justice issues related to Latino/a and Chicano/a race, class, and gender experiences (Mahmud, Mutua, & Valdes, 2015). Asian critical race theory scholars challenge negative and ubiquitous perceptions of Asians and interrogates issues related to national identity, language, accent, and discrimination (Delgado & Stefancic, 2001). Tribal critical race theory researchers address issues of indigenous peoples in the United States (Brayboy, 2005). Critical White studies seeks to dismantle White privilege while investigating power and the role of the wage of whiteness (Du Bois, 1971) in relationship to people of color (Delgado & Stefancic, 2001). The creation of CRT has led the charge for many different fields that are impacted by race gender and culture, especially the field of education.

Gloria Ladson-Billings and William Tate were influential in introducing CRT to education with an article entitled "Toward a Critical Race Theory of Education" (1995). For Ladson-Billings and Tate, CRT is appropriate to examine inequalities in education because (1) race continues to be significant in the United States; (2) U.S. society is based on property rights rather than human rights; and (3) the intersection of race and property creates an analytical tool for understanding inequity (p. 47). The topics that CRT is uniquely suited to focus on—history, economics, equity, constitutional law, and, of course, racism—are particularly salient in this chapter, as they are intertwined in a matrix that affects educational outcomes for all children, especially minority children. Simply put, CRT uses race as a theoretical lens for examining social inequality in education (Ladson-Billings & Tate, 1995). Since race is a social construct, a theory that encompasses social implications has value for understanding the social dynamics behind issues related to schooling for Black students in America.

History of Education in America for Blacks

While reading this section that highlights the first tenet of CRT history and its effects on African American education, it is important to keep in mind that, while there has been systematic opposition to educating minorities in America for centuries (Ransaw, 2013), there have also been efforts by both Black and White teachers to teach Blacks at great risk. For example, Prudence Crandall was placed in jail for educating Blacks in 1834, and Mrs. Margaret Douglass of Norfolk, Virginia, was placed in prison for teaching Blacks to read in 1853 (North Carolina Digital History, 2010). Mickelson (2003) and Oakley, Stowell, and Logan (2009) chronicle numerous examples where Blacks advocated for the right to be educated and did so at great personal risk. Hotchkiss (2016) shares that at one time in American history it was a corporal offense for a Black person to teach a fellow Black person to read.

Sometimes discussed as a moral issue or an economic issue, the rationale for denying Blacks an education, and the resulting effects of lack of education leading to incarceration, was based on the European sixteenth-century belief that Blacks were descendants of Ham, which, according to select readings of the Bible (*Genesis 9:24–27*), allowed enslavement of those who had dark skin (*Goldenberg, 2003*). Jones (2007) and Reiland (2009) argue that there are many Black males who are still victims of these sixteenth-century beliefs, first suspended from school and later incarcerated to serve sentences and perform low-wage labor in prisons on the same land where their ancestors were enslaved (Jones, 2007; Reiland, 2009). Ransaw (2013) asserts that low literacy rates are to blame for Black males' high incarceration rates, poor educational outcomes related to detentions, and suspensions for nonviolent offenses based on teacher racism.

Minority, low-SES males have a history of low academic performance in the United States. In the 1870s, it was ethnic White males from Ireland and Italy, not males of color, who were thought of as uneducable and feared as violent gang members (Grant, 2014). Irish and Italian boys suffered from the same social barriers to success then as African American, Latino, Native American, and Whites males in impoverished neighborhoods do today. However, some say that Black poverty in the United States is different from almost any other kind (Delgado & Stefancic, 2005). The color of Black skin has led to redlining, denial of loans, inflated rates for mortgages and car loans, as well as discrimination in employment. However, it was the same gender-based historical social conditions and lack of employment that previously led White males to gang involvement that steer minority males into gang involvement today (Grant, 2014). CRT's tenet regarding economics is particularly relevant with regard to ethnic minorities since many of them suffer from racial oppression in a way that affects their SES.

The point is that racism in the United States historically is tied to both race and SES. Racism has also played a historically influential role in the field of American education. For example, the right to educate Black Americans was officially denied in the 1857 *Dred Scott v. Stanford* court case. This U.S. Supreme Court case ruled that people of African descent imported as slaves and their descendants—free or not—were not considered citizens of the United States. Therefore, enslaved Blacks at one time in the United States were not treated equally compared to Whites and had no legal right to be educated. Historically, SES and racial equality have all been barriers to positive outcomes for minorities that were influenced by another component of CRT, constitutional law.

While physical enslavement of Blacks ended with the Emancipation Proclamation in 1863, barriers to education in the United Stated still persisted. For example, while the U.S. Constitution's Thirteenth Amendment, Section 1 states, "Neither slavery nor involuntary servitude, except as a punishment for crime whereof the party shall have been duly convicted, shall exist within the United States," more laws were created that made it legal to restrict interactions between Blacks and Whites. Known as the Jim Crow laws, between 1876 and 1965 racially based restrictions maintained racial separation between Whites and Blacks, including in schools authorized by state and local governments. Jim Crow laws made the spread of substandard education due to racial bias easily concealable and poorly funded Black schools common practice. In 1896 racial segregation was upheld under the idea of separate but equal by the *Plessy v. Ferguson* ruling. It was not until 1954 that the *Brown v. Board of Education of Topeka* case ruled that separate education of Black and White children was unconstitutional. The *Brown v. Board of Education* ruling made segregating children solely on the basis of race a violation of the Fourteenth Amendment, overturning *Plessy v. Ferguson.* However, while not *officially* legal, education in the United States at that time was still *unofficially* separate and unequal. The *Brown v. Board of Education* landmark case that introduced the term "desegregation" by definition (if not practice) was one of the most controversial policies in American school history.

Persistent educational inequities and lagging reform response time related to *Brown v. Board of Education* led to the "Brown II" decision of 1955. "Brown II" was an attempt to have *Brown v. Board of Education*'s ruling implemented quickly. Milner and Howard (2004) report, "With no clear outlines, means of implementation, or timetable to desegregate schools, many White schools refused to implement the Supreme Court's ruling" (pp. 292–93). After *Brown*, the U.S. district court ruled that Prince Edward County, Virginia, did not have to desegregate its schools immediately and included the language "with all deliberate speed." Essentially, this ruling allowed courts the flexibility to impose subjective interpretations concerning the timing of the implementation—speed—of desegregation. In plain language, "all deliberate speed" meant that schools could take their time to desegregate schools despite the best intentions of the ruling. The phrase "all deliberate speed" paved the way for White students in Prince Edward County to be given monetary assistance to attend White-only "private academies" that were taught by teachers formerly employed by the public school system, while Black students had no education at all unless they moved out of the county, making desegregation unlikely. This, in turn, lead to the 1978 "Brown III" case, which upheld that open enrollment for schools had the potential to continue to divide Black and White schoolchildren unfairly (Wishart, n.d.).

Michelson (2003) looked at the modern effects of desegregation and made the following observations after controlling for individual-, family-, and school-level covariates of achievement:

> First, students—both black and white—who have experienced desegregated schools and classrooms have benefited academically in significant and substantive ways. Second, racially identifiable black schools *and* classrooms exert significant negative effects on both black and white students' academic outcomes. Third, even in desegregated middle and high schools, tracking helps to maintain white privilege by placing whites disproportionately into higher tracks than their comparably able black peers. This practice increases whites' access to better teachers and other resources, while it diminishes access to superior opportunities to learn for students in racially identifiable black tracks. (Mickelson, 2003, p. 1560)

Delgado and Stefancic (2001) argue that civil rights litigation was motivated more by the interests of high-social-class Whites than by an interest in helping

Blacks. For Michelson (2003), the 1954 achievement gaps between Black and White students still prevail despite best efforts. She may have a point.

Research about the positive effects of eliminating majority same-race student and teacher classrooms through desegregation is mixed. On the one hand, critics argue that students in desegregated schools have higher long-term educational outcomes and occupational attainment (Michelson, 2003). On the other hand, some research says the positive effects of desegregated schools are minimal with no consistent academic short-term grade and test score benefits for Blacks (Michelson, 2003). Milner and Howard (2004) interviewed one desegregation expert who contends that desegregation just moved Black students from one school or classroom to another and did nothing to improve the resources, learning opportunities, or educational outcomes of Black students. However, Milner and Howard (2004) interviewed another desegregation expert who asserted that segregated schools created nurturing and supportive environments where Black students were better off because Black teachers cared more about them. They also note that Black students were not tracked into special education and White students were not labeled as gifted until after desegregation (Milner & Howard, 2004). Clearly, classroom merits of same-race students and teachers warrant further conversation.

In summation, originally Blacks were legally forbidden to go to school in many parts of the United States. Then they were legally restricted from attending the same schools as White students, and later, when laws were enacted to end same-race schools, those rules were circumvented to allow states to refuse to do so and then later to establish private schools that only allowed Black students to attend if they could afford to live in the right neighborhoods or to pay for the schooling. Currently, in some cities, we have a system of public education where students of color can attend better schools than low-performing schools in their neighborhoods. These are called "choice" or magnet schools, and they are typically in White neighborhoods. When parents do have opportunities to enroll their children in choice schools, they must ask "permission" for their children to attend schools outside their neighborhoods instead of having better schools created in the areas where they already live. The United States has legally enforced racially segregated same-race classrooms. Legally sanctioned racial restrictions in U.S. schools have resulted not only in same-race classrooms, but in same-race classrooms with predominantly White female teachers. During 2012, students of color in the United States made up more than 45 percent of the preschool and K–12 student population, while teachers of color made up only 17.5 percent of the education workforce (Deruy, 2016).

Since NAEP data collection didn't start till the early 1960s, it seems as if achievement gaps between Black and White students happened almost immediately after desegregation and the proliferation of Black students with White teachers (Milner & Howard, 2004). While unintentional, the effects of desegregation resulted in fewer Black educational professionals, many of whom left teaching due to mistreatment in White schools, a loss of positive professional self-identity, and failing community support in Black neighborhoods (Comer & Poussaint, 1992; Milner & Howard, 2004).

For example, after *Brown v. Board of Education,* various nonfavorable actions toward predominantly Black schools resulted in the loss of predominantly Black teachers in Black classrooms by 1986 (Oakley, Stowell, & Logan, 2009). Racially biased acts included reassigning Black teachers to White schools, while White teachers had free choice to pick whichever schools they wanted, eliminating Black teacher tenure; firing Black teachers without cause and not replacing them with other Black teachers, and assigning teachers to teach outside of their content fields (Oakley, Stowell, & Logan, 2009). Currently, America still has a deficit of Black teachers in most schools. The Albert Shanker Institute (2012) reports that in some of America's largest cities—including Boston, New York, Los Angeles, Chicago, Cleveland, New Orleans, Philadelphia, San Francisco, and Washington, D.C.—there has been a 9 percent decline in the number of Black teachers in both traditional and charter schools. While America is hiring more minority teacher than it has in the last two and a half decades, from 325,000 in 1987 to 666,000 in 2012, minority teachers are leaving the education profession at even higher rates (Albert Shanker Institute, 2012). The reason? Teacher dissatisfaction with administration was at 81 percent due to lack of voice in decision-making and lack of professionalism (Albert Shanker Institute, 2012).

Personal Bias Statement

Since this chapter addresses issues and arguments that are not only in my research field of interest, but also of personal interest to me, I thought it would be prudent to include a story about my educational background. People learn through the use of information presented in story form (Newkirk, 2014), and it is also important for people to tell their stories because it creates a psychic safe place where listeners can more readily accept ethnocentric views of socially constructed narratives they may not be otherwise ready to comfortably engage (Delgado, 1989).

As a young child, I attended a predominantly Black Head Start and kindergarten school in a predominantly Black middle-class neighborhood in South Side Chicago. I attended Head Start because my grandmother was a teacher in a Head Start school and she dragged me along to her classroom. Both of my grandmothers were Black teachers; one had a master's degree. One of my grandmothers got her teaching degree in 1929 from the Hickory Colored School in Newton, Mississippi. My kindergarten teacher was Black. She was also my mother's kindergarten teacher. My mother, aunts, godmother, and many cousins were all teachers, and most attended that same school. The school I attended in elementary school was predominantly Black and also had a Black male principal, although my first-grade teacher was White. My father was in the armed services, so I attended second and third grade at a military base school in the United Kingdom. As you would imagine, the racial composition of students in an American military base in a foreign country is extremely diverse. I could not begin to recount all the different ethnic groups with which I attended school. There were also many teachers from different backgrounds. My family did, however, live off base in a small English (all White) town.

After a few years, my family moved to Albuquerque, New Mexico, where I attended another military base school for one year in fourth grade and then a Catholic school for fifth, sixth, seventh, and eighth grades. The military base school was, again, multicultural. The Catholic school was a predominantly White and Latino upper-class student population. There I was one of three Black students out of 315, and the only Black male in my class.

During my high school years, we moved to Las Vegas, Nevada, where I attended a mixed Black, Latino, and White high school. After my baccalaureate degree, I became a guest teacher. As a guest teacher, I taught in upper-, middle-, and lower-SES schools. However, most of my long-term assignments were in low-SES urban special education classrooms. Currently, in my higher-education career, I have taught at a community college, a state university, and a land-grant university.

So, although I have lived in two countries, attended a predominantly Black school as well as racially mixed schools and even lived in a majority-White country, I had only one K–12 Black teacher. I did, however, have two Black professors, both male, one in undergraduate and one in graduate school. Between substitute teaching and being a college instructor, I have taught every grade, at least one time, from K–12 all the way through college sophomore students in both low- and high-SES neighborhoods.

Same-Race Student and Teacher Classrooms

This section begins with a discussion of the pros and cons of same-race student and teacher classrooms. Using data collected from Project Student Teacher Achievement Ratio (STAR, a randomized field trial conducted in Tennessee), Dee (2004) found that Black students learn more from Black teachers, and White students learn more from White teachers. Project STAR followed students from seventy-nine schools as they progressed from kindergarten to third grade. One might think that predominantly Black schools in the study would be more likely to have lower-performing or lower-quality Black teachers since those schools are typically the most economically disadvantaged. However, Desimone and Long (2010) and Anderson (2014) rationalize that predominantly Black schools that have few resources may be more likely to attract quality Black teachers who are motivated to make a positive difference, and less likely to attract quality White teachers because quality White teachers may not be as interested in working in a school with fewer resources. Unfortunately, the rule of thumb is that low-achieving students tend to get lower-performing teachers (Goldhaber, Lavery, & Theobald, 2015; Desimone & Long, 2010). Research suggests that positive outcomes based on student and teacher race bear further investigation.

For example, supporting the argument that Black students with Black teachers have better outcomes, Black students from disadvantaged neighborhoods seem to benefit from having Black teachers more than all other students (Dee, 2004). Dee used STAR data of roughly 11,600 students, with 2,200, 1,600, and 1,200 students entering in the first, second, and third grades, respectively, for his study. The results suggest that Black students from disadvantaged neighborhoods benefit from Black teachers based on the possibility of low-quality White teachers who work in disadvantaged schools and larger populations of Black students. For White students, the school demographics and teacher race did not seem to affect educational outcomes, and White students still seem to have higher educational outcomes regardless of school neighborhood location (Dee, 2004). However, in the United Kingdom, Coughlan (2014) reports that White students who attend school in high-SES neighborhoods do perform better than their White peers in low-SES schools because they have supplemental support that fosters resilience regardless of teacher disconnects. It would seem that race and social class are interrelated factors in both the United States and United Kingdom.

Research on same-race teacher and student classrooms also sheds light on the relationship between ethnicity and educational outcomes. In a comprehensive study that looked at both subjective essay questions and objective true-and-false questions of community college instructors, minority students performed better in classes where instructors were of the same race or ethnicity (Fairlie, Hoffmann, & Oreopoulos, 2014). This is similar to Villegas and Irvine's (2010) study, which agrees that minority students perform better with minority teachers, stating that even the mere presence of a teacher of color has positive benefits that are reflected in educational outcomes. These positive effects are reflected in community colleges, where underrepresented minority students are 1.2–2.8 percentage points more likely to pass classes, 2.0–2.9 percentage points less likely to drop out of classes, and 2.4–3.2 percentage points more likely to get a grade of B or higher in classes with underrepresented instructors (Fairlie, Hoffmann, & Oreopoulos, 2014, p. 2588). These are concrete statistics which support the idea that minority students fare better with minority teachers.

Ideological and Conceptual Debates

Not all the evidence of educational outcomes for same-race classrooms is positive. Gay (2000) reports that it is a mistake to assume that shared ethnic membership is the sole answer to educating minority students. However, Gay (2000) also feels that students learn better when they receive information based on their own cultural experience. It would not be unreasonable to assume that a student will have higher educational outcomes from a teacher who has the same cultural background. However, one quantitative study by Driessen (2015) that examined cognitive and noncognitive effects of teacher and student ethnicity in the Netherlands, Belgium, Germany, and the United Kingdom revealed that

> there is as yet little unambiguous empirical evidence that a stronger degree of ethnic match, be it in the form of a one-to-one coupling of teachers to students with the same ethnic background, or a larger share of minority teachers at an ethnically mixed school, leads to predominantly positive results. (Driessen, 2015, p. 188)

In a study that examined the impact of African American teachers on African American eighth graders in Texas Title I schools, results indicate that African

American students do not necessarily fare better when taught by African American teachers. Gay (2005) asserts that "similar ethnicity between students and teachers may be potentially beneficial, but it is not a guarantee of pedagogical effectiveness" (p. 205). In fact, Hunt's (2012) study showed that achievement gaps between Black and White eighth-grade students were *greater* on campuses with *larger* populations of Black teachers, indicating that teacher race alone is not a determining factor in closing achievement gaps for Black students, since other factors such as teacher quality also matter. Goldhaber, Lavery, and Theobald (2015) define teacher quality as comprised of both input and output. Teacher quality input consists of experience, licensees, and certifications; teacher quality outputs are performance estimates such as grades and tests scores (Goldhaber, Lavery, & Theobald, 2015). Gaps between inputs and outputs are called teacher quality gaps.

Mickelson (2003) asserts that Black schools and classrooms (which are more likely to be in disadvantaged neighborhoods) have significant negative educational outcomes for both Black and White students. Low SES, a critical component analyzed in CRT, may also be an interlaced factor with same-race students and teachers, since the testing gap in standardized test scores of affluent and low-income students is double the gap between Blacks and Whites (Tavernis, 2012). In other words, achievement gaps persist between high academically achieving White students in affluent neighborhoods and high academically achieving White students from low-SES schools (Plucker, Hardesty, & Burroughs, 2014). Negative outcomes of low-SES neighborhoods seem to persist regardless of teacher race.

According to Schmidt (2015):

> Affluent students are consistently provided with greater opportunity to learn more rigorous content, and students who are exposed to higher-level math have a better ability to apply it to real-world situations of adult life, such as calculating interest and estimating the required amount of carpeting for a room. (p. 1)

By the time high-income children start school, they have spent about four hundred hours more than poor children in literacy–related activities (Tavernis, 2012). Unfortunately, low SES and lack of opportunity to take advanced classes go hand in hand for all students, regardless of race (Schmidt, 2015). Additionally, Alexander, Entwisle, and Olson (2001) assert that students from low-SES neighborhoods are less likely to be able to take advantage of access to libraries and museums during summer recess. Low-SES students start the following year even farther behind students who attend school in more affluent neighborhoods.

Boggs and Dunbar (2015) argue that, with regard to urban education, schools merely reproduce social class, which is also a reflection of American racial preferences. All too often the lens of Whiteness serves as the perspective through which other ethnic groups are viewed (Boggs & Dunbar, 2015). Only when students and teachers are exposed to different points of view and multicultural experiences are valued in the classrooms do schools begin to disrupt racial bias and have truly meaningful educational outcomes.

In both arguments—same-race student and teacher classrooms and mixed-race student and teacher classrooms—teacher quality is an important variable in learning outcomes for students. The next section will expound on key concepts related to the influence of student and teacher race on educational outcomes: teacher quality, high expectations, positive feedback, empathy, connectedness, and student racial/ethnic identification.

Arguments Related to Race and Student/Teacher Outcomes

Measures of teacher quality can include experience, degree level, certifications, professional development, and student achievement (Desimone & Long, 2010; Hanushek & Rivkin, 2010). It would be natural to conclude that teacher quality may be more important to student outcomes than the racial composition of students and teachers. However, Desimone and Long (2010) found evidence that "lower achieving students are initially assigned to teachers who emphasize basic instruction, and higher achieving students are assigned teachers who emphasize more advanced instruction" (p. 3024). As a result, Desimone and Long (2010) assert that teacher quality and type of instruction have little or no effect because low-achieving students are assigned teachers who give fewer instructional minutes, a factor that increases achievement gaps regardless of student race. Time spent on instruction, also known as opportunity to learn, and type of instruction were more significant to closing achievement gaps than was teacher quality.

Hattie's work (2009), which includes a synthesis of over eight hundred meta-analyses (a meta-analysis is a large, qualitative study of smaller similar studies), reports that teacher subject matter knowledge has only a $d = 0.09$ effect and teacher training has only a $d = 0.11$ effect size. These numbers are insignificant: Hattie asserts that an effect size has to be over $d = 0.40$ to be of a positive measurable value. However, teacher-student relationships have an effect size of $d = 0.72$, and teacher credibility in the eyes of the student has an effect size of $d = 0.90$, while teacher high expectations only have an effect size of $d = 0.43$. It is reasonable to assume that, based on these numbers, student/teacher relationships and student trust have measurable benefits in the classroom.

Why do student/teacher relationships and trust appear to have more positive results than subject matter knowledge, teacher training, and high expectations? Teachers who have deep content rarely teach beyond a surface level because they have little choice in instructional methods or curriculum (Hattie, 2009). Hattie also recounts that there is no difference in teacher quality when teachers are from different backgrounds as analyzed by same-race students and teachers: effect sizes are $d = 0.02$ for reading and $d = 0.03$ for mathematics (p. 118). It would seem that teachers who are adept at building relationships, commanding credibility, and helping to facilitate students' belief in themselves through exhibiting high expectations are the most effective teachers.

High Expectations

High expectations have been described as the belief that *all* students can achieve (Green, 2014). Dweck (2013) contends that, while seemingly obvious, high expectations are important to the development of Black males and subsequent teacher interactions with them, since having positive beliefs increases the amplitude of brainwaves and increases productivity. Racial bias and low teacher expectations based on gender, ethnicity, and social class have limited learning opportunities for minority students in other countries such as New Zealand (Jones, 2014; Rubie-Davis, Hattie, & Hamilton, 2007). In fact, Coughlan (2014) reports that White working-class students in the United Kingdom suffer from lack of high expectations in low-SES neighborhoods.

However, high teacher expectations may be a factor in why American Asian students tend to outperform White students, despite having predominantly White female teachers. For example, Asian American test-takers outperform Whites in the quantitative math subtest by an effect size of nearly 0.38 (Hsin & Xie, 2014). Assumptions about the educational achievement of Asian American persist in at least three areas: SES, cognitive ability, and work/ethic and motivation. However, SES rates are not uniform for all American Asians (poverty rates for Vietnamese and

Chinese Americans are higher than for American Whites), little evidence suggests that there is a cognitive difference between White and Asian students, and little empirical evidence actually supports the perceptions that Asian American students are more focused and motivated by education (Hsin & Xie, 2014). Consequently, Hsin and Xie (2014) do assert that teachers' high expectations may motivate Asian students to perform higher academically and that as a result Asian American students exert greater effort in the classroom.

Hattie and Timperley (2007) report that one practice that has shown promise for all students, and that demonstrated more positive effects for Black students, was teacher use of positive feedback.

Positive Feedback

Yeager et al. (2014) conducted three double-blind, randomized field experience tests to measure Black and White middle and high school student response to positive feedback. Studies 1 and 2 were conducted with seventh-grade students who were given critical feedback on essays from their teachers matched with teacher high standards and the belief that the students were capable of meeting those standards—a method called wise feedback. Wise feedback has the advantage of increasing a student's likelihood of submitting a paper revision and of improving the quality of final drafts. Positive effects of wise feedback were the strongest for African American students who previously felt distrust toward school. The final study was conducted in a low-income public high school using attributional retraining. Attributional retraining focuses on critical feedback coupled with teacher belief in student potential. Together, wise feedback and critical feedback fostered a positive classroom culture of trust (Yeager et al., 2014). The results of the final study indicated a significant increase in African American student grades and a slight but statistically significant increase in White student grades (Yeager et al., 2014). It would seem that wise feedback alone is not sufficient to improve educational outcomes for Black students. What was shown to be effective was establishing a positive view of constructive feedback through using attributional retraining, which allowed Black students opportunities to improve with guided support as an effective way to eliminate feelings of teacher bias, and, in turn, increased grades.

McGrady and Reynolds's (2013) research on Asian, Black, Hispanic, and White tenth graders in the 2002 Education Longitudinal Study suggests that White teachers usually view Asian students more positively than White students, view Black students more negatively, and view Hispanic students similar to White students. It would stand to reason that a teacher's ability to eliminate conscious bias would increase educational outcomes. Teacher mindfulness with regard to bias may be one way to help build and maintain student teacher relationships.

An often-forgotten common denominator for student success, building strong relationships has been proven to have positive effects for both K-12 and college students of color (Warren, 2012; Allen, 2010). According to Hattie (2009), "Building relationships implies agency, efficacy, [and] respect by the teacher for what the student brings to the class (from home, culture, and peers) and recognition of the life of the student" (p. 118). Building strong student and teacher relationships is also known as a key factor in culturally responsive teaching (Hyland, 2005). Effective student-teacher relationships help bolster student self-esteem and self-efficacy.

A student's sense of self-efficacy is one way to increase resiliency. Resilience has been defined as "the strengths that people and systems demonstrate that enable them to rise above adversity" (Van Breda, 2001, p. 14). Marsh, Chaney, and Jones's research (2012) suggests that high-achieving Black students in diverse high schools find resilience to oppression through forming and joining social groups. Hill's research (1972) asserts that family kinship bonds (the strength of family) can never be overlooked with regard to Black student success. Additionally, Griffin and Allen's (2006) research suggests that resilience is the most salient factor for Black students who attend both well-resourced suburban high-schools and low-resourced urban schools to combat negative racial climates and other barriers, such as lack of resources, to positive academic outcomes. High future expectations are an indicator of resilience (Slaughter-Defoe & Rubin, 2001; Wyman et al., 1993).

However, according to Milner and Howard (2004), for Black students, high expectations alone are not enough. Having high expectations is more powerful when you believe in and identify with your students based on shared common experiences (Milner & Howard, 2004). Empathy with students is one instance where cultural and ethnic affiliation of same-race teacher and student classrooms has persuasive benefits.

Empathy

In a study of two largely predominantly Black high school districts that looked at empathic concern and perspective-taking, Warren (2012) found that empathy is most useful for helping teachers establish trusting relationships and build strong classroom communities. Empathy may also be a beneficial way to increase teacher willingness to take risks, make emotional investments and connections, and be flexible with students (Warren, 2012). Teacher empathy may also help establish connectedness in a manner that helps to increase academic engagement.

Connectedness

Conchas and Rodriguez (2008) found that connectedness and a sense of community are key ingredients in the academic engagement of African American students. Teachers who are able to help provide a sense of community are viewed more favorably by Black students (Coleman, 2007). It may be that positive effects on Black students in classrooms of Black teachers before desegregation were beneficial from cultural connectedness. Bendroth and Brereton (2002) report that five years after the Thirteenth Amendment was passed in 1865, 80 percent of African Americans were illiterate; but by 1910, the numbers had declined to 50 percent. Part of the reason for the increase in literacy for African Americans in the early nineteenth century was the social groups created by Black American church members that helped build a sense of community based on shared experiences of people of African descent (Barnes, 2005; Smith, 2004). The Black church, in particular, encouraged the idea that education is the first step toward freedom (Lincoln & Lawrence, 1990). The social support provided by the Black church through education was so influential that, between 1861 and 1890, most African Americans in higher-education institutions were enrolled in schools that were categorized as church-affiliated (Leavell, 1970). The majority of those religious schools that supported Blacks getting an education were taught by Black teachers.

Student Racial/Ethnic Identification

Racial socialization, often conceptualized as the implicit and explicit messages parents convey about race, helps African American youth to develop a positive racial identity, particularly in the face of racial bias and adversity (Stevenson, 1995). However, Black boys and girls develop the highest levels of self-esteem independent of how they are performing in school (Patterson, 2006). In other words, self-esteem does not necessarily translate into good grades. In fact, racial socialization from parents is positively associated with all student educational outcome variables *except* school belonging and valuing education (Wang & Huguley, 2012). Davies,

Spencer, and Steele (2005) call the affinity of race over schooling the disidentification of education. Alternately, preparation for possible racial bias from teachers and students is positively correlated with school identification and cognitive engagement, but not with GPA or educational aspirations (Wang & Huguley, 2012). In fact, some might say that Black racial identity may be a negative relational factor in academic experience of Black students because, in some schools, being seen as intelligent is seen as acting White.

Acting White is a negative connotation that intelligence is only associated with White people, and that modeling the behavior, speech, and actions of your oppressor is culturally unfavorable. Much of the negative sentiment surrounding acting White has more to do with the perception that "White" cultural norms and history are seen as the standard lens through which to view the world and that people of color are not given equal standing. School textbooks, curriculum, suspensions, and expulsions, as well as media influences, leave some students with a feeling their unique cultural experiences are not valued. Often called oppositional culture (Ogbu, 2008), attitudes about acting White are a phenomenon described as resulting from a combination of societal and school discrimination, instrumental community factors such as perception of lack of jobs, and Black oppositional culture. These three interrelated factors may contribute to the role of racial identity in Black students' low academic outcomes. It would seem that a strong sense of racial identity has the potential to be both good and bad.

It is also worth noting that racial identity may affect gender identity differently. For example, Taylor's article "Go Sisters Go! Black Women Are the Most Educated Group in the United States" (2014) shares the fact that despite the misconceptions and stereotypes about African American women, half of all Black women between the ages of eighteen and twenty-four are now pursuing degrees. Additionally, 2011 data shows that 9.7 percent of all Black women are enrolled in colleges; the number of African American women earning master's degrees between 1991 and 2001 rose 150 percent (Taylor, 2014; Catalyst, 2004). Since the majority of students in the United States are taught by White females, the achievement of Black female students does not seem to be restricted by race.

Academic achievement of African American women makes it difficult to argue that helping to establish a sense of Black racial/gender identity (or that teacher racial identity alone) is a catalyst for academic achievement of Black students. For example, while students with a positive view of their ethnicity demonstrate enhanced academic performance, they also show an increase in positive developmental adjustment, and a decline in participation in delinquency as well as improved sociability (Hattie, 2009, p. 56). Positive behavioral effects are hard to measure by the race of a teacher alone.

It may be that all of the above attributes, including teacher quality, resilience, high expectations, positive feedback, empathy, connectedness, and ethnic and racial identity are just examples of culturally responsive good teaching (Ladson-Billings, 1995). Ladson-Billings and Tate (1995) describe culturally responsive teachers as educators who practice seven principles: (1) effective communication of high expectations, (2) a pedagogy of active teaching methods, (3) treating the role of a teacher as facilitator, (4) inclusion of students who are culturally and linguistically diverse, (5) awareness of cultural sensitivity, (6) teaching a curriculum that is reshaped to include student-controlled classroom discourse, and (7) implementing small-group instruction and academically related discourse. The aforementioned are all pedagogical behaviors of both *good Black* and *good White* teachers. However, good teaching by both good Black and White teachers may be mitigated by the fact that teachers are very rarely involved in curriculum decisions, which suggests that research should focus more on the effects of having more diverse education administrators.

Discussion

This chapter focused largely on Black/White student/teacher differences. It began with a brief overview of the history of education for Blacks in America using critical race theory. CRT was a useful lens through which to examine laws that serve as barriers to people of color in their pursuit of an education. This is true for national, state, and local laws that deny or restrict opportunities for minority students, including desegregation laws. Legal policies that restrict educational access to schooling are no less damaging to both Black and White students than school and district policies that do not serve all students equally. Next followed a brief literature review that synthesized arguments for and against same-race teachers and schools. It would seem as if inequities of educational outcomes in the United States encompass more than issues of student and teacher race. Many education policies still segregate students by income, both in the classroom through tracking and pedagogy and in the building through detention and placement in special education. Finally, arguments related to the debate of same-race students and teacher classrooms were included. If traits such as professional quality, empathy, and cultural competency are becoming more valued in the corporate world while the teaching profession is losing its economic and social status, it may be, as Desimone and Long (2010) suggest, that the best teachers may no longer be in the classroom but in other places like the boardroom where they feel valued.

Questions to ponder: What happens to the cultural gains of students who attend same-race student and teacher classrooms after they graduate from high school and either work or go to school with members of other cultures? Are students who attend same-race student and teacher classrooms effectively prepared to work in multicultural environments? Longitudinal outcomes of same-race classrooms at this writing have yet to be conducted.

It may be shortsighted to overlook the benefits of predominantly multiracial student and teacher classrooms. Single-race student and teacher classrooms miss learning opportunities: White students can learn from Black teachers and vice versa. In the words of Anderson (2015), "Anecdotal and empirical evidence suggests that teachers of color can help disrupt what are often one-sided portrayals of the world and offer invaluable insight to students from different backgrounds" (p. 4). Same-race student and teacher classrooms may restrict opportunities for students to learn from other cultures.

Does it make sense to say that Black students learn differently than White students depending on the race of the teacher? Rimer (1988) reported a story about a debate between New York officials and educators that broke into heated arguments over opinions that Blacks and Whites have different learning styles. Georgia State University's Asa Hilliard (in Rimer, 1988) suggested that teachers "tend to treat the stylistic mismatch (learning style discrepancies) between some students and schools as a student deficiency or problem requiring the students to change. We fail to see the potential for enriching the school experience for all children." Alternatively, Kenneth B. Clark said: "If kids are respected and taught, they will learn" (Rimer, 1988). Richard Buery, the deputy mayor of New York, announced the city's plan to hire one thousand Black, Latino, and Asian male teachers by 2017 (Layton, 2015). The reason? "We think white students will benefit as well from having diverse teachers because it breaks down stereotypes" (Buery, quoted in Layton, 2015). Are students just students, or are students fundamentally different because of, and not in spite of, their race?

Clearly, the argument over same-race student and teacher classrooms is nuanced and complex, and not as black and white as it seems. The overarching theme from the selected research articles seems to be that many of the laws that deny Blacks education opportunities, like zero-tolerance laws, also restrict them from access to higher social classes. Barriers to social classes are reflected in many policies that affect low-SES families both Black and White. For example, parents in Connecticut, Kentucky, Ohio, and Missouri have been arrested for sending their children to better public schools outside of their districts (Flaherty, 2011). Smith (2012) reports that in 2012 a homeless mother was given a combined twelve-year sentence, seven years in prison and five years' probation, for enrolling her six-year-old son in a better school district that she did not officially reside in. While restricting access to a better school outside a district is not the same thing as segregation, placing a parent in jail for doing so is inequitable and oppressive.

Sadly, Flaherty (2011) also reports that school districts in California and Massachusetts hire special investigators to follow children home to make sure they actually live in the high-achieving districts in which their parents say they live. Other school districts use high-tech services such as Verifyresidence.com to covertly videotape, photograph, and document children from house to school (Flaherty, 2011). Since living close to a good school is a key factor in buying a home for both owners who have children and those who do not (National Association of Realtors, 2012), being unable to afford a home in a better school/neighborhood reduces a family's chances of opportunities for a better education. In fact, the 2016 Distressed Communities Index suggests that family zip code is an indicator of positive life outcomes. Racial segregation by race or income level intersects economics, equity, *and* racism, all critical components of analyses by CRT. The ability to live in a quality neighborhood and access to a good school for one's children are issues that were compounded for African Americans after desegregation.

Additionally, the benefits of desegregation suggested during the 1960s overlook the importance of Black neighborhoods, Black families, and kinship networks found in Black communities before the civil rights acts integrated neighborhoods and reduced the economic vibrancy of Black neighborhoods. This in turn contributed to the decline of educational outcomes due to decreased economic power to support Black schools. Bell (1983) encourages implementing plans to improve the quality of schools in Black neighborhoods instead of opposing racial balancing plans for positive educational outcomes.

Interestingly, providing equal academic resources, including books, was the intent of the *Brown v. Board of Education* court case, not bussing Black students out of Black neighborhoods into White schools in White neighborhoods (Milner &

Howard, 2004). Then as now, same-race classrooms seem to have almost as many disadvantages as advantages. All too often, benefits of cultural affiliation of all-Black schools are intertwined with funding inequalities of low-SES neighborhoods. This is true in the United States and abroad. Additionally, a critical analysis of school hiring practices, school textbooks, curriculum design, and school policies is necessary before any effective long-term changes can be implemented by teachers in the classroom. In a review of Derrick Bell, Delgado and Stefancic (2005) share that Bell asserts effective school policies that include

> publication of and prompt enforcement of school rules and penalties; daily principal visits to classrooms and rigorous supervision of staff; meaningful parent participation in the school program; close monitoring of students' progress; criterion-referenced tests to determine reading groups; teaching assignments determined on the basis of expertise, not preference; highly structured, self-contained classrooms modified by some teaching and tempered with affection and consideration; using effective teaching materials not approved by the board, especially phonics, mathematics word problems, and black history, culture, and literature. (p. 124)

To be clear, the problem with schools is not segregation but racism (Bell, 1992). It would seem that race, class, gender, and cultural competency are an interrelated matrix in good teaching and effective classrooms regardless of student/teacher ethnicity. CRT is a suitable framework with which to examine educational outcomes of same-race students and teacher classrooms.

Challenges of Doing Same-Race Student Teacher Research

This chapter looked at arguments pertaining to same-race student and teacher classrooms and included further discussion of teacher quality, the SES of the school, resilience, high expectations, positive feedback, empathy, and connectedness, as well as the merits and limitations of ethnic and racial identity of same-race student and teacher classrooms. On either side of the argument, those who favor of same-race student and teacher classrooms and those who do not, the overall conclusions are less than definitive. For example, after controlling for student SES and other student, teacher, and school characteristics (within-school differences and between-school differences) of varied racial compositions, the causes of racial achievement gaps are often indeterminate (NAEP, 2015). Additionally, while many of the variables of same-race student and teacher classrooms are measurable, some are not. A large part of the mixed findings of same-race student and teacher classrooms stem from lack of cohesive research questions and designs. For example, in same-race student and teacher arguments, despite being intertwined, very little of the research examines the variables of economics, equity, legal issues, and race the same way. To solve this dilemma, very specific research needs to be conducted.

Recommendations for Future Research

To make the arguments about Black students with Black teacher classrooms more compelling would require multiple studies, both quantitative and qualitative, that look at student race, student gender, student achievement, student SES, teacher race, teacher gender, teacher quality, teacher training, and school demographics such as SES and racial composition as both dependent and independent variables related to educational outcomes. School demographic and racial composition is especially relevant since where a student lives is often an indicator of life outcomes (Distressed Communities Index, 2016), White students are no longer the majority in American schools (Wong, 2015), and White students are also more likely to attend majority-White schools (Dwyer, 2014). An additional aspect of K–12 same-race student and teacher classroom outcomes that may benefit from more study is the effects of summer recess between advantaged and disadvantaged students who do and do not attend year-round schools. This is especially relevant since SES is more of a predictor of educational outcomes than race (Tavernis, 2012). It will not be until studies such as the ones above are conducted that arguments related to same-race student and teacher classrooms and cultural responsive pedagogy will be answered.

Highlighting the pros and cons of same-race students and teacher classrooms has been challenging as well as rewarding. In the words of Bell (1992), the challenge of using CRT to examine issues of race, class and gender has been to tell the truth without "causing disabling despair" (p. ix). However provoking it may be, research that outlines arguments pertaining to educational outcomes helps to inform practice and advance research surrounding teacher pedagogy and practice, and there needs to be more of it.

REFERENCES

Alexander, K. L., Entwisle, D. R., & Olson, L. S. (2001). Schools, achievement, and inequality: A seasonal perspective. *Educational Evaluation and Policy Analysis 25*, 171–91.

Allen, W. R. (2010). The color of success: African-American college student outcomes at predominantly White and historically Black public colleges and universities. *Harvard Educational Review 62*(1), 26–45.

Anderson, M. D. (2014, September). America's unspoken education issue: Black kids need Black teachers. *The Root.* Retrieved from http://www.theroot.com/articles/culture/2014/09/the_teacher_wars_book_provides_more_evidence_that_teachers_of_color_matter.html.

Anderson, M. D. (2015, August). Why schools need more teachers of color—for White students: Nonwhite educators can offer new and valuable perspectives for children of all backgrounds. *The Atlantic.* Retrieved from http://www.theatlantic.com/education/archive/2015/08/teachers-of-color-white-students/400553/.

Albert Shanker Institute. (2012, September). The state of teacher diversity. Washington, DC: Albert Shanker Institute.

Baker, J. A., Cookson, P., Gay, G. Hawley, W., Jacqueline J. I., Sonia, N., Janet. W. S., & Walter, G,. S. (2005). Education and Diversity. *Social Education 69*(1), 36–40.

Barnes, S. L. (2005). Black church culture and community action. *Social Forces 84*(2): 967–94.

Bell, D. (1983). Time for the teachers: Putting educators back into the brown remedy. *Journal of Negro Education 52*(3), 290–301.

Bell. D. (1992). *Faces at the bottom of the well.* New York: Basic Books.

Bell, D. (2003). *Ethical ambition.* Bloomsbury Publishing PLC.

Bendroth, M. L., & Brereton, V. L. (2002). *Women and twentieth-century Protestantism.* Urbana: University of Illinois Press.

Blackdemographics.com. (2015). *Black educational attainment by the numbers.* Retrieved from http://blackdemographics.com/education-2/education/.

Boggs, B., & Dunbar, C. (2015). An interpretive history of urban education and leadership in an age of perceived racial invisibility. In M. Khalifa, C. Grant, & N. Arnold (eds.), *Handbook for Urban Educational Leadership.* Lanham, MD: Rowman & Littlefield.

Bohrnstedt, G., Kitmitto, S., Ogut, B., Sherman, D., and Chan, D. (2015). *School composition and the Black-White achievement gap* (NCES 2015-018). U.S. Department of Education, National Center for Education Statistics. Retrieved from http://nces.ed.gov/pubsearch.

Brayboy, B. M. J. (2005). Toward a tribal critical race theory in education. *Urban Review 37*(5), 425–46. doi:10.1007/s11256-005-0018-y.

Camera, L. (2015, December). Despite progress, graduation gaps between whites and minorities persist: A new report shows schools still have work to do to get more students to toss their caps. *US News & World Report.* Retrieved from http://www.usnews.com/news/blogs/data-mine/2015/12/02/college-graduation-gaps-between-white-and-minority-students-persist.

Catalyst (2004). *Advancing African-American women in the workplace: What managers need to know.* New York: Catalyst Publications.

Coleman, B. (2007). Successful White teachers of Black students: Teaching across racial lines in urban middle school science classrooms. Ed.D. diss., University of Massachusetts.

Comer, J. P., & Poussaint, A. P. (1992). *Raising Black children: Two leading psychiatrists confront the educational, social and emotional problems facing Black children.* New York: Penguin.

Conchas, G. Q., & Rodriguez, L. F. (2008). *Small schools and urban youth: Using the power of school culture to engage students.* Thousand Oaks, CA: Corwin.

Cottman, M., H. (2015, September). Do Black students really need Black teachers? Blackamericanweb.com. Retrieved from http://blackamericaweb.com/2015/09/17/do-black-students-really-need-black-teachers/2/.

Coughlan, S. (2014, June). Poor White pupils "need best teachers and long days." *BBC News.* Retrieved from http://www.bbc.com/news/education-27886925.

Davies, P. G., Spencer, S. J., & Steele, C. M. (2005). Clearing the air: Identity safety moderates the effects of stereotype threat on women's leadership aspirations. *Journal of Personality and Social Psychology 88*(2), 276–87. doi:10.1037/0022-3514.88.2.276.

Dee, T. (2004, Spring). The race connection. *Education Next 2*(2), 53–59.

Delgado, R. (1989). Storytelling for oppositionists and others: A plea for narrative. *Michigan Law Review 87*(8), 2411–41.

Delgado, R., & Stefancic, J. (2001). *Critical race theory: An introduction.* New York: New York University Press.

Delgado, R., & Stefancic, J. (2005). *The Derrick Bell reader.* New York: New York University Press.

Deruy, E. (2016). Student diversity is up but teachers are mostly White. American Association of Colleges for Teacher Education. Retrieved from https://aacte.org/news-room/aacte-in-the-news/347-student-diversity-is-up-but-teachers-are-mostly-white.

Desimone, L., & Long, D. (2010). Teacher effects and the achievement gap: Do teacher and teaching quality influence the achievement gap between Black and White and high- and low-SES students in the early grades? *Teachers College Record 112*(12), 3024–73.

Distressed Communities Index. (2016). The 2016 Distressed Communities Index: An analysis of community well being across the United States. Economic Innovation Group. Retrieved from http://eig.org/research.

Driessen, G. (2015). Teacher ethnicity, student ethnicity, and student outcomes. *Intercultural*

Education 26(3), 179–191. doi:10.1080/14675986.2015.1048049.

Du Bois, W. E. B. (1971/1935). *Black Reconstruction in America, 1860–1880.* New York: Harcourt Brace.

Dweck, C. (2013). Changing mindsets: Motivating students with Carol Dweck. Webinar *Education Week*. Retrieved from edweek.org/media/2012-02-16_changingmindsets.pdf.

Dwyer, L. (2014). 6 shocking facts about public school segregation: Today is the 60th anniversary of the *Brown v. Board of Education* decision, yet many of our campuses are separate and unequal. *Takepart*. Retrieved from http://www.takepart.com/article/2014/05/17/shocking-facts-about-school-segregation.

Fairlie, R., Hoffmann, F., & Oreopoulos, P. (2014). A community college instructor like me: Race and ethnicity interactions in the classroom. *American Economic Review* 104(8), 2567–91. doi:10.1257/aer.104.8.2567.

Flaherty, M. (2011, October). The latest crime wave: Sending your child to a better school. *Wall Street Journal.* Retrieved from http://www.wsj.com/articles/SB10001424053111903285704576557610352019804.

Gay, G. (2000). *Culturally responsive teaching: Theory, research, and practice.* New York: Teachers College Press.

Gay, G. (2005). Politics of multicultural teacher education. *Journal of Teacher Education 56*(3), 221–228.

Goldenberg, D. (2003). *The curse of Ham: Race and slavery in early Judaism, Christianity, and Islam.* Princeton, NJ: Princeton University Press.

Goldhaber, D., Lavery, L., & Theobald, R. (2015) Uneven playing field? Assessing the teacher quality gap between advantaged and disadvantaged students. *Educational Researcher 44*(5), 293–307. doi:10.3102/0013189X15592622.

Grant, J. (2014). *The boy problem: Educating boys in urban America, 1870–1970.* Baltimore: John Hopkins University Press.

Green, R. L. (2014). *Expect the most, provide the best: How high expectations, outstanding instruction, and curricular innovations help all students succeed.* New York: Scholastic Books.

Griffin, K., & Allen, W. (2006). Mo' money, mo' problems? High-achieving Black high school students' experiences with resources, racial climate, and resilience. *Journal of Negro Education 75*(3), 478–94.

Hattie, J. (2009) *Visible learning: A synthesis of over 800 meta-analyses relating to achievement.* New York: Routledge.

Hattie, J., & Timperley, H. (2007). The power of feedback. *Review of Educational Research 77*(1), 81–122.

Hanushek, E. A., & Rivkin, S. G. (2010). The quality and distribution of teachers under the No Child Left Behind Act. *Journal of Economic Perspectives 24*(3), 133–50.

Hill, R. B. (1972). *The strength of Black families.* New York: Emerson Hall.

Hotchkiss, W. A. (2016). Slave codes of the State of Georgia, 1848. Race, racism and the Law: No struggle, no progress. Retrieved from http://racism.org/index.php?option=com_content&view=article&id=454:slavelaw&catid=118&Itemid=243.

Hsin, A., & Xie, Yu. (2014). Explaining Asian Americans academic advantage over Whites. *Proceedings of the National Academy of Sciences of the United States of America 111*(23), 8416–8421.

Hunt, W. C., Jr. (2012). The relationship between African-American teachers and 8th grade student achievement on Title I campuses. Ed.D. diss., University of Houston.

Hyland, N. E. (2005). Being a good teacher of Black students? White teachers and unintentional racism. *Curriculum Inquiry 35*(4), 429–59.

Johnson, C., & Kritsonis, W. A. (2006). The national dilemma of African American students: Disparities in mathematics achievement and instruction. *National Forum of Applied Educational Research Journal 19*(3), 1–8.

Jones, N. (2014, May), Teachers' bias against Maori pupils revealed in study. NZherald.co.nz. Retrieved from http://www.nzherald.co.nz/nz/news/article.cfm?c_id=1&objectid=11249785.

Jones, V. (2007, January). Van Jones at the NCMR. *YouTube*. Retrieved from https://www.youtube.com/watch?v=n2z6nOOO-2Y&list=PLE065B0A498C79451.

Krogstad, J. M. (2016, July). Five facts about Latino and education. Pew Research Center. Retrieved from http://www.pewresearch.org/fact-tank/2016/07/28/5-facts-about-latinos-and-education.

Ladson-Billings, G. (1995). *The dreamkeepers: Successful teachers of African American children.* San Francisco: Jossey Bass.

Ladson-Billings, G., & Tate, W. (1995). Toward a critical race theory of education. *Teachers College Record 97*(1), 47–68.

Layton, L. (2015, December 11). Wanted in New York City: A thousand Black, Latino and Asian male teachers. *Washington Post*. Retrieved from https://www.washingtonpost.com/local/education/wanted-in-new-york-city-a-thousand-black-latino-and-asian-male-teachers/2015/12/11/a8cc0f52-9f7f-11e5-a3c5-c77f2cc5a43c_story.html.

Leavell, U. W. (1970). *Philanthropy in Negro education.* Westport, CT: Negro Universities Press.

Lincoln, C. E., & Lawrence, H. M. (1990). *The Black church in the African American experience.* Durham, NC: Duke University Press.

Mahmud, T., Mutua, A. D., & Valdes, F. (2015). LatCrit praxis @ XX: Toward equal justice in law, education and society. *Chicago-Kent Law Review 90*(2), 361–427.

Marsh, K., Chaney, C., & Jones, D. (2012). The strengths of high-achieving Black high school students in a racially diverse setting. *Journal of Negro Education 81*(1), 39–51.

Martin, R. (2012, March). Are Black students better off with Black teachers? *Clutch*. Retrieved from http://www.clutchmagonline.com/2012/03/are-black-students-better-off-with-black-teachers/.

McGrady, P. B., & Reynolds, J. R. (2013). Racial mismatch in the classroom: Beyond Black-White differences. *Sociology of Education 86*(1), 3–17. doi:10.1177/0038040712444857.

Mickelson, R. A. (2003). The academic consequences of desegregation and segregation: Evidence from the Charlotte-Mecklenburg schools. *North Carolina Law Review 81,* 1513–62.

Milner, H. R., & Howard, T. C. (2004). Black teachers, Black students, Black communities, and brown: Perspectives and insights from experts. *Journal of Negro Education 73*(3), 285–97.

National Assessment of Educational Programs (NAEP). (2015). *School composition and the Black-White achievement gap*. Washington, DC: National Assessment of Educational Programs.

National Association of Realtors. (2012). *Profile of home buyers and sellers 2012*. Washington, DC: National Association of Realtors.

National Center for Education Statistics. (2012). *Improving the measurement of socioeconomic status for the national assessment of educational progress: A theoretical foundation.* Retrieved from https://nces.ed.gov/nationsreportcard/pdf/researchcenter/Socioeconomic_Factors.pdf.

Newkirk, T. (2014). *Minds made for stories: How we really read and write informational and persuasive texts.* Portsmouth, NH: Heinemann.

North Carolina Digital History (2010). A bill to prevent all persons from teaching slaves to read or write, the use of figures excepted (1830). Legislative Papers, 1830–31, Session of the General Assembly. Retrieved from http://www.learnnc.org/lp/editions/nchist-newnation/4384.

Oakley, D., Stowell, J., & Logan, J. R. (2009). The impact of desegregation on Black teachers in the metropolis, 1970–2000. *Ethnic and Racial Studies 32*(9), 1576–98. doi:10.1080/01419870902780997.

Ogbu, J. (2008). *Minority status, oppositional culture, and schooling: Sociocultural, political, and historical studies in education*. New York: Routledge.

Patterson, O. (2006, March 25). A poverty of the mind. *New York Times.* Retrieved from http://www.nytimes.com/2006/03/26/opinion/26patterson.html?pagewanted=1.

Plucker, J. A., Hardesty, J., & Burroughs, N. (2014). *Talent on the sidelines: Excellence gaps and*

America's persistent talent underclass. Storrs, CT: Center for Education Policy Analysis, University of Connecticut. Retrieved from http://cepa.uconn.edu/mindthegap.

Ransaw, T. (2013). *The art of being cool: The pursuit of Black masculinity*. African American Images: Chicago.

Razack, S., Smith, M., & Thobani, S. (2010). *States of race: Critical race feminism for the 21st century*. Toronto: Between the Lines.

Reiland, R. (2009, September 17). Van's line. *New Spectator.* Retrieved from https://spectator.org/40888_vans-line/.

Rimer, S. (1988, June). Do Black and White children learn the same way? *New York Times.* Retrieved from http://www.nytimes.com/1988/06/24/nyregion/do-black-and-white-children-learn-the-same-way.html.

Rubie-Davis, C., Hattie, J., & Hamilton, R. (2007). Expecting the best for students: Teacher expectations and academic outcomes. *British Journal of Educational Psychology 20*(1), 429–44.

Sanzone, J., Aylward, A., Ahram, A., Donchick, L., Flamm, A., & Noguera, P. (2014). *The state of Black and Latino students in education.* Cambridge, MA: Schott Foundation for Public Education.

Schmidt, W. (2015, September 30). Failed mission: How schools worsen inequality. Michigan State University, College of Education. Retrieved from http://msutoday.msu.edu/news/2015/failed-mission-how-schools-worsen-inequality/.

Slaughter-Defoe, D. T., & Rubin, H. (2001). A longitudinal case study of Head Start eligible children: Implications for urban education. *Educational Psychologist 36*(1), 31–44.

Smith, G. (2012, March 1). Homeless mother who sent six-year-old son to a better school in the wrong town jailed for five years. *Daily Mail.* Retrieved from http://www.dailymail.co.uk/news/article-2108733/Homeless-mother-Tanya-McDowell-sent-son-6-better-school-wrong-town-jailed-years.html.

Smith, Y. (2004). *Reclaiming the spirituals: New possibilities for African American Christian education.* Cleveland: Pilgrim Press.

Stevenson, H. C. (1995). Relationship of adolescent perceptions of racial socialization to racial identity. *Journal of Black Psychology 21*(1), 49–70. doi:10.1177/00957984950211005.

Tavernis, S. (2012, February 9). Education gap grows between rich and poor, studies say. *New York Times.* Retrieved from http://www.nytimes.com/2012/02/10/education/education-gap-grows-between-rich-and-poor-studies-show.html.

Taylor, A. V. (2014, July). Go sisters go! Black women are the most educated group in the United States. *Naturally Moi.* Retrieved from http://naturallymoi.com/2014/07/go-sisters-go-black-women-the-most-educated-group-in-the-united-states/#.Vj01H7_0eag.

Van Breda, A. D. (2001). *Resilience theory: A literature review*. Pretoria: South African Military Health Service. Retrieved from http://www.vanbreda.org/adrian/resilience.htm.

Vanneman, A., Hamilton, L., Baldwin Anderson, J., and Rahman, T. (2009). *Achievement gaps: How Black and White Students in public schools perform in mathematics and reading on the National Assessment of Educational Progress* (NCES 2009-455). U.S. Department of Education, National Center for Education Statistics, Institute of Education Sciences.

Villegas, A. M., & Irvine, J. J. (2010). Diversifying the teaching force: An examination of major arguments. *Urban Review 42*(3), 175–92. doi:10.1007/s11256-010-0150-1.

Wang, M., & Huguley, J. P. (2012). Parental racial socialization as a moderator of the effects of racial discrimination on educational success among African American adolescents. *Child Development 83*(5), 1716–31. doi:10.1111/j.1467-8624.2012.01808.x.

Warren, C. A. (2012). Empathic interaction: White female teachers and their Black male students. Ph.D. diss., University of Illinois Chicago.

Wishart, D. J. (N.d.). *Brown v. Board of Education of Topeka. Encyclopedia of the Great Plains.* Retrieved from http://plainshumanities.unl.edu/encyclopedia/doc/egp.law.011.

Wong, A. (2015, September). The subtle evolution of Native American education: Compared to their peers, "American Indian" and "Alaska Native" students aren't seeing the same growth in enrollment or attainment. *The Atlantic.* Retrieved from http://www.theatlantic.com/education/archive/2015/09/native-american-education/402787/.

Wyman, P. A., Cowen, E. L., Work, W. C., & Kerley, J. H. (1993). The role of children's future expectations in self-system functioning and adjustment to life-stress. *Development and Psychopathology 5*, 649–61.

Yeager, D. S., Purdie-Vaughns, V., Garcia, J., Apfel, N., Brzustoski, P., Master, A., & Cohen, G. L. (2014). Breaking the cycle of mistrust: Wise interventions to provide critical feedback across the racial divide. *Journal of Experimental Psychology* 143(2), 804–824.

Yosso, T. (2005). Whose culture has capital? A critical race theory discussion of community cultural wealth. *Race, Ethnicity and Education 8*(1), 69–91.

Zorn, D., Noga, J., Bolden-Haraway, C., Louis, V., Owens, N., & Smith, S. (2004, March). *Family Poverty and Its Implications for School Success: Issues Facing Cincinnati's Families* (Executive summary). Cincinnati: University of Cincinnati Evaluation Services Center.

PART 2.

Policy, Leadership, and Innovation

Defining High-Quality Education through the Eyes of Policymakers in American Indian Tribal Governments

Christie M. Poitra

> In our every deliberation, we must consider the impact of our decisions on the next seven generations.
>
> —Iroquois saying

This chapter is concerned with how policymakers holding high-level leadership roles in American Indian tribal governments define the term *high-quality education* (in regard to crafting educational policy, and providing educational programming to their Native youth).[1] Additionally, how do these policymakers, operating within different governmental, cultural, and societal contexts, value different types of educational knowledge, skills, and experiences? Using descriptive case study data from three American Indian tribal governments, this chapter will demonstrate that policymakers within these governments hold diverse beliefs about education, and therefore define the concept of *high-quality education* differently. Even with the differing notions of quality expressed by the policymakers, there are some strong thematic similarities across the cases. This text advances the argument that the similarities in definition of *high-quality education* result from the broader desire of the policymakers to ensure the current and future socioeconomic well-being of their tribal societies.

My motivations for writing this chapter materialized after attending an education department meeting at the Blue River government.[2] The purpose of the meeting was to discuss merging two tribally managed reservation schools into one school, in order to meet the government's fiscal goals. The difficulty in merging the two buildings was due to the serious pedagogical differences between the two schools (in the types of educational knowledge and experiences they wanted to provide to their students). One building was a language immersion school that exclusively taught the tribal language, and the other school was focused on providing students with academic rigor. The foundation of the struggle identified during the education department meeting was that leadership from each of the schools had wildly different beliefs about what constituted a *high-quality education* for Native youth. In turn, these differences made the logistics of merging the two buildings into a political struggle. Unfortunately, the meeting concluded without a clear course of action. My observations led me to believe that there is not necessarily a clear definition of high-quality education within tribal governments.

My experience at the education department meeting demonstrates that perspectives on education "do not speak with a single voice" (Green, 1983, p. 318). Individuals with different knowledge, professional expertise, and value systems will come to the table with different definitions of high-quality education. This chapter theorizes that definitions of high-quality education[3] are informed by multiple inputs (i.e., social, economic, and political) and vary from policymaker to policymaker, as well as tribal government to tribal government. This piece is a descriptive case study of the perspectives of five policymakers from three tribal governments located in California. This chapter is guided by three research questions: (1) how do American Indian policymakers working in tribal governments define high-quality education for Native youth, (2) in what ways are their definitions of high-quality education reflected in tribal education programs, and (3) what factors (whether social, political, economic, or other) shape their definitions of high-quality education?

To better situate my thinking about how high-quality education is defined throughout Indian Country, I looked at the way academic literature frames educational quality. Education research has equated educational quality with correcting the educational inequities that are prominent among Native youth (Belgrade & Lore, 2003; Benjamin, Chambers, & Reiterman, 1993; Guillory & Wolverton, 2008; Huffman, 2009, 2010; Aguilera-Black Bear & Tippeconnic, 2015). Another trend in American Indian education research has been to highlight the need for Native youth to have access to tailored educational programming that is culturally appropriate, and that recognizes the cultural distinctiveness of tribal societies (Fletcher, 2008; Hinton & Hale, 2001; Hinton, Vera, & Steele, 2002; Reyhner, 1988; Ward, 2005; Aguilera-Black Bear & Tippeconnic, 2015; Knowles & Lovern, 2015).

Next, I examined the policy advocacy platform of the National Congress of American Indians (NCAI) and the National Indian Education Association (NIEA) to understand the types of educational experiences, skills, and knowledge that these political-minded organizations value most for Native youth (as conveyed through their policy reports and memos). An analytical reading of the NCAI *2015 Native Children's Policy Agenda: Putting First Kids First*; the NIEA *2013 Policy Agenda Standing for High-Quality Native Education Advocacy Brief*; and the 2012 *An NIEA Brief: Advocacy, Research and Capacity-Building* revealed that there is a clear need for more expansive forms of collaboration between tribal governments and schools systems, that reservation teachers need access to adequate resources, and that states need to create systems of support to meet the unique needs of Native youth. Both organizations described the need for expanded opportunities for schools to engage in tribal language and culture revitalization, and to expand forms of academic accountability in Bureau of Indian Education schools (National Indian Education Association, 2012, 2013; National Congress of American Indians, 2015).

Lastly, I examined the federal Indian policy arena by looking at the most recent hearings and bills coming out of the United States Senate Committee on Indian Affairs, including the 2014 oversight hearing "Bureau of Indian Education: Examining Organizational Challenges in Transforming Educational Opportunities for Indian Children," the 2015 Senate bill S.1419, Native Language Immersion Student Achievement Act, the Senate bill S.1163, Native American Languages Reauthorization Act of 2015, and the 2015 Senate bill S.410, Building Upon Unique Indian Learning and Development Act. Granted, I reviewed only a handful of documents, which is a limited sample. Given the focus of this chapter, this snapshot of the most recent bills and hearings is more than appropriate. The government documents revealed several themes around the definition of high-quality education, including the need to (1) increase the academic achievement among Native youth, (2) increase the tribal cultural and language presence in schools serving large Native student populations, and (3) expand and deepen the state and tribal interactions and partnerships around the educational needs of Native youth. From a federal policy perspective, it appears that the definition of high-quality education is focused on providing Native youth with a culturally and linguistically responsive educational experience, and on expanding the collaboration between reservation schools and tribes in order to meet the unique needs of Native youth.

Who Participated in This Study?

This is a collective case study of three American Indian tribal governments. A collective case study is done to examine multiple cases "in order to investigate a phenomenon, populations, or general condition" (Stake, 2000, p. 437). The study of several cases also adds validity and supports the generalizability of the findings to theory (Miles & Huberman, 1994; Firestone, 1993). The analysis presented in this chapter relies on interview data generated from five policymakers serving in three tribal governments. All of the policymakers held positions at the highest levels of their respective tribal governments, and four out of the five had served their government for over twenty years. All of the interviewees volunteered to speak with me at the request of their tribal councils. The second source of data (used to provide context for each of the cases) were primary documents generated by the participating governments, including (1) newsletters, (2) program information geared toward parents and youth, and (3) mission and vision statements of government and education programs.

California was an ideal setting for this study because it has the second largest population of American Indians in the United States (DeVoe, Darling-Churchill, & Snyder, 2008), spread over a state that is highly diverse in geography, regional economic opportunities, and population size and density. Over one hundred tribes, with similar reservation sizes and enrollments, reside within the boundaries of California (Tiller, 2006). Given the nature of the research questions, it was important to select cases that had governmental institutional arrangements that were similar to each other, and represented the prominent trends existing across California. That is, each case had (1) a council, (2) a tribally managed business, (3) an educational department, and (4) educational programming.

To further narrow the pool of 110 California tribes (Federal Register, 2013) to three, this study used a two-stage sampling method, with a *discovery phase* and a *focus phase*. The discovery phase included examining tribal newspapers and websites to get a larger sense of the diversity in types of tribal governments existing in California. The goal of the focus phase was to select three governments that had similar bureaucratic arrangements and were also representative of the economic and governmental trends present among the population of California tribes (as identified during the discovery phase). Ultimately, the Rock Rancheria, the River Indian Tribe, and the Sawville Indian Rancheria governments agreed to participate in this study.

Rock Rancheria is a small tribe of about 889 members located in Northern California. The Rock Rancheria government maintains a number of businesses located on and off of the reservation. The government operates a gaming establishment. Rock Rancheria also owns several off-reservation businesses, including a gas station and minimarket (called Red Rock Mini Mart), a fine dining restaurant, a hotel, a storage company, and an eighteen-hole golf course. Although the Rock Rancheria own a number of successful businesses, a significant amount of the government's revenue comes from the gaming establishment.

The governing council is composed of six elected policymakers. The council positions are chairperson, vice-chairperson, secretary, treasurer, and two alternative members. The principal responsibility of the council is to generate policy and oversee tribal businesses. The tribal government also has an executive team composed of three policymakers (the chief operations officer, the chief executive officer, and the chief financial officer). This team oversees all of the administrative operations of the businesses and departments.

When the Rock Rancheria was approached about participating in this study, the council met and selected two policymakers from the executive team to represent the government. The first interviewee was Delcie. She had worked in the tribal government as an elected and appointed policymaker since 1996. Upon graduation, she was appointed to the position of tribal attorney by the council. Later, Delcie was elected as the vice-chairperson, a position she held for several years. Later she was elected as the chairperson, a position she held for four years. After that, she has transitioned into the chief executive officer (CEO) role. Her principal responsibility is to ensure the integrity of the tribal operations. The second interview was with Jessica, the chief operations officer (COO). In 1991, at age nineteen, Jessica began serving as a council member. After a year on council, she transitioned into the role of public information specialist. In 1994, Jessica became COO while completing her bachelor of arts degree, and continues to serve as COO today.

The River Indian Tribe has 1,425 members and is located in Southern California. The River government maintains a number of businesses located on and off of the reservation, including convenience stores, a steakhouse, and a gaming establishment. The government is led by a council of nine policymakers, including chairman, vice-chairman, treasurer, secretary, and five tribal citizens. The principal responsibility of the council is to oversee the day-to-day operations of the government, including the development of policy and management of the tribal businesses. The government has multiple departments including Administration, Department of Public Safety, Education Department, Environmental Department, Fire Department, Forestry Department, Indian Child Welfare Department, General Counsel, Public Works Department, River Alcoholism Program, Water Rights, Workforce Development, and Archaeological Advisory Team.

When the River Indian Tribe was approached about participating in the study, individual policymakers volunteered to participate. A council member (Seana) and general legal counsel (Farah) were interviewed. Seana has served on council for thirty-nine years, and worked for the tribal health clinic for two years. Seana's career in the River government began while she was in high school. She started supporting the council as an administrative assistant and was later appointed to the executive assistant role. Later, Seana became the contracts director. In 2013, she was elected to the council. The second interviewee was Farah. After finishing her undergraduate degree, she worked for the tribal government. Upon learning about the unique relationship between the tribe and the federal government, she decided to go to law school. Upon completion of her law degree, Farah was appointed as general legal counsel for the government.

The Sawville Indian Rancheria has 1,066 members and is located in Northern California. The Sawville Indian Rancheria government maintains a gaming establishment and a gas station/minimarket. The general council is composed of seven policymakers. The positions on the council include tribal chairman, vice-chairman, secretary-treasurer, District 1 councilman, District 2 councilman, at-large representative on-trust land, and at-large county representative. The principal responsibility of the council is to oversee the day-to-day operations of the tribe (e.g., the development of policy and overseeing the businesses). The government also includes a number of subcommittees that support the work of the council (such as the Election Board, Health Board, Housing Board, Mini-Mart Board of Directors, Gaming Commission, Education Committee, Education Committee, ICWA Committee, Parent Advisory Committee, and Tribal Government Liaison Committee).

When the Sawville Rancheria was approached about participating in this study, the council chairman volunteered to be interviewed. Chairman James was elected to the council in 1994 and served until 1997. At the end of his term in 1997, James decided that he did not want to continue in tribal politics. It was not until the early

2000s that he again considered running for elected office. In the summer of 2003, a group of elders from the tribe approached him to run for the chairman position. James said that he felt hesitant because it was a "big responsibility to lead" his community. Armed with his family's support, he decided to mount a campaign. In November 2003, James won the chairman election, and he was reelected in 2012.

How Do Policymakers Define High-Quality Education?

This analysis borrows from the theoretical work of Thomas Green in the paper "Excellence, Equity and Equality" (1983) to examine how policymakers from the three California tribes define high-quality education, and what factors influence these definitions. The act of defining quality requires individuals to make judgments (based upon their beliefs about the larger purposes of education to identify the education outcomes that they find most desirable). Arguably, defining educational quality is closely related to defining its purpose. Green advances the idea that the purpose of education requires a complex definition because it reflects a multitude of goods, ideals, and understandings. An implication of this complexity is that the purpose of education is often simplistically described, even though it represents a conglomerate of societal values. The principal characteristic of Green's theory is that the purpose of education is usually described through the policy aims of (1) excellence, (2) equity, and (3) equality. *Equality* is defined as equal treatment and distribution of rewards to individuals, without consideration for fairness. In contrast, *equity* denotes a "just treatment," where distribution of rewards and treatment to individuals are directly tied to recognizing the differences in need. Lastly, *excellence* means a pursuit of academic rigor for all individuals (Green, 1983). Achieving any of these aims (i.e., excellence, equity, and equality) requires a number of educational goods (e.g., quality instruction and curriculum, bilingual programming, teacher-student relations, college readiness opportunities). The combination of the goods necessary to achieve any of these policy aims will vary according to (1) the level of the governmental system that the policy aim intends to influence, (2) the policymaker's definition of the policy aim, and (3) the policymaker's perception of the value of the policy aim. It is not presumptuous to assume that in the eyes of different policymakers (operating in different institutional contexts), some policy aims (and educational goods) will hold a higher value than others. This difference in opinion among policymakers about the value of each of the policy aims creates inconsistencies in the educational system and educational policy. Moreover, Green argues that there exist ideological differences between the three policy aims that make them ideologically incompatible, meaning these aims cannot be equally pursued at the same time.

This study found that tribal policymakers defined high-quality education through Green's policy aim of *equity*. As illuminated by the interview data, the differences in definitions are influenced by the fact that policymakers are functioning in different governmental contexts. These definitions were influenced by the perception of the (1) current and future human capital needs of the government, and (2) weaknesses existing in the education system serving Native youth.

A Need for Human Capital through Educational Excellence

Across the three governments, the policymakers often formed their definitions of high-quality education according to their perceptions of the government's current and future human capital needs—as defined by students' ability to be academically successful in school (i.e., be college and career ready). These definitions were further filtered through the long-term governmental strategic plans to strengthen self-governance and support economic development. An example of this phenomenon is a quote from Chairman James from Sawville Indian Rancheria. James describes how he views economic development and the tribal government changing in the future:

> We're progressing fairly fast. We did a master plan in 2003 and we just exceed[ed] those expectations. . . . This tribe, you know, started out small, and now we're almost like 180% progressing forward. . . . Ten years from now, I just see our government's going to be, the tribe's going to be, sustainable and diversifying jobs, creating jobs for our tribal citizens. 'Cause that's one thing you always hear whenever you go to general council meetings. . . . I see a high expectation of economic development with this tribe.

James expresses the long-term goals of the Sawville government and highlights the success that the government has already achieved. He believes that Sawville's economy will continue to grow, strengthen, and diversify. A result of this perception of future economic growth is an increased need for the Sawville government to have access to human capital. However, James followed up his discussion of the future of the Sawville economy with a commentary about the larger struggle with tribal citizens' low skill levels:

> They can't even pass the basic test, as for typewriting and math, English, all of that And we have our HR department, Human Resources. If you don't, if you can't pass the test . . . we're here to help you.

The human capital gap becomes a policy problem when the tribal economy is growing and providing jobs for tribal citizens, but tribal citizens do not have the basic skills to fill those jobs. From James's perspective, Sawville has a talent gap that may continue over time if the Sawville government does not intervene through policy.

CEO Delcie and COO Jessica also said that Rock Rancheria will continue to develop economically. When asked to describe the Rock Rancheria's future economic plans, they mentioned the goal of moving away from relying on the casino to produce revenue for the government and provide jobs. These policymakers expressed the fear that gaming is not a long-term economic solution because of the political and legal instability of the gaming industry for California tribes. As Jessica described:

> I just see the tribe getting even more aggressive and trying to diversify away from—not away from the casino, but in conjunction—so that we're not relying totally on the casino. . . . [Renegotiating] our compact [is] right around the corner. . . . We need to get those funds replaced in a different way.

These two quotes provide a glimpse into the way these policymakers think about the next steps that these governments need to take in order to protect and promote the interests of their societies, which include being strategic about business expansion and diversification, and exercising sovereignty through economic stability.

According to the policymakers interviewed, Native youth are key to strengthening the government and society and ensuring a positive economic future. In Rock Rancheria, Native youth are described as being an important factor in future economic endeavors, according to Jessica:

> I think the education of Native youth sort of leads to everything, economic development being one of them. I mean, if they're not educated and don't understand why you would want to diversify your businesses or how to even get there, then

> obviously that's not going to happen. . . . If they're not educated about those things, then . . . our tribe may not move forward as fast as we want it to or be as successful as we want them to be.

Jessica describes two types of knowledge. The first type of knowledge is that Native youth must attain a level of business savvy that equips them with the knowledge to build upon a successful organization. This knowledge includes having a general grasp on "best business practices." The second type of knowledge is that youth must be able to adapt and apply general business knowledge in a tribal context. Additionally, Jessica highlights the value of cultivating the skills and talents of Native youth to ensure the long-term welfare of the community.

In the River Indian Tribe, Native youth hold a prominent place in the government's long-term strategic plans. General Counsel Farah described the role of Native youth as steering economic development by bringing innovation to the tribal economy:

> [The government] gives out $60,000, and all they [applicants] have to have [is] a business plan, and the council will give them the money. And so what I've seen is that more and more young people are applying for these loans and going into business for themselves. . . . I think as more and more youth find out about this opportunity . . . they'll take advantage of it and come up with some ideas that us older people . . . and tribal council [don't have], and they'll have more fresh ideas and be able to bring these things into our community.

Farah theorized that Native youth will play a larger role in the future economy by applying for business start-up grants. This increased participation will create a more diverse economy and will cultivate a more diverse pool of human capital and job opportunities.

A Need for Equality

Concerns about the quality of education that Native youth are receiving in schools were frequently framed in a lens of Green's *equality*, such as parents having equal access to school programs, services, and support (i.e., parents having an equal access to knowledge about the school system, productive relationships with schools, and knowledge about college and career readiness). Delcie related the lack of college readiness to the difficulties of Native youth in meeting basic college requirements:

> An issue in general is just keeping kids in the classes that they need to go on to college. . . . So the big discussion up here is, once you're a freshman, everybody's in college prep, but then we go through high school and we're not in the classes that allow us to go on to college. We have to go to a junior college or remedial just to get caught up, to go to college. And then you don't do it because, by then, you're so far behind.

Jessica also highlighted larger inequities in the school system around planning for college. Without the correct classes, Native youth will be at a disadvantage in gaining admission into a university. Delcie related this inequity to parents' general lack of knowledge about college readiness:

> In our case, we've got a lot of parents who haven't been to school or been to college, so they don't know. So I don't know whose job that is to educate them, if it's the schools. I think it's counselors—high school counselors in the school is a big problem, too.

James echoed similar remarks as the other policymakers about it being difficult f or parents in Sawville to feel comfortable engaging schools on behalf of their children's learning: "That's one thing that's hard about our community. There's a lot of single parents . . . And that's where we're trying to get our parents involved with our kids."

All of the policymakers interviewed indicated that high-quality education for Native youth would include a stronger relationship between the tribal government and schools around supporting Native youth' needs to be academically successful. Many of the policymakers expressed that it is difficult to develop relationships with schools (i.e., superintendents, principals, and teachers). For Rock Rancheria, one cause for the lack of a relationship between the government and the schools serving Rock Rancheria students was due to logistics. Students are spread across three small districts that are located off of the Rock reservation, with each school enrolling only a handful of Native youth. As a result, schools are sometimes unaware that they have Rock Rancheria students in their schools. CFO Delcie also described mixed feelings about when a school becomes aware that they have a Rock Rancheria student because of the broader public's negative perception of the tribe's gaming establishment:

> And then other than that, I think because by virtue that we're in a small town, I think that we'll sort of get wind that a tribal member kid, you know, is at their school and that can be good and bad. You know, depending on the perceptions that they think about the tribe.

CFO Delcie continued by describing that the public perception of the surrounding non-Native community about the tribal government is both positive and negative (due to the success of the tribal businesses, including its casino). This perception might have an impact on the tribal government's relationship with the local off-reservation schools that youth attend. However, she also went on to describe a positive experience with a local charter school that requested her to come into the school and talk about the Rock Rancheria government and its history. Delcie was also able to share the documentary about the tribe with the school, which was later shown school-wide. She stated that she has been going into the school and sharing about the tribal government for several years, and enjoys it because the school is recognizing the presence of Rock Rancheria.

For Sawville Indian Rancheria, the struggle to forge a relationship with the local off-reservation schools that most youth attend is an ongoing difficulty, but it has improved over time. James stated that the relationship with schools changed as a result of an awards ceremony put on by the Sawville council to recognize the academic achievements of Native youth, as well as the support of the teachers and principals. Chairman James said that along with youth, parents, and families, the council reached out to teachers, principals, district administrators, and the local community college president to attend the ceremony. Since the ceremony, the relationship and lines of communication between the government and schools have improved dramatically. As James remarks:

> I think we're finally getting . . . more collaboration, you know, what goes on in the school districts. Before we really weren't getting that info [on] our kids. That's one thing that my brother . . . and I get in working with the high school and the elementary schools monthly, just talking about what's our expectations, from the tribe to the school district.

He views fostering a relationship with the local schools as important because it opens a line of communication between the council and the schools for the purposes of conveying tribal desires for education. From the perspective of the Sawville government, this provides another opportunity to influence human capital development of Native youth.

The policymakers that were interviewed also asserted that schools need to break away from dominant culture's learning norms, and be more willing to recognize the cultural background of Native youth. Moreover, schools need to be more welcoming of the cultural differences existing among these populations. James pointed out that teachers are starting to recognize the cultural differences prevalent among Native youth in a meaningful way that promotes positive learning outcomes:

> It's really helping us out, focusing on our kids, too, at the same time. And they really talk about these kids, how they're so silent and quiet and now they're really speaking out. And they feel confident now. That's one thing that's breaking that barrier, advancing these kids to the next level.

The policymakers from Rock Rancheria also stressed that high-quality education for their Native youth would include recognizing the Rock Rancheria's culture and students' cultural difference in the classroom. Delcie stated that Rock Rancheria is willing to support schools attempting to incorporate tribal culture into the classroom:

> We can always come in and do cultural stuff, a cultural day. Actually, there was a few years, in fourth grade, they study California Indian tribes, I think, and we had a person here who would go in their regalia and bring a bunch of stuff, so that we can also provide that to a school, as a tribal member.

Farah points out that when schools fail to recognize Native youths' cultural differences, it breeds cultural conflict, which ultimately alienates students in the classroom:

> If you think about how we lived traditionally, a tribal group, you lived in a tribal unit. You contributed to the tribe as a whole. But when you get out there and go to school, they teach you you need to be individuals. You need to do this or this—to hell with

> everybody else, basically. Then you come back home to the reservation, you still kind of have that mentality if you're not taught that it's like this up here. . . . Almost all the kids, they're bused off the reservation, taken off the reservation to school even though the society's here. It's kind of like you go outside your community, learn whatever out there, stuff that doesn't really apply to the community, come back, and it's not culturally relevant. It doesn't make sense in a way. And I think because of that, a lot of kids lose interest in school.

To some degree, all of the policymakers indicated that it is a struggle for schools to acknowledge and honor tribal culture. The lack of cultural responsiveness in schools fosters cultural conflict because the goals and knowledge being taught in the classrooms clash with the norms and knowledge of the tribe. One political actor theorized that the implication for cultural conflicts in schools is that Native youth will become alienated and disengaged from their learning. Moreover, students being disengaged in the classroom can impede tribal governmental interests in long-term human capital development.

A Need for Equity

As highlighted previously, a theme across the interviews was that Native youth are the key to supporting the future economic and political endeavors of their respective tribal governments. It is important that students gain the appropriate knowledge and skills to assume roles in tribal businesses and government. However, some policymakers said that there is a gap in skill levels among tribal citizens. According to these policymakers, the academic struggles of Native youth come from a need for equity-focused policy aims. One political actor said that parents do not have a background in preparing or attending college, and schools are not great at providing detailed information about the college application process. Another issue mentioned was that schools have failed to provide a culturally responsive environment for youth, which has produced conflict between the youth and the school. Related to the issue of cultural responsiveness is the struggle of tribal governments to forge relationships with local schools. Even though one of the governments had successfully opened lines of communication with the school district, it was a relationship that developed over time and was not positive in the past. The policymakers from Rock Rancheria also struggled with developing relationships with local schools, and they were not as successful as Sawville.

Policymakers' definitions of high-quality education were couched in Green's category of equity—where the distribution of resources and investment is directly tied to recognizing difference. These policymakers noted low-quality characteristics in their educational systems, including the lack of cultural responsiveness, insufficient tribal-school interactions and communication, and a lack of knowledge about how to navigate the educational system. Thus, definitions of educational quality came out of what was perceived as *lacking* quality. It is important to highlight this because inequities limit the choices of individuals (Green, 1983). Native youth functioning in an educational system that is riddled with inequities will limit their long-term choices, and shrink the pool of human capital available to tribal governments. To illustrate the concept of choice, Green used the example of a child never seeing a violin and therefore not becoming a violinist (Green, 1983). Not becoming a violinist is not the result of the child's conscious choice; it is, rather, a reflection of the environment that had no real choice (Green, 1983). The same point can be made about the situations described by the tribal policymakers. For example, Native youth who are unaware that they need to take certain classes to prepare for college admissions do not have a real choice to attend college. At the core of the policymakers' definitions of quality education is having a choice that is not limited by the inequities existing in the educational system.

In What Ways Are Policymakers' Definitions of High-Quality Education Reflected in Education Programs?

Although the policymakers conveyed their definitions of educational quality through the policy aim of *equity* and *equality*, tribal educational programs focused on pursuing the policy aim of *educational excellence*. The educational programming provided across the three tribal governments included tutoring and supplementary academic support, public recognition for academic achievement, use of academic mentors, technical support for preparing and applying for college, funding for college, internship opportunities, and youth leadership development and investment. The trend across the educational programs was achieving *academic excellence* to further human capital development.

Because these programs were formulated at the highest levels of tribal government, they were designed to foster equality. Specifically, these programs are presented to Native youth as pools of resources, investments and opportunities (i.e., goods) that are open to all Native youth. Native youth are given a choice to utilize these opportunities or not. These goods are presented as equally accessible for the whole community.

College Scholarships

All three tribal governments offer funding to attend college. All of the scholarship opportunities are funded by revenue produced by tribal businesses. These scholarships range from a few thousand dollars to all costs associated with attending college. The requirements for receiving a college scholarship vary slightly across these communities. For the River Indian Tribe, scholarships cover costs for up to fifteen semesters of college course work. This opportunity is open to anyone who is a tribal member. Sawville Rancheria recently instituted college scholarships for tribal citizens. To receive a scholarship, members must apply for the funds. Rock Rancheria offers scholarships that cover all costs associated with attending college. These funds are available to all tribal citizens.

Vocational Training

Rock Rancheria offers a youth employment program that enables youth to work in any tribal governmental office or businesses. The program runs year around. The only requirement to participate in the youth employment program is to be a tribal member and to be old enough to apply for a work permit. As one political actor mentioned, the program hopes to spark interest in youth to work in the tribe, and also to develop a strong work ethic at a young age. The River Indian Tribe also offers a youth employment program that operates every summer and during the holiday season. There is also an internship program that provides employment during the year. Both programs offer full-time employment and a stipend.

Tutoring and School Advocacy

The River Indian Tribe operates an education center on the reservation, which funds teachers and has multiple classrooms. The tribal government also operates a study center off the reservation. Both centers offer after-school programming for kindergarten through high school. The tribe offers transportation for students to go to the study center. At the center, Native youth are provided with tutors and are expected to work on their homework. During school breaks, the center offer special activities that include field trips to museums and other activities. During these breaks, programming lasts the entire day. The center staff also track students' grade point average, and they contact schools on parents' behalf to check in about progress. Rock Rancheria provides tutoring to all Native youth. The tribe pays for parents to get their own tutor and receive tutoring at their home. If parents prefer, the tribe will hire a tutor, and the youth can come to the tribal government office to meet with the tutor. Rock Rancheria also provides SAT prep course for Native youth and private SAT prep tutoring. Sawville Rancheria has chosen to employ an education mentor who supports and monitors the academic progress of the Native youth. When a student is doing poorly, the mentor approaches the teacher and connects the tribal education department with the school to ensure an open line of communication and help the student catch up.

Leadership Development and Investment

Sawville Rancheria has a youth leadership council. The youth council is encouraged to come to attend tribal business council meetings to learn more about the Sawville government. Rock Rancheria offers a youth leadership development program for ages eleven to fifteen. The program meets monthly. A handful of tribal council members build a curriculum that is revised every year. Programming consists of presentations and events from people inside and outside of the tribe. The council members are also involved in the program presentations. The program focuses on culture and basic life skills, such as budgeting, balancing a checkbook, and investing in the stock market. The program concludes with a three-day group trip. The hope of the program is to provide youth with an opportunity to become closer earlier in life, so that when they serve on the council later, they already know each other. Another hope of the program is to "pave the way for [youth] to work together in the future" (Jessica, Personal Communication, March 19, 2013). Once students are above the age of fifteen, they become mentors, and they help with the sessions. The River Indian Tribe does not offer a youth leadership program, but it does offer opportunities for youth to develop business start-ups through a tribal business grant program. The grant is $60,000, and the tribe only requires that they have a business plan. As one political actor remarked, she has seen that "more and more young people are applying for these loans and going into business for themselves."

What Factors Shape These Understandings of High-Quality Education?

Interviews with tribal policymakers made it clear that equity is the main criterion for quality education for Native youth. However, the educational programs that are present in these communities are not focused on equity, but rather on excellence. You might ask yourself why that is. Where does the ideological mismatch come from? The answer is human capital development. Tribal policymakers consistently identified the importance of youth supporting larger economic and political endeavors. For tribal governments, pursuing educational excellence seems like the most direct path to cultivating human capital. Providing Native youth with pools of resources to select from is the simplest policy solution. It requires staff to ensure implementation, without the messiness of low-aggregate program differentiation for individual needs.

What would Green's theoretical lens say about these policy solutions? It would say that "policy is a crude instrument to ensure social ideals" (1983, p. 322). Namely, policy is limited by its tools to achieve certain aims. Policy focuses on gross values (or high levels of aggregation) and strives to satisfy common societal ideals by sorting ideals and goods on a macro scale (Green, 1983, p. 3). Policy cannot advance "specific benefits," but rather fosters "the prevention of specific evils" (p. 322). Tribal governments provide pools of resources for Native youth in hopes of creating opportunity (or choice). Although Green argued that excellence is best achieved at a low level of social aggregation, conceptually excellence is a universalistic pursuit. As a result, the "pursuit of educational excellence is likely to produce gains in equity" (Green, 1983, p. 331). In pursuing educational excellence, tribal governments will indirectly impact the policy problem of inequity.

The policymakers demonstrated that definitions of high-quality education are steeped in issues of human capital development (e.g., economic development, and maintaining the health and welfare of tribal societies). The success of tribal governments relies on their ability to address these complex policy problems in ways that align with their respective capacities, needs, and values. The literature has identified human capital as a key ingredient for many tribal governments in mitigating policy problems related to governance and economic development (Coffey & Tsosie, 2001; Champagne, 2006; Kemper, 2013). To cultivate human capital requires that tribal governments prioritize educational issues and make strategic financial and political investments in educational policy and programs.

The governments that participated in this study prioritized educational policy problems related to two broader themes: (1) a general concern about the quality of education received by their children (e.g., having access to technology, educational enrichment programming, culturally responsive and academically focused childcare, after-school programming and tutoring, and academic and financial support for postsecondary education endeavors); and (2) the impacts that the quality of children's education have on their life prospects, and on the future economic and political health of the tribe. All of the policymakers who were interviewed discussed the relationship between educational quality and the cultivation of human capital for the tribal society. The need to cultivate human capital was reflected in the interviewees' perceptions of the obligation to expand business enterprises and protect tribal sovereignty.

What Is the Value in Understanding How Tribal Governments Define High-Quality Education?

Understanding the way that tribal governments make decisions about educational policy (i.e., programs, resources, opportunities, and investments) is an interesting and largely unexplored topic. It is invaluable to have a grasp of the processes that contemporary tribal governments go through to define high-quality education to make educational investments in their societies. It is equally important to understand tribal governments' perceptions of their societies' human capital needs. This chapter is only an introduction to this area of study, but hopefully it will draw attention that might be useful intellectually and from a policy perspective.

This research views tribal governments as nation-states operating in, and governed by, their unique political, social, and economic contexts. Investigating what policymakers desire for their youth provides a basis for academic and policy communities to understand better the diversity that exists among policymakers across different governments. In turn, this allows for understanding how to produce research that is relevant to the current needs and values expressed by policymakers, which in its own right is a valuable intellectual endeavor.

■ ■ ■

A limitation of this work is that this analysis is based on a handful of policymakers from three tribal governments. There are over one hundred tribes in California, and over five hundred tribes across the United States. Each represents a different governmental structure, culture, history, and political climate. As a result, it is not possible to draw broad conclusions about the population of tribal governments based upon the limited scope of this data. To make larger assertions about the way tribal governments define high-quality education requires data collected from policymakers operating across multiple communities. However, these findings are generalizable for the purpose of a broader theoretical understanding of the ways that governments select, define, and pursue high-quality education for their societies. Generalizing to theory does not rely on sample sizes; instead, it relies on fostering a clearer understanding of the phenomena present in a case study (Firestone, 1993; Yin, 1989). These findings are also valuable in their case-to-case transferability (i.e., when the characteristics of a case are applicable to the circumstances of another case) (Glesne, 2006). Thus, these findings are valuable in understanding the way tribal governments think about education in relation to their unique political, economic, and social contexts.

Many aspects of the functions and actions of tribal governments have been understudied or not studied. There are numerous ways to explore the topic of high-quality education using a variety of qualitative and quantitative methods—all of which could add significant value to the field of American Indian studies. A larger-scale qualitative study can provide a more expansive set of data to analyze. This can be achieved by (1) having a number of policymakers participate from a single tribal government, or (2) interviewing multiple actors across a number of governments. Either research schema can produce interesting information about the ways policymakers define educational quality. A more quantitative study (e.g., a survey of tribal policymakers from multiple governments) would allow researchers to control the particular characteristics of the policymakers (e.g., education level and income), as well as the characteristics of the broader tribal government and society (e.g., wealth of the community, distance from an urban area, and language fluency).

NOTES

1. The term Native youth denotes tribal citizens that are under the age of eighteen.
2. The tribal governments and policymakers that are discussed in this chapter have been

given pseudonyms. In some cases, the gender label of the policymaker has been changed in order to further mask his or her identity.

3. For the purposes of this chapter, the term high-quality education is defined by (1) how the participating policymakers convey concepts of educational quality through their interviews and the texts produced by the tribal government, and (2) what actions policymakers take to provide high-quality educational programming, policies, or services to Native youth. The term education is confined to K–12 educational policies, programs, or initiatives operating within a reservation context. Although adding this boundary to the definition of education will constrain the number of definitions of quality that can be discussed in this chapter, it will allow for a more focused discussion of quality.

REFERENCES

Aguilera-Black Bear, D., & Tippeconnic, J. (2015). *Voices of resistance and renewal: Indigenous leadership in education*. Norman: University of Oklahoma Press.

Belgrade, M., & Lore, R. (2003). The retention/intervention of Native American undergraduates at the University of New Mexico. *Journal of College Student Retention 5*(2), 175–202.

Benham, M. (ed.). (2008). *Indigenous educational models for contemporary practice: In our mother's voice*. Vol. 2. New York: Routledge Taylor & Francis Group.

Benjamin, D., Chambers, S., & Reiterman, G. (1993). A focus on American Indian college persistence. *Journal of American Indian Education 32*(2), 24–40.

Canby, W. (2006). *American Indian law in a nutshell*. 5th ed. St. Paul, MN: West Publishing.

Castile, G. (1998). *To show heart: Native American self-determination and federal Indian policy, 1960–1975*. Tucson: University of Arizona Press.

Champagne, D. (2006). In search of theory and method in American Indian studies. *American Indian Quarterly 31*(3), 353–72.

Coffey, W., & Tsosie, R. (2001). Rethinking the tribal sovereignty doctrine: Cultural sovereignty and the collective future of Indian nations. *Stanford Law and Policy Review 12*(2), 191–221.

DeVoe, J., Darling-Churchill, K., & Snyder, T. (2008). *Status and trends in the education of American Indians and Alaska Natives: 2008*. NCES 2008-084. Washington, DC: National Center of Educational Statistics.

Evans, L. *Power from powerlessness: Tribal governments, institutional niches, and American federalism*. New York: Oxford University Press.

Federal Register. (2013). Indian entities recognized and eligible to receive services from the United States Bureau of Indian Affairs. 78 *Federal Register* 87 (May 6, 2013), 26384–89.

Firestone, W. (1993). Alternative arguments for generalizing from data as applied to qualitative research. *Educational Researcher 22*(4), 16–23.

Fletcher, M. L. (2008). *American Indian education counternarratives in racism, struggle, and the law.* New York: Routledge Taylor & Francis Group.

Glesne, C. (2006). *Becoming qualitative researchers: An introduction.* Boston: Pearson.

Green, T. F. (1983). Excellence, equity and equality. In L. Shulman & G. Sykes (eds.), *Handbook of Teaching and Policy*. New York: Longman.

Guillory, R., & Wolverton, M. (2008). It's About Family: Native American Student Persistence in Higher Education. *The Journal of Higher Education 79*(1), 58–87.

Hinton, L., & Hale, K. (eds.). (2001). *The green book of language revitalization in practice.* San Diego: Academic Press.

Hinton, L., Vera, M., & Steele, N. (2002). *How to keep your language alive: A commonsense approach to one-on-one language learning*. Berkeley, CA: Heyday.

Huffman, T. (2009). *American Indian higher educational experiences: Cultural visions and personal journeys.* New York: Peter Lang.

Huffman, T. (2010). *Theoretical perspectives on American Indian education: Taking a new look at academic success and the achievement gap.* New York: AltaMira Press.

Kemper, K. R. (2013). Tribal sovereignty means competition, broadband access, and economic development for Indian Country: A law and economics analysis of the efficiency of the FCC's Standing Rock Sioux case. *Journal of Information Policy 3*, 442–63.

Knowles, F. & Lovern, L. (2015). *A critical pedagogy for Native American education policy: Habermas, Freire, and emancipatory education.* Basingstoke, UK: Palgrave Macmillan.

Miles, M., & Huberman, A. (1994). *Qualitative data analysis: An expanded sourcebook.* Thousand Oaks, CA: Sage.

National Congress of American Indians. (2015, August). 2015 Native children's policy agenda: Putting first kids 1st. Retrieved from http://www.ncai.org/resources/ncai-publications/Aug_2015_Native_Childrens_Policy_Agenda.pdf.

National Indian Education Association. (2012). An NIEA brief: Advocacy, research and capacity-building. Retrieved from http://niea.org/data/files/niea_brief_2012.pdf.

National Indian Education Association. (2013). Standing for high-quality Native education: Policy agenda. Retrieved from http://niea.org/data/files/policy/briefingbook2013_mobile.pdf.

O'Brien, S. (1993). *American Indian tribal governments.* Norman: University of Oklahoma Press.

Reyhner, J. (ed.) (1988). *Teaching American Indian students.* Norman: University of Oklahoma Press.

Stake, R. (2000). Qualitative case studies. In N. K. Denzin and Y. S. Lincoln (eds.), *The Sage*

Handbook of Qualitative Research. 3rd ed. Thousand Oaks, CA: Sage Publications.

Tiller, V. (2006). *Tiller's guide to Indian country: Economic profiles of American Indian reservations*. Albuquerque, NM: Bow Arrow Publishing.

Ward, C. (2005). *Native Americans and the school system: Family, community, and academic achievement*. New York: AltaMira Press.

Yin, R. (1989). *Case study research: Design and methods*. 2nd ed. Newbury Park, CA: Sage.

Distributed Leadership and Educator Attitudes

A Multilevel Analysis of TALIS 2013

Yan Liu and Susan Printy

> In a real sense all life is inter-related. All men are caught in an inescapable network of mutuality, tied in a single garment of destiny. Whatever affects one directly, affects all indirectly.
>
> —Rev. Dr. Martin Luther King Jr.

Research suggests there are elements that are vital to shaping a successful school: academic capacity and culture (Heck & Hallinger, 2009), teachers' job satisfaction and organizational commitment (Angelle, 2010; Hulpia et al., 2012), academic optimism (Chang, 2011; Mascall et al., 2008); and indirect impact of student achievement (Bryk et al., 2010; Leithwood & Seashore-Louis, 2012; Marks & Printy, 2003). Additionally, among both researchers and practitioners, there is unprecedented international interest in the role leadership plays in crafting a successful school (OECD, 2014). For example, an Organization for Economic Cooperation and Development (OECD) report asserts:

> There is increasing evidence that within each individual school, school leaders can contribute to improved student learning by shaping the conditions and climate in which teaching and learning occur. (Pont, Nusche, & Moorman, 2008, p. 19)

Current literature suggests that a principal's leadership is especially influential when principals foster trust (Bryk et al., 2010; Edwards, 2011; Fitzsimons, James, & Denyer, 2011) and build a cooperative climate where participation from staff and community is welcome (Hargreaves & Shirley, 2012; Heck & Hallinger, 2009; Leithwood & Seashore-Louis, 2012). Principal's leadership might succinctly be defined as influence that brings others to collectively work toward desired goals of the school.

Research on school-level leadership has long sought to determine whether or not principals have an influence on student-level outcomes, particularly student achievement. When research focuses on the activities and behaviors of principals as measures of leadership, results suggested that principals have indirect influence on students through teachers and instructional cultures (Heck & Hallinger, 2009). In the last decade, there has been further focus on investigating the involvement of teachers and other stakeholders in school management and operation (Bolden, 2011; Elmore, 2000; Leithwood et al., 2007; Spillane, 2005). Researchers agree that participation from shareholders and cooperative leadership improves staff satisfaction while increasing commitment to school goals (Angelle, 2010; Hartley, 2010; Hulpia et al., 2012), as well as cohesion among faculty (Heck & Hallinger, 2009; Price, 2012; Printy, 2008). The research suggests that stakeholder involvement in leadership tasks includes a broad range of beliefs and attitudes. This includes distributed leadership.

In practice, distributed leadership is a process of synergistic interaction among the leader, the followers, and the situations (Gronn, 2002; Spillane & Diamond, 2007). In addition, various people with expertise and organizational characteristics are involved in many school functions (Harris et al., 2008; Heck & Hallinger, 2009; Lashway, 2006; Leithwood et al., 2007). The research cited above offers evidence that distributed leadership accrues positive leverage to a school's organizational capacity and student outcomes, and suggests that positive work relationships between the leader and subordinates improve both principals' and teachers' perception of job satisfaction, cohesion and commitment (Price, 2012). However, some research findings are mixed (Bolden, 2011; Thorpe, Gold, & Lawler, 2011; Tian, Risku, & Collin, 2015). The current study investigates the extent to which stakeholders' involvement in leadership creates a kind of virtuous or upward spiral of positive perceptions within the school.

This chapter seeks to understand whether stakeholders' participation in school leadership responsibilities is related to principal and teacher satisfaction, cohesion, and commitment in schools. We treat principals' perceived cohesion, commitment, and satisfaction first as dependent variables and investigate the relation of these attitudes to distributed leadership involvement. Next we use the measures of principal attitudes as mediators in the investigation of the relationship of distributed leadership to teachers' attitudes. Specifically, this research explores how the variation in stakeholders' participation in different leadership roles manifests in differentiated levels of job satisfaction, cohesion among people, and organizational commitment for principals and teachers.

Literature Review

The framework for this study synthesizes theories regarding stakeholders' participation in school functions and how the proactive involvement of broad sets of stakeholders promotes positive attitudes of educators. Because principals have been identified as central to what happens among adults in schools, this study focuses on the mediator effect of the principal on teachers' attitudes.

Distributed Leadership and Its Impact on People and Schools

Since 1954, when Gibb initially articulated the specific term *distributed leadership* (Gronn, 2002), researchers have offered similar conceptualizations using different terms, such as "shared" (Marks & Printy, 2003) or "collective" (Leithwood et al., 2012) leadership. Much of the literature focuses on the conceptual development of distributed leadership (Gronn, 2008; Harris et al., 2008; Leithwood et al., 2007; Spillane, 2005); the description of the necessary practices (Harris & Gronn, 2008; Leithwood, Mascall, & Strauss, 2009; Spillane, 2006); and analytic models for leadership distribution (Gronn, 2011; Leithwood et al., 2007; Spillane & Diamond, 2007).

Evidence-based studies detailing the effects of distributed leadership on schools have only recently begun to emerge. Evidence-based research, both qualitative and quantitative, has focused on the consequence of distributed leadership on people, including staff's organizational commitment (Hulpia et al., 2012), organizational affiliation, trust, job satisfaction, teacher retention (Angelle, 2010), and teachers' academic optimism (Chang, 2011; Mascall et al., 2008). Distributed leadership has also been shown to increase academic capacity, including teachers' knowledge and pedagogical skills as well as student achievement (Heck & Hallinger, 2009; Leithwood & Seashore-Louis, 2012; Marks & Printy, 2003). Most findings on the impacts of distributed leadership on the attitudinal dimensions of social capital (e.g., trust, satisfaction, collegiality, commitment, and organizational affiliation) have been positive when the principal reports taking up supportive roles, though findings on the correlation between distributed leadership and student achievement have been mixed (Heck & Hallinger, 2009). Overall, research confirms the idea that principals have direct influence on various elements of school culture, in large part working through teachers and other adults. As a result, this present study includes many variables related to school social conditions and educator attributes.

Researchers take varied approaches to the measurement of distributed leadership. Some investigate who is involved in collaborative decisions, such as those related to school vision or direction (Heck & Hallinger, 2009; Leithwood et al., 2007). Other research seeks to measure collective influence of individuals involved in reaching shared goals, including, for instance, measures of shared accountability and collective school culture (Heck & Hallinger, 2009; Boudreaux, 2011; Davis, 2009). Research also aims to understand the influence of teachers and others working with principals to improve teaching and learning (Gordon, 2005; Marks & Printy, 2003). The study reported here seeks to add to the knowledge base of how involvement of a broad set of stakeholders is related to educators' attitudes about their schools and professions. We assert that the evidence will provide guidance to both principals and teachers about the relative importance of distributed leadership to satisfying careers for educators.

Distributed Leadership Involves People in a Synergistic Way

Distributed leadership expands the practice of leadership beyond the responsibility of principals and other formal leaders (such as district leaders) by recognizing personnel with expertise and skills (such as instructional specialists, grade-level leaders, or other school employees (Leithwood et al., 2007; Spillane & Diamond, 2007; Harris, 2009; Lashway, 2006). Spillane and Diamond (2007) use the metaphor of leadership being stretched over leaders and followers in varied situations. Distributed leadership, conceptually, is organic in that who is leading at a particular time can shift from situation to situation. Accordingly, leadership can come from many individuals, as needed.

Distributed Leadership as Recognition of Expertise

Some research points to expertise as individuals' warrant for leadership (Bennett et al., 2003). Schools are financially, instructionally, and managerially complex organizations and therefore beyond the expectation that a principal can provide sufficient leadership for success (Hargreaves & Fink, 2006; Thorpe, Gold, & Lawler, 2011). Certainly where the core technology of schools is concerned, teachers provide critical expertise to lead in matters directly related to matters of instruction and student performance (Elmore, 2000). Elmore recognizes that people will have varied skills and competencies developed due to their interests, predispositions, aptitudes, prior experiences, and dedicated roles. Distributed leadership theory acknowledges "multiple sources of guidance and direction, following the contours of expertise in an organization, made coherent through a common culture" (Elmore, 2000, p. 15). Further, Elmore (2000) argues that, in a school, "the roles and activities of leadership flow from the expertise required for learning and improvement, not from the formal dictates of the institution" (p. 15). Recognizing expertise at various sites within the school allows for a more fluid approach to leadership than assigning formal roles and positions. Depending on the task at hand, teachers, with or without formal positions of responsibility, can introduce new initiatives and influence the practice of colleagues. Recognizing that expertise exists throughout the school can contribute to creating a robust school culture, which can be a powerful motivating force for teachers, helping them to feel valued in their work and encouraging their participation in matters beyond their classrooms.

Distributed Leadership Suggests Openness of Boundaries

While distributed leadership is generally concerned with collaborative leadership activity among the principal and teachers, it could also include students, parents, and those involved in site-based governance and management (Harris, 2003, 2006). Harris takes up the argument that all teachers are suited for leadership: "All teachers harbor leadership capabilities waiting to be unlocked and engaged for the good of the school" (Harris, 2003, p. 78). She develops this point further by stressing the need for professional development that will create communities of learning and link professional development and leading. "Teachers who are engaged in learning with their peers are most likely to embrace new initiatives and to innovate" (Harris, 2003, p. 78). The rationale for distributed leadership is grounded in the concept of sustainable leadership (Hargreaves & Fink, 2006). Leadership promotes school improvement that needs to be embraced by the teachers who are responsible for implementation in classrooms (Hargreaves & Fink, 2006; Marks & Printy, 2003). Also critical, reactions of parents and students can shape the outcomes of the change, whether in a positive or negative way (Lashway, 2006; Leithwood & Mascall, 2008). Thus, distributed notions of leadership can include a broad set of stakeholders who have the potential to exert influence on the situations present in the school.

Leadership Functions in the School

Schools are organizations that have the goal of helping students learn (Tschannen-Moran & Barr, 2004). To achieve the purpose, principals, teachers, and others share the responsibilities of managing and teaching. Traditional views separate the responsibility of teaching from leadership, but recent research argues that leading the school toward success is accomplished in a collective manner, in which both the leaders and the teachers play essential roles (Bryk et al., 2010; Firestone & Martinez, 2007; Harris & Gronn, 2008). This view builds on theory that a school is a loosely coupled organization in which formal leaders cannot closely monitor every teacher (Weick, 1976).

Particular leadership functions have been identified in the school (Bryk et al., 2010; Hallinger & Murphy, 1985; Marks & Printy, 2003). Leithwood and his colleagues (2007) proposed four leadership functions in the school: setting the school vision, developing people, managing instructional practice, and redesigning schools so that the school purpose can be achieved. This line of research shows that inclusion of the teachers in the school decision-making, operation, and development help maintain coherence to shared norms and values in order to improve the school (Goddard, Goddard, & Tschannen-Moran, 2007). Distributed leadership reduces teachers' seclusion and increases dedication to the collective good of the school by involving more people in school processes (Heikka, Waniganayake, & Hujala, 2013; Leithwood, Mascall, & Strauss, 2009). Distributed leadership is particularly helpful in providing widespread quality management of the instructional program in schools where multiple groups guide and mobilize staff in instructional change and improvement (Bennett et al., 2003; Spillane, Halverson, & Diamond, 2004). Instructional leadership and effective school improvement processes include areas such as decisions about staffing, monitoring school improvement strategies, and allocating resources that foster school improvement (Lashway, 2006; Leithwood et al., 2007; Spillane & Diamond, 2007). Leithwood and his colleagues (Leithwood &

Mascall, 2008; Leithwood & Seashore-Louis, 2012) moved even further and claimed a collective leadership model that includes the parents and students in the school leadership roles.

Teacher and Principal Attitudes

A person's attitude toward his or her job, including satisfaction, commitment, and cohesion, is related to the content and the process of the job (Spector, 1997). School climate also plays a vital role in predicting both teachers' and the principal's attitude (Cohen et al., 2009; Desai et al., 2014). Individual dispositions precede and condition the extent to which a person perceives satisfaction, cohesion, and commitment. When a principal provides supportive leadership and develops a positive relationship with the teachers and a collaborative culture develops, teachers' contributions to school decision-making are positively related to increased teacher commitment and satisfaction (Fusarelli, Kowalski, & Petersen, 2011; Hulpia et al., 2012; Price, 2012; Angelle, 2010; Firestone & Pennell, 1993). Research suggests that the central position of the principal in the school influences the attitudes of others (Price, 2012; Printy, 2010). Price (2012) asserts that interpersonal factors emerging between the principal and teachers are highly variable and play a role in shaping both the principal's and teachers' attitudes. As a result of these findings, we investigate the mediating role of principals' attitudes on the same attitudes of teachers.

Distributed Leadership as an Antecedent of Attitude

School leadership has been shown to have an impact on teachers' organizational commitment and other attitudes (Randeree & Ghaffar Chaudhry, 2012; Sleegers, Nguni, & Denessen, 2006; Wahab et al., 2014). Harris (2008) claimed that there are positive effects of distributed leadership on teachers' self-efficacy and levels of morale, which are conceptually related to their organizational commitment. Related research premised the positive impact of distributed leadership on teachers' satisfaction and commitment to the supportive leadership of the principal and to collaboration among the leadership team (Hulpia et al., 2012; Rosseel, Devos, & Hulpia, 2009). It appears that teachers respond more to supportive principal leadership and cooperation among informal leaders than they do to formal leadership distribution arrangements, such as shared decision-making.

Distributed leadership has also been shown to have a relationship to teachers' satisfaction, commitment, and academic optimism, as well as a hopeful attitude about a school's chances for success (Angelle, 2010; Mascall et al., 2008). Mascall and his colleagues (2008) explored the importance of alignment across sources of leadership and whether leadership was planned, emergent, or uncoordinated. They found planned and aligned leadership distribution is positively associated with teachers' academic optimism.

Conceptual Framework

The studies reviewed to this point have offered solid evidence that teachers in schools where leadership is distributed have more positive attitudes than teachers in schools without leadership distribution. None of the studies mentioned, however, actually measured the extent to which each group from a school community participates in different leadership functions and how the varied level of contribution and influence from different levels impacts the attitude of teachers. Moreover, the research reviewed did not seek to detect the mediating effect the principal's attitudes have on the attitude of teachers. Given the evidence that the principal is vital to the school and that interaction between the principal and teachers has an impact on the attitude of both the school and teachers (Leithwood & Seashore-Louis, 2012; Price, 2012), this study remedies that identified gap.

The study detailed in this chapter answers the following research questions:

1. What is the relationship of distributed leadership participation to principals' sense of school cohesion, their reported commitment, and their satisfaction with their job?
2. What is the relationship of distributed leadership participation to teachers' sense of school cohesion, their reported commitment, and their satisfaction with their job?
3. To what extent do principals' attitudes mediate teachers' attitudes?

The conceptual model for the study is presented in figure 1. The configurations of participation in various leadership tasks are displayed in the gray box. The various models evaluate the relationships between distributed leadership and principal and teacher attitudes. All models include school controls and controls for principals' and teachers' characteristics.

FIGURE 1. Conceptual Model of Distributed Leadership and Individual Attitudes

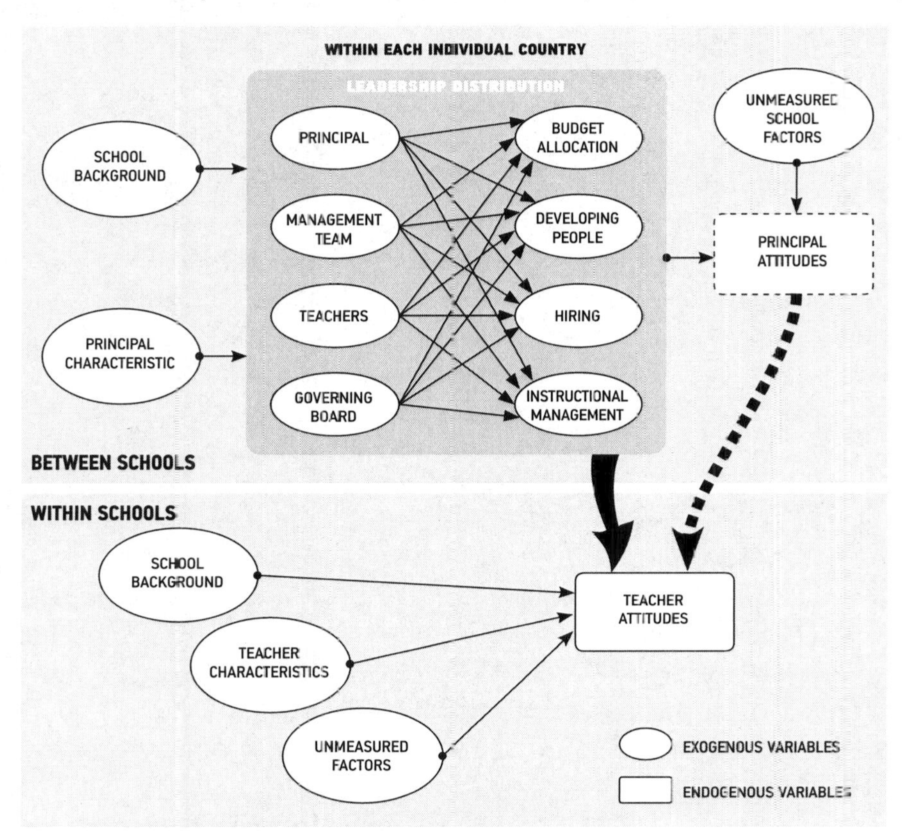

Data and Method

Data Source

The research reported in this chapter uses data from the Teaching and Learning International Survey (TALIS) 2013, specifically, the second round of the study conducted by the OECD. The TALIS study intends to provide policymakers, researchers, and educational leaders with insights from school administrators and teachers (OECD, 2014). TALIS includes significant information regarding school characteristics and education systems, and extensive data about the learning environment and working condition of teachers and school principals. The TALIS data also include intensive information on various key issues across countries, such as appraisal, feedback, job satisfaction, self-efficacy, professional development, leadership style, autonomy, and so on.

TALIS 2013 involves elementary, lower secondary, and high secondary schools. This study uses data for the lower secondary level because most participating countries have data at this level. The first cycle of TALIS was conducted in 2008 with twenty-four countries (regions). In 2013, the number of participant countries (regions) in lower secondary level went up to thirty-four. TALIS 2013 used a stratified cluster sampling method that firstly randomly selected two hundred schools from each country, then randomly selected twenty teachers from each participating school. TALIS had separate questionnaire to collect data from the principal and from teachers. This study uses data from both the principal and the teacher questionnaires to investigate the influence of participation by both groups in leadership functions on the attitude of both the principal and teachers. With the primary attention paid to teacher attitudes, the principal's attitudes serve as mediating effect in the teacher model. Due to the complex feature of the sampling frame, a multilevel model was applied to reduce the error caused by sampling (Lee & Forthofer, 2006). We use the entire set of usable responses from teachers and principals in the countries that participated in TALIS and did not conduct any subgroup analysis for this study. The 2013 TALIS data used in this study included the following thirty-two countries: Australia; Brazil; Bulgaria; Chile; Croatia; Czech Republic; Denmark; Estonia; Finland; France; Israel; Italy; Japan; Korea; Latvia; Malaysia; Mexico; Netherlands; Norway; Poland; Portugal; Serbia; Singapore; Slovak Republic; Spain; Sweden; United States; England (United Kingdom); Flanders (Belgium); Dhabi (United Arab Emirates); Alberta (Canada); and Romania. A detailed list of the 2013 TALIS data used in this study can be found in the appendix.

Latent Variable Construction

Dependent Variables

The primary interest of the current research is to estimate the relationship of distributed leadership to the attitudes of school educators, both principals and teachers. In each case, attitudes are measured as reported job commitment, perception of school cohesion, and personal satisfaction. Both latent variables of interest are constructed from Likert-type responses using the Latent Trait Method that generates continuous latent variables using categorical manifestations (Langeheine & Rost, 2013). The degree of job commitment by teachers and the principal is captured by their ratings of their willingness to stay in the same school and same profession even if they have the chance to change. Teacher and principal satisfaction measures are constructed from several indicators on the respective surveys assessing whether or not teachers or principals enjoy working at the current school and are satisfied with the profession. Teachers' perceived cohesion is measured using a set of questions asking the teachers' perspectives on collaborative activities in the school. Principal perceived cohesion assesses the principals' perceptions of teacher solidarity, sharing, and cooperation on the school issues. To ensure that the values for items used in measures go in same direction, two questions for both teachers (TT2G46C TT2G46D) and the principal (TC2G39C TC2G39D) were reverse coded before constructing the latent variables.

TALIS used complicated stratified sampling that may amplify the estimate error; therefore, OECD calculated sample weights to compensate for any error due to sampling design error and data collection in order to accurately represent the population for each country (OECD, 2014). Most statistical software can handle sample weight for estimation, and Mplus 7 was used for this study. Table 1 details the model fit indices for the study. The overall model fit for the six latent constructs (i.e., three for principals and three for teachers) is satisfactory according to the rule of thumb that the CFI (comparative fit index) and TLI (Tucker-Lewis index) are above 0.95, and the RMSEA (root mean squared error of approximation) is less than 0.06 (Bowen & Guo, 2012; Hu & Bentler, 1999; Kline, 2011). For the principal model, the CFI is 0.977, the TFI is 0.967, and the RMSEA is 0.041; for the teacher attitude model, the CFI is 0.948, the TFI is 0.953, and the RMSEA is 0.077.

Independent Variables

The independent variable of primary interest in this research is leadership distribution. TALIS 2013 contains a set of questions asking about the participation of varied stakeholders, including the principal, the management team, the teachers, and the governing board or the mentors, in different leadership responsibilities. We conducted an exploratory factor analysis and found the data were allied well for four leadership roles: staff hiring, budgetary allocation decision, instructional management, and teacher development. We call these *participant-by-function* variables. We also included one latent variable to measure stakeholders' participation

TABLE 1. Model Fit Statistics for Latent Variables

VARIABLE	ITEMS	CFI	TFI	RMSEA	OBS	MEAN	SD	MIN	MAX
Principal-cohesion	TC2G30A, TC2G30C TC2G30D, TC2G30E	0.977	0.967	0.041	6,080	−0.013	0.878	−3.523	1.680
Principal-commit	TC2G39B, TC2G39C TC2G39D				6,080	−0.019	0.819	−2.998	1.433
Principal-satisfaction	TC2G39F, TC2G39H TC2G39I				6,080	−0.020	0.859	−3.292	1.592
Teacher-cohesion	TT2G33A, TT2G33B TT2G33C, TT2G33D TT2G33E, TT2G33F TT2G33G, TT2G33H	0.928	0.913	0.077	101,404	−0.001	0.882	−2.880	2.782
Teacher-commit	TT2G46B, TT2G46C TT2G46D				101,404	−0.014	0.842	−3.094	1.711
Teacher-satisfaction	TT2G46B, TT2G46C TT2G46D				101,404	−0.015	0.883	−3.336	1.888

TABLE 2. Model Fit Parameters and Descriptive Outcomes for Distributed Leadership Variables

VARIABLES	ITEMS (TC2G)	CFI	TFI	RMSEA	OBS	MEAN	SD	MIN	MAX
BUDG_P	18C1,D1,E1				6,038	0.109	0.666	−0.803	1.654
BUDG_MT	18C2,D2,E1	0.955	0.949	0.011	6,038	0.146	0.687	−0.650	1.987
BUDG_T	18C3,D3,E3				6,038	0.113	0.526	−0.453	2.728
BUDG_GB	18C4,D4,E4				6,038	0.104	0.525	−0.424	1.789
DEPEO_P	28A2-F2				5,468	−0.013	0.788	−1.683	1.631
DEPEO_MT	28A3-F3	0.987	0.982	0.020	5,468	−0.011	0.789	−1.367	1.396
DEPEO_M	28A4-F4				5,468	0.132	0.693	−0.712	2.040
DEPEO_T	28A5 F5				5,468	0.051	0.755	−1.076	2.052
HIR_P	18A1, B1				6,042	−0.017	0.616	−0.779	1.539
HIR_MT	18A2, B2	0.996	0.992	0.010	6,042	0.161	0.600	−0.463	1.818
HIR_T	18A3, B3				6,042	0.156	0.587	−0.457	2.302
HIR_GB	18A4,B4				6,042	0.189	0.550	−0.283	1.568
INSTR_P	18G1,I1,J1,K1				6,045	0.021	0.752	−1.255	1.432
INSTR_MT	18G2,I2,J2,K2	0.928	0.912	0.020	6,045	0.021	0.733	−1.168	1.289
INSTR_T	18G3,I3,J3,K3				6,045	0.023	0.719	−1.225	1.398
INSTR_GB	18G4,I4,J4,K4				6,045	0.112	0.647	−0.583	1.969
SHAREDECIS	22A,B,C	1.000	1.000	0.000	6,073	−0.016	0.849	−3.030	1.613

in decision-making (though these data report the perceptions of the principal, not teachers). The Latent Trait Method was applied using Mplus 7 to construct a latent variable responding to each group's participation in one leadership responsibility respectively. Therefore, there were five models fitted in total for distributed leadership. It is important to notice that all items coded in TALIS as 2 (indicate no participation) were recoded as 0 for consistent direction of the variables. Table 1 details the individual indicators included in each latent variable construct, and the model fit parameters. The variables use the abbreviations BUDG = budget; DEPEO = developing people; HIR = hiring; INSTRU = managing instruction; SHAREDECIS = sharing decision-making; P = principal; MT = management team; GB = governing board.

Mediating Variable

A key research interest is investigating whether principals' attitudes make a contribution to teachers' attitudes toward their work. In the second stage of analysis, with teacher commitment, teacher sense of cohesion, and teacher satisfaction as the dependent variables, the principal attitudinal variables were entered into the models to test for a mediation effect.

Control Variables

Along with the main independent variables (distributed leadership responsibility shared among four groups of stakeholders), several other school, principal, and teacher characteristics are included, with the aim of controlling for the context. The school-level control variables consist of principals' gender, age, educational level, experience as a principal, and employment status; as well as school type (public vs. private), school location (rural, village, small town, town, city, and large city), funding recourse (50 percent or more of the school's funding comes from the government), size (the number of students enrolled), and socioeconomic status. The teacher-level controlled variables include gender, age, education, experience as a teacher, employment status as a teacher, and tenure. Table 3 details the coding and the descriptive outcomes for the controlled variables.

Data Analysis

The Impact of Distributed Leadership on Principals' Attitudes

To answer research question 1, we applied a multivariate linear regression model based on standard ordinary least square (OLS) assumptions. Regression models were fitted by pooling all of the observations across thirty-two countries (countries with data usable for this study), with the school and principal backgrounds controlled. However, given expected variation across thirty-two countries, we believe cultural, political, and educational backgrounds for individual countries are likely antecedents for principals' attitude (Den Hartog et al., 1999). Therefore, we include country variation as fixed dummy variables in the model. This method of including dummy variables in the international comparative study has been frequently used by researchers (Chudgar, Luschei, & Zhou, 2013; Zhou, 2014).

$$\begin{aligned}(PA)_{0j} = {} & \beta_{00} + \beta_{01}(SHAREDDECISION) + \beta_{02}(BUDGET\_GROUPS) + \beta_{03}(DEVEPEO\_GROUPS) \\ & + \beta_{04}(HIRING\_GROUPS) + \beta_{05}(INSTRU{+}GROUPS) + \beta_{06}(PGENDER) + \beta_{07}(PAGE) \\ & + \beta_{08}(EDUCATION) + \beta_{09}(PEXPERIENCE) + \beta_{10}(PEMPLOYMENTSTATUS) \\ & + \beta_{11}(LOCATION) + \beta_{12}(MANAGETYPE) + \beta_{13}(PUBLICFUND) + \beta_{14}(SIZE) \\ & + \beta_{15}(IMMIGRANT) + \beta_{16}(LOWSES) - i.country + r_{0j}\end{aligned}$$

Where $(PA)_{0j}$ is the value on one of the three attitudes (satisfaction, commitment, cohesion) for principal j, β_{00} is the average score of principal attitude, r_{0j} is the random effect for the individual teacher, and σ^2 is the variability of the principal's attitude. β_{01} to β_{16} are the effects of independent variables and controls and *i.country* is fixed dummy variable for country effect.

The Impact of Distributed Leadership on Teacher Attitudes

As discussed earlier, TALIS administers questionnaires to the principal and the teachers, respectively, in the same school. The analytic interest and data structure make a hierarchical model appropriate for answering research question 2, related to the relationship of leadership distribution to teachers' attitudes. When data has a cluster structure because teachers are nested in the school, the responses within a school become dependent because they share commonalities due to the same context (Garson, 2013; Raudenbush & Bryk, 2002). The challenges to analyzing the

TABLE 3. Coding and Descriptive Outcomes for Control Variables

CONTROL VARIABLES		OBS	MEAN	SD	MIN	MAX
School Level: Principal Characteristics						
Gender	TC2G01 Female=1, Male=0	6,122	0.519	0.500	0	1
Age	TC2G02 How old are you?	6,103	50.577	8.221	23	73
Education	TC2G03 Highest formal education. 1 <Below ISCED Level 5> 2 <ISCED Level 5B>(Associate) 3 <ISCED Level 5A>(Bachelor) 4 <ISCED Level 6>(Masters)	6,091	2.991	0.301	1	4
Experience as a principal	TC2G04B Year(s) working as a principal in total.	5,735	8.671	7.186	1	45
Employment status	TC2G05 1=Full-time, 0=Part-time	5,907	20.044	10.262	1	49
School Level: School Factors						
Location	TC2G09 o 1 [Hamlet or rural area] (1,000 people or fewer) 2 [Village] (1,001 to 3,000 people) 3 [Small town] (3,001 to 15,000 people) 4 [Town] (15,001 to 100,000 people) 5 [City] (100,001 to 1,000,000 people) 6 [Large city] (more than 1,000,000 people)	6,094	3.762	1.431	1	6
Publicly or privately managed	TC2G010 1=Publicly managed, 0=Privately managed	6,116	0.858	0.350	0	1
Government funded	TC2G011A 50% or more of the school's funding comes from the <government> 1=Yes, 0=No	6,097	0.869	0.337	0	1

Size	TC2G014 The number of students enrolled	6,025	658.305	493.801	1	4335
Proportion of immigrant students	TC2G015A Percentage of immigrant students 1=None, 2=1% to 10%, 3= 11% to 30%, 4=31% to 60%, 5=More than 60%	6,002	1.873	1.046	1	5
Low SES	TC2G015C Percentage of students from socioeconomically disadvantaged homes 1=None, 2=1% to 10%, 3= 11% to 30%, 4=31% to 60%, 5=More than 60%	6,032	2.839	1.085	1	5
Teacher Level: Teacher Characteristics						
Gender	TT2G01 Female=1, Male=0	104,355	0.680	0.466	0	1
Age	TC2G02 How old are you?	104,269	42.512	10.538	18	76
Employment status	TT2G03 What is your current employment status as a teacher? 1=Full-time, 0=Part-time	102,136	0.796	0.403	0	1
Experience as a teacher	TC2G05B Year(s) working as a teacher in total	97,773	16.139	10.382	0	58
Tenure	TC2G06 Tenure status 1=Permanent employment (an ongoing contract with no fixed end-point before the age of retirement) 0=Fixed-term contract for a period of time	102,464	0.816	0.388	0	1
Education	Highest degree finished 1 <Below ISCED Level 5> 2 <ISCED Level 5B>(Associate) 3 <ISCED Level 5A>(Bachelor) 4 <ISCED Level 6>(Masters)	102,910	2.907	0.393	1	4
Training	Complete a teacher training? Yes=1, No=0	102,578	0.884	0.320	0	1

nested data include within-cluster dependencies, homogeneity, and within-cluster covariance, as well as sources of variation within and across clusters predicted from samples (Garson, 2013; Raudenbush & Bryk, 2002). More researchers are using multilevel modeling to account for the nested structure of data in a school system (Raudenbush & Bryk, 2002). This study uses Hierarchical Linear Modeling (HLM) that simultaneously investigates relationships within and between hierarchical levels of stratified data and makes it more efficient to account for variance among variables at different levels (Garson, 2013; Raudenbush & Bryk, 2002).

As mentioned before in the principal model, we included country-level dummy variables to account for the country uniqueness. When dealing with the data with the feature of nesting that teachers are nested in the school, and the schools are nested in the country, there are two options for running the multilevel models. One is to fix a three-level model in which the country-level variation is included as the third level. This approach considers country-level effect as random; the second option is to run a two-level model in which country-level variation is controlled as dummy variables to repent country variation. This way considers country-level variation as fixed. This approach allows us to account for all the variation in teacher attitude due to observed and unobserved attributes at both the school and country levels, or in other words, compare teachers within schools of one country rather than across diverse schools and countries (e.g., Chudgar & Luschei, 2009; Dewan & Kraemer, 2000). The second reason for selecting a two-level model with dummy rather than a three-level model was that we could control the country effect as fixed and compare the variance it added to explain the variance of teacher attitude by running the model step by step.

In the model, Level 1 represents teachers and Level 2 represents schools. Models were built sequentially: (1) the baseline model or unconditional model; (2) the distributed leadership model that includes distributed leadership variables along with control variables; (3) the principal mediation model that includes variables of principal attitudes as the mediator at the school level. Specifically, the *teacher-level model* for the baseline model (Model 1) is

$$(TA)_{ij} = \beta_{0j} + r_{ij}$$
$$r_{ij} \sim N(0, \sigma^2),$$

where $(TA)_{ij}$ is the value on one of the three teacher distal outcomes (satisfaction, commitment, cohesion) for teacher i in school j, β_{0j} is the average score of teacher attitude in school j, r_{ij} is the teacher level random effect, and σ^2 is the variability within schools. The corresponding *school-level model* is

$$\beta_{0j} = \gamma_{00} + \mu_{0j}$$
$$\mu_{0j} \sim N(0, \tau_{00}),$$

where γ_{00} is the grand mean (or intercept), μ_{0j} is the school-level random effect, and τ_{00} is the variability of teacher attitude across schools.

The *teacher-level model* for the distributed leadership model (Model 2) is as follows:

$$\begin{aligned}(TA)_{ij} = \beta_{0j} &+ \beta_{1j}(TGender) + \beta_{2j}(TAge) + \beta_{3j}(TEmploymentStatus)\\ &+ \beta_{4j}(PExperience) + \beta_{5j}(TTenured) + \beta_{6j}(TEducation)\\ &+ \beta_{7j}(Tpreparation) + r_{ij}\end{aligned}$$

$$r_{tij} \sim N(0, \sigma^2),$$

where β_{1j} to β_{5j} are the coefficients of controls for teacher backgrounds.

The responding distributed leadership school-level model is as follows: γ_{01} to γ_{02} coefficients of the stakeholders' participation in each of the leadership responsibilities, γ_{06} to γ_{16} are coefficients of the controls for the school contexts and principal characteristics, and *i.country* is country fixed dummy variables.

$$\begin{aligned}\beta_{0j} = \gamma_{00} &+ \gamma_{01}(SHAREDDECISION) + \gamma_{02}(BUDGET\_GROUPS) + \gamma_{03}(DEVEPEO\_GROUPS)\\ &+ \gamma_{04}(HIRING\_GROUPS) + \gamma_{05}(INSTRU\_GROUPS) + \gamma_{06}(PGENDER) + \gamma_{07}(PAGE)\\ &+ \gamma_{08}(PEDUCATION) + \gamma_{09}(PEXPERIENCE) + \gamma_{10}(PEMPLOYMENTSTATUS)\\ &+ \gamma_{11}(LOCATION) + \gamma_{12}(MANAGETYPE) + \gamma_{13}(PUBLICFUND) + \gamma_{14}(SIZE)\\ &+ \gamma_{15}(PROIMMIGRANT) + \gamma_{16}(LOWSES) + i.countrt + \mu_{0j}\end{aligned}$$

$$\mu_{0j} \sim N(0, \tau_{00})$$

The teacher-level model for Model 3 remains the same as Model 2. The *school-level principal mediation model* builds on the distributed leadership model by including three principal attitude variables in the model. While the other coefficients remain the same, γ_{17} to γ_{19} are the effects of the principal's attitudes on the teacher's attitude.

$$\beta_{0j} = \gamma_{00} + \gamma_{01}(SHAREDDECISION) + \gamma_{02}(BUDGET\_GROUPS) + \gamma_{03}(DEVEPEO\_GROUPS) + \gamma_{04}(HIRING\_GROUPS) + \gamma_{05}(INSTRU\_GROUPS) + \gamma_{06}(PGENDER) + \gamma_{07}(PAGE) + \gamma_{08}(PEDUCATION) + \gamma_{09}(PEXPERIENCE) + \gamma_{10}(PEMPLOYMENTSTATUS) + \gamma_{11}(LOCATION) + \gamma_{11}(LOCATION) + \gamma_{12}(MANAGETYPE) + \gamma_{13}(PUBLICFUND) + \gamma_{14}(SIZE) + \gamma_{15}(PROIMMIGRANT) + \gamma_{16}(LOWSES) + \gamma_{17}(PCOHEN) + \gamma_{18}(PCOMIT) + \gamma_{19}(PCOMIT) + i.country + \mu_{0j}$$

$$\mu_{0j} \sim N(0, \tau_{00})$$

Findings

The Impact of Distributed Leadership on Principals' Attitudes

The first question asked in this research is how the implementation of distributed leadership impacts principals' attitudes. Results of this stage of analysis are in table 4. When principals' perceived cohesion is dependent on the included predictors, shared decision-making has a strong positive impact on it ($\beta = 0.301$, $p < 0.001$), as does the principal's ($\beta = 0.133$, $p < 0.05$) participation in instructional management. Teachers' participation in instructional management is negatively related to the principal's perceived school cohesion ($\beta = -0.182$, $p < 0.01$).

For the principal's commitment, in general, the extent to which the varied stakeholders, including the staff, parents, and students, participate in school decision-making ($\beta = 0.220$, $p < 0.001$) is positively related to the principal's commitment. In addition, the management team's active participation in developing people ($\beta = 0.083$, $p < 0.05$) and the teacher's involvement in hiring ($\beta = 0.415$, $p < 0.01$) predict higher levels of the principal's commitment. On the other hand, the government board's leading role in hiring ($\beta = -0.222$, $p < 0.01$) and teachers' active involvement in instruction ($\beta = -0.127$, $p < 0.05$) are negatively related to the principal's commitment.

For the principal's job satisfaction, once again, shared decision-making by the staff, the parents, and the students has a positive association ($\beta = 0.265$, $p < 0.001$). Moreover, the management team's participation in developing teachers ($\beta = 0.096$, $p < 0.05$) and teachers' participation in hiring ($\beta = 0.464$, $p < 0.001$) predict a satisfied principal in the school, but the governing board's leading role in hiring ($\beta = -0.190$, $p < .005$) and teacher leader involvement in instructional decisions ($\beta = -0.143$, $p < 0.05$) actually dissatisfy the principal. For all three principal attitude variables, shared decision-making is a relatively strong and positive predictor that the principal is more satisfied and committed and reports higher cohesion in the school where the staff's, parents', and students' participation in school decision-making is welcome. Note that we did not find the participation by stakeholders in the budgetary allocations associated with the principal's attitude to be significant. Interestingly, the participation from teachers in hiring is a very strong predictor of principals' commitment and satisfaction.

For the school and principal background controls, principals' gender and experience are the significant predictors for principal perceptions of school cohesion, commitment, and job satisfaction. Female leaders report a higher level of perceived school staff cohesion and are more committed to their jobs. Older principals serving longer in the school demonstrate more commitment and satisfaction and report higher levels of school cohesion. Additionally, schools with more immigrant students and students from low socioeconomic backgrounds have less committed and satisfied principals.

The country dummy variables were not included in the final results table, but many countries reveal a strong effect of the country's uniqueness on the principal's attitudes. (Readers interested in these tables should contact the first author.) The model in total explained 18.8 percent, 26.5 percent, and 27.1 percent of the principal's perceived school cohesion, commitment, and satisfaction.

The Results for Impact of Distributed Leadership on Teacher Attitude in HLM

The results from the unconditional model of teacher attitude, the first step in hierarchical linear modeling, are presented in Table 5. The intraschool correlation is 25.4 percent for teacher perceived cohesion; thus approximately 25 percent of the variance in teachers' perceived cohesion lies between schools. Approximately 19.6 percent of the variance in teachers' commitment is explained by school variation, and 21.6 percent of the variance in teachers' satisfaction is explained by between-school differences.

Distributed Leadership as Antecedent of Teachers' Attitudes with or without Principals' Attitudes

Building on the unconditional model, Model 2 and Model 3 (see table 6) test the effect of stakeholders' participation in school leadership responsibilities on teachers'

TABLE 4. Results for the Influence of Distributed Leadership on Principal Attitudes

	PRINCIPAL-COHESION	PRINCIPAL-COMMIT	PRINCIPAL-SATISFACTION
Intercept	−0.053 (0.440)	−0.118 (0.380)	−0.045 (0.391)
Predictors			
SHARED_DECISION	**0.301***** (0.035)	**0.220***** (0.032)	**0.265***** (0.033)
BUDGET_PRINCIPAL	0.025 (0.098)	0.093 (0.085)	0.088 (0.091)
BUDGET_MANTEAM	−0.022 (0.092)	−0.125 (0.092)	−0.128 (0.098)
BUDGET_TEACHER	0.045 (0.150)	−0.038 (0.088)	−0.017 (0.103)
BUDGET_GOVBOARD	−0.097 (0.062)	0.016 (0.067)	−0.003 (0.068)
DEVPEO_PRINCIPAL	0.043 (0.054)	0.024 (0.045)	0.039 (0.050)
DEVPEO_MANTEAM	0.073 (0.047)	**0.083*** (0.042)	**0.096*** (0.045)
DEVPEO_TEACHER	0.006 (0.040)	0.029 (0.036)	0.028 (0.038)
DEVPEO_GOVBOARD	0.080 (0.047)	0.061 (0.046)	0.049 (0.049)
HIRING_PRINCIPAL	−0.119 (0.128)	−0.074 (0.129)	−0.123 (0.124)
HIRING_MANTEAM	0.138 (0.111)	−0.101 (0.106)	−0.098 (0.106)
HIRING_TEACHER	−0.075 (0.207)	**0.415**** (0.152)	**0.464***** (0.140)
HIRING_GOVBOARD	0.121 (0.096)	**−0.222**** (0.082)	**−0.190*** (0.084)
INSTRU_PRINCIPAL	**0.133*** (0.068)	0.027 (0.066)	0.047 (0.070)

INSTRU_MANTEAM	−0.095	0.004	−0.030
	(0.072)	(0.075)	(0.079)
INSTRU_TEACHER	**−0.182****	**−0.127***	**−0.143***
	(0.058)	(0.064)	(0.068)
INSTRU_GOVBOARD	0.049	0.022	0.024
	(0.068)	(0.060)	(0.061)
School Level Control			
Gender	**0.144****	**0.126***	0.087
	(0.056)	(0.055)	(0.057)
Age	0.006	0.007	0.004
	(0.005)	(0.005)	(0.005)
Education	0.008	−0.005	0.022
	(0.106)	(0.113)	(0.115)
Experience	**0.010***	**0.011***	**0.012****
	(0.005)	(0.004)	(0.005)
Employstatus	0.103	0.212	0.213
	(0.114)	(0.131)	(0.139)
Location	0.010	0.041	0.037
	(0.023)	(0.021)	(0.022)
Managetype	−0.064	−0.065	−0.027
	(0.087)	(0.082)	(0.090)
Publicfund	0.080	−0.105	−0.081
	(0.075)	(0.068)	(0.073)
Size	−0.000	0.000	0.000
	(0.000)	(0.000)	(0.000)
Immigrant	−0.034	**−0.066***	**−0.074***
	(0.043)	(0.033)	(0.034)
LowSES	−0.032	−0.036	**−0.055***
	−0.053	−0.118	−0.045
N	4857	4857	4857
R2	0.188	0.265	0.271

Note: Standard errors in parentheses. $^{*}p < 0.05$, $^{**}p < 0.01$, $^{***}p < 0.001$

TABLE 5. Hierarchical Linear Modeling (HLM) Results of the Unconditional Model

	TEACHER-COHESION	TEACHER-COMMIT	TEACHER-SATISFACTION
Intercept	−0.012* (0.006)	−0.005 (0.005)	−0.001 (0.005)
Variance Component			
Between School	0.217*** (0.004)	0.143*** (0.003)	0.177*** (0.003)
Within School	0.636*** (0.011)	0.587*** (0.008)	0.643*** (0.009)
ICC Between School	0.254	0.196	0.216
N	101404	101404	101404

*$p < 0.05$, ***$p < 0.001$

attitude (research question 2), and whether the principal's attitude and perception mediate the effect (research question 3). The estimates provide information about the impact of different groups' participation in leadership responsibilities on teachers' perceived cohesion, commitment, and satisfaction. In general, Model 2 added approximately 4 percent of the explained variance toward teacher cohesion over Model 1, 5 percent toward teacher commitment, and 6 percent toward satisfaction, respectively, at school level. In addition, Model 3 added 4 percent, 5 percent, and 7 percent over Model 1 regarding teacher cohesion, commitment, and satisfaction that could be explained by the predictors. The results indicated that the varied level of participation from different groups of stakeholders did not explain much of the variance in teachers' perceived cohesion, teachers' commitment, and teachers' satisfaction. In answer to the question about principals' attitudes mediating teachers' attitudes, Model 3 in each case explained some additional variance of teachers' attitudes but not significantly. The remaining between-school variance, 11 percent, 10 percent, and 12 percent, is still significant ($p < 0.001$), which suggests the presence of unmeasured between-school factors that account for discrepancies in teachers' attitude between schools.

Model 2, which includes distributed leadership dimensions, indicates that shared decision-making is a consistent predictor for teachers' perceived cohesion ($\beta = 0.014$, $p < 0.05$), commitment ($\beta = 0.016$, $p < 0.05$), and satisfaction ($\beta = 0.019$, p

< 0.01). In addition, principals' ($\beta = 0.026, p < 0.05$) and mentors' ($\beta = 0.023, p < 0.05$) participation in teacher development has a positive effect on teacher cohesion, as does management team participation in instructional management ($\beta = 0.030$ $p < 0.05$). However, the governing board's role in budget allocation indicates a negative impact on teacher perceived cohesion ($\beta = -0.031, p < 0.05$). For teacher commitment and satisfaction, governing board participation in hiring and teachers' leading in instructional management have significant positive effects.

Model 3 did not show much difference relative to effect size and significance for the impact of the distribution of leadership functions on teacher attitude, with one exception. Principals' perceived cohesion, however, is positively related to teachers' perceived cohesion ($\beta = 0.050, p < 0.001$), commitment ($\beta = 0.060, p < 0.001$), and satisfaction ($\beta = 0.083, p < 0.001$). As evidence of a possible mediation effect, however, principals' sense of school cohesion reduced the magnitude of the prior effects of shared decision-making and related significance. It might be the case that both of these variables—principals' attitude about the cohesion in the school and principals' beliefs about shared decision-making in the school—actually measure the same dynamics among school members. Principals' satisfaction is also positively related to teachers' satisfaction ($\beta = 0.045, p < 0.05$).

At the school level, female principals have a stronger relationship to teachers in terms of their perceptions of school cohesion. Even given that finding, schools with female leaders have less committed and satisfied teachers. Principals' age is a consistent significant predictor for teachers' attitudes, all in a negative direction. Public schools have more teacher solidarity, but teachers in the public schools possess less commitment and satisfaction. Another predictor that has been found to be important is a school's proportion of students from low-income families. These schools with more disadvantaged students have more cohesion among teachers, but the teachers have a lower level of commitment and less satisfaction in their job.

Discussion

Distributed leadership is increasingly advanced as an approach to remedy isolation, dissatisfaction, and disappointing school outcomes (Harris & Gronn, 2008; Spillane, 2006; Thorpe, Gold, & Lawler, 2011). Research has provided evidence on the favorable effect of distributed leadership on schools' social capital (Heck & Hallinger, 2009), and intellectual capital (Leithwood & Seashore-Louis, 2012; Marks & Printy, 2003).

TABLE 6. Relationship of Distributed Leadership to Teacher Attitudes and Mediation Model

	TEACHER-COHESION		TEACHER-COMMIT		TEACHER-SATISFACTION	
	MODEL 2	MODEL 3	MODEL 2	MODEL 3	MODEL 2	MODEL 3
Intercept	0.336** (0.121)	0.338** (0.121)	0.458*** (0.124)	0.473*** (0.122)	0.654*** (0.131)	0.670*** (0.129)
Predictors						
Principal-Cohesion		0.050*** (0.009)		0.060*** (0.007)		0.083*** (0.008)
Principal-Commit		0.007 (0.020)		−0.006 (0.019)		−0.017 (0.020)
Principal-Satisfaction		−0.018 (0.021)		0.033 (0.020)		0.045* (0.022)
SHARED_DECISION	**0.014*** (0.007)	0.003 (0.007)	**0.016*** (0.006)	−0.008 (0.006)	**0.019**** (0.007)	−0.012 (0.007)
BUDGET_PRINCIPAL	−0.009 (0.017)	−0.010 (0.017)	0.002 (0.016)	−0.000 (0.016)	−0.002 (0.018)	−0.005 (0.017)
BUDGET_MANTEAM	0.011 (0.016)	0.012 (0.016)	0.008 (0.014)	0.011 (0.013)	0.018 (0.015)	0.022 (0.015)
BUDGET_TEACHER	−0.012 (0.019)	−0.013 (0.019)	−0.024 (0.017)	−0.025 (0.017)	−0.027 (0.019)	−0.028 (0.018)
BUDGET_GOVBOARD	**−0.031*** (0.015)	**−0.032*** (0.015)	−0.010 (0.013)	−0.011 (0.012)	−0.019 (0.014)	−0.019 (0.014)
DEVPEO_PRINCIPAL	**0.026**** (0.009)	**0.023*** (0.009)	0.002 (0.009)	−0.004 (0.008)	0.005 (0.010)	−0.003 (0.009)
DEVPEO_MANTEAM	0.012 (0.009)	0.010 (0.009)	0.004 (0.009)	0.001 (0.009)	0.005 (0.010)	0.001 (0.009)
DEVPEO_TEACHER	**0.023*** (0.009)	**0.021*** (0.009)	0.006 (0.008)	0.003 (0.008)	0.001 (0.009)	−0.002 (0.009)
DEVPEO_GOVBOARD	0.005 (0.008)	0.003 (0.008)	−0.001 (0.008)	−0.006 (0.008)	0.001 (0.009)	−0.004 (0.009)
HIRING_PRINCIPAL	−0.014 (0.023)	−0.011 (0.023)	0.007 (0.020)	0.010 (0.019)	0.001 (0.022)	0.006 (0.021)
HIRING_MANTEAM	−0.003 (0.020)	−0.004 (0.020)	0.023 (0.018)	0.019 (0.018)	0.020 (0.020)	0.015 (0.019)
HIRING_TEACHER	0.018 (0.025)	0.018 (0.025)	−0.023 (0.021)	−0.024 (0.021)	−0.020 (0.024)	−0.022 (0.023)
HIRING_GOVBOARD	0.025 (0.017)	0.024 (0.017)	0.030* (0.015)	0.030* (0.015)	0.039* (0.017)	0.039* (0.016)
INSTRU_PRINCIPAL	−0.012 (0.014)	−0.015 (0.014)	0.005 (0.012)	−0.003 (0.012)	0.008 (0.014)	−0.002 (0.014)
INSTRU_MANTEAM	**0.030*** (0.014)	**0.030*** (0.014)	−0.014 (0.013)	−0.012 (0.013)	−0.016 (0.014)	−0.014 (0.014)
INSTRU_TEACHER	−0.011 (0.011)	−0.008 (0.011)	**0.031**** (0.010)	**0.039***** (0.010)	**0.029**** (0.011)	**0.039***** (0.011)
INSTRU_GOVBOARD	0.010 (0.011)	0.012 (0.011)	−0.011 (0.010)	−0.008 (0.010)	−0.004 (0.011)	−0.000 (0.011)

School Level Control						
Gender	**0.038*****	**0.036****	**−0.023***	**−0.030****	−0.013	**−0.022***
	(0.011)	(0.011)	(0.010)	(0.010)	(0.011)	(0.011)
Age	**−0.002***	**−0.002****	−0.001	**−0.002***	**−0.002***	**−0.003****
	(0.001)	(0.001)	(0.001)	(0.001)	(0.001)	(0.001)
Education	0.009	0.009	−0.025	−0.025	−0.023	−0.023
	(0.018)	(0.018)	(0.018)	(0.018)	(0.019)	(0.019)
Experience	0.000	−0.000	0.001	0.001	0.001	0.001
	(0.001)	(0.001)	(0.001)	(0.001)	(0.001)	(0.001)
Fulltime	0.042	0.038	−0.021	−0.031	−0.016	−0.029
	(0.032)	(0.032)	(0.027)	(0.026)	(0.029)	(0.028)
Location	0.008	0.008	−0.003	−0.004	−0.006	−0.008
	(0.005)	(0.005)	(0.004)	(0.004)	(0.005)	(0.005)
Public	**0.047***	**0.052****	**−0.066*****	**−0.056****	**−0.057****	**−0.045***
	(0.019)	(0.019)	(0.018)	(0.017)	(0.020)	(0.019)
Publicfund	0.007	0.008	−0.030	−0.025	−0.026	−0.020
	(0.018)	(0.018)	(0.015)	(0.015)	(0.017)	(0.017)
Size	0.000	0.000	0.000	0.000	0.000	0.000
	(0.000)	(0.000)	(0.000)	(0.000)	(0.000)	(0.000)
ImmigrantStudent	−0.008	−0.008	−0.003	−0.002	−0.012	−0.011
	(0.007)	(0.007)	(0.006)	(0.006)	(0.007)	(0.007)
LowSES	**0.014***	**0.015***	**−0.034*****	**−0.032*****	**−0.046*****	−0.043***
	(0.007)	(0.007)	(0.006)	(0.006)	(0.006)	(0.006)
Teacher Level Controls						
Gender	**0.085*****	**0.085*****	**0.060****	**0.060****	0.033	0.033
	(0.017)	(0.017)	(0.019)	(0.019)	(0.020)	(0.020)
Age	**−0.008*****	**−0.008*****	0.004	0.004	0.004	0.004
	(0.002)	(0.002)	(0.002)	(0.002)	(0.002)	(0.002)
Employstatus	**0.149*****	**0.149*****	0.007	0.007	0.022	0.022
	(0.019)	(0.019)	(0.023)	(0.023)	(0.023)	(0.023)
Experience	**0.005****	**0.005****	−0.002	−0.002	−0.002	−0.002
	(0.002)	(0.002)	(0.002)	(0.002)	(0.002)	(0.002)
Tenured	0.027	0.027	−0.033	−0.033	−0.030	−0.030
	(0.030)	(0.030)	(0.025)	(0.025)	(0.027)	(0.027)
Education	−0.005	−0.005	**−0.056***	**−0.056***	**−0.075****	**−0.075****
	(0.025)	(0.025)	(0.025)	(0.025)	(0.028)	(0.028)
Professional Preparation	**0.127****	**0.127****	0.039	0.039	0.027	0.027
	(0.041)	(0.041)	(0.027)	(0.027)	(0.028)	(0.028)
Variance Components						
Between School	0.114***	0.113***	0.096***	0.092***	0.121***	0.114***
	(0.004)	(0.004)	(0.002)	(0.002)	(0.003)	(0.003)
Within School	0.611***	0.611***	0.596***	0.596***	0.651***	0.651***
	(0.013)	(0.013)	(0.010)	(0.010)	(0.012)	(0.012)
N	72906	72906	72906	72906	72906	72906

Note: Standard errors in parentheses. $^{*}p < 0.05$, $^{**}p < 0.01$, $^{***}p < 0.001$

However, most available evidence-based research measured distributed leadership dimensions through the extent to which either the principal or the teacher perceives existing distributed leadership in the school. No available research has measured the direct participation from different groups of stakeholders in school leadership roles. No research has examined how the variation of stakeholders' participation in different leadership functions explained the dimensions of social capital represented as school cohesion, teachers' commitment, and teachers' satisfaction in their job. This study fills this identified gap and provides direct evidence of operational nuances of distributed leadership and its varied impacts on both the principal's and the teacher's attitudes. Even in models specifying particular roles and participation patterns, shared decision-making by the teacher, the parent, and the student showed a consistent, significant, and positive impact on both principals' and teachers' attitudes. It might be that this strong effect is due to the synergy reflected in the decision-making variable, in short, that many individuals work together for the good of the school. The relatively lesser effects for individual sets of participants in various functions suggest that the power of distributed leadership truly rests in interactions among many individuals. That said, particular results are worthy of more consideration.

Relatively few participant-by-function variables made a difference in principals' attitudes. Principals' sense of school cohesion increases when they report their involvement in managing instruction, yet it decreases when they report that teachers manage instruction. This finding might be indicative of an authority struggle and warrants further study. Principals' commitment and satisfaction are enhanced when members of the management team invest in developing people and when teachers participate in hiring. The findings suggest, however, that the governing board's participation in hiring is detrimental to principals' commitment and satisfaction, as is teachers' participation in managing instruction. It is quite surprising that teachers' participation in managing instruction has negative consequences for all three of the principals' attitudes, yet this kind of distributed involvement is, perhaps, the most frequent type of participation advocated. Again, this rather counterintuitive finding warrants further analysis.

Significant effects of participant-by-function variables are also relatively infrequent when investigating teachers' attitudes. Teachers' sense of school cohesion is enhanced by principals' and teachers' investment in developing people and by a management team's involvement in instruction. However, budget decisions made by the governing board reduce this attitude. Teachers' commitment to the school is enhanced by the governing board's involvement in hiring (perhaps because they are spending money to do so) and by teachers' participation in managing instruction. Teachers are more satisfied when principals report high levels of satisfaction, when the governing board invests in hiring, and when teachers share the responsibility for managing instruction. From the teachers' perspective, it appears that teachers appreciate the opportunity to be involved in two key functions related to school intellectual capital—hiring new personnel and closely monitoring instructional work.

Study Limitations

This study explains that the varied levels of stakeholders' participation in leadership plays a role in variations in individual attitudes. However, caution should be applied when considering the scope of this study. Leadership distribution is only one aspect influencing people's attitude. Schools are organizations that involve different processes, resources, conditions, and social relationships, which all simultaneously impact people in the setting. This study included a number of individual and contextual conditions in models as controls, but the between-school variance is still significant ($p < 0.001$), which suggests that there remain unmeasured between-school variables that account for unexplained variation in the models.

A second limitation to this study is that the processes described here have a nonrecursive nature where stakeholders' participation in leadership roles affects individual attitudes, and the individual attitudes, in turn, influence the extent to which the stakeholders participate in school functions. TALIS does not currently permit the requisite nonrecursive analysis. Future research that examines such mutual influence would strengthen theoretical and empirical arguments in support of leadership participation by a broad set of stakeholders and the relationship of such leadership to educators' attitudes.

Third, this study has not included the intrinsic psychological elements that may also exogenously impact the individual attitudes. For example, studies have offered evidence regarding the effect of teachers' self-efficacy on their commitment (Bogler & Somech, 2004; Rosenholtz, 1989). We could not include self-efficacy as a control in our study because it is not present in TALIS. The findings of this study also revealed unexplained factors that account for teacher attitudes beyond the included variables.

Policy Implications and Conclusions

For administrators and teachers in schools worldwide, positive attitudes about school cohesion and their own commitment and satisfaction are important indicators of their continued employment in their schools. The findings of this study offer evidence about the extent to which participant-by-function variables and shared decision-making contribute to those attitudes held by educators. While we offer no evidence of the importance of these attitudinal outcomes to school outcomes, much research reported in the review at the beginning of this chapter supports those relationships.

The strongest and most consistent finding of this study is that principals and teachers around the world appear to enjoy working in schools where many stakeholders are involved in shared decision-making and report stronger school cohesion, higher commitment, and greater satisfaction under these conditions. Given the complexity of navigating a successful schooling experience in modern society and the competition for adequate resources, it is not surprising that school personnel report stronger attitudes about their situation when there are more oars rowing the boat. Indeed, qualitative research conducted by Hargreaves and Shirley (2012) offers evidence that schools are more likely to prosper when a broad range of stakeholders are engaged. Contrary to conditions where an emphasis on accountability pulls professionals and external agents in separate and antagonistic directions, collaborative work toward shared goals results in quality instruction, high achievement, and satisfying working conditions.

Notwithstanding that finding, the results using these international data indicate that principals and teachers do not always see things in the same way and that separate domains for principals and teachers sometime manifest in connection with instruction. For all three of the principals; attitudes, there is a significant negative effect of teachers' involvement in managing instruction. While there are variations in this effect in countries, on average, principals want to have primary responsibility for monitoring instructional processes. A quite different perspective is seen from teachers, on average, who report higher levels of commitment and satisfaction when they or their colleagues play a role in instructional supervision or management. Follow-up studies will explore these country—or geographic subgroup—differences to seek clearer explanations. Policymakers may also need to heed the contextual differences when making policies about who should—or should not—be involved in various responsibilities related to schools.

TABLE 7. Countries of the Second Round of TALIS Used for This Study

COUNTRY	FREQUENCY	PERCENT	CUMULATIVE
Australia	123	1.91	1.91
Brazil	1,070	16.58	18.48
Bulgaria	197	3.05	21.53
Chile	178	2.76	24.29
Croatia	199	3.08	27.37
Czech Republic	220	3.41	30.78
Denmark	148	2.29	33.08
Estonia	197	3.05	36.13
Finland	146	2.26	38.39
France	204	3.16	41.55
Israel	195	3.02	44.57
Italy	194	3.01	47.58
Japan	192	2.97	50.55
Korea	177	2.74	53.29
Latvia	116	1.80	55.09
Malaysia	150	2.32	57.41
Mexico	187	2.90	60.31
Netherlands	127	1.97	62.28
Norway	145	2.25	64.52
Poland	195	3.02	67.54
Portugal	185	2.87	70.41
Serbia	191	2.96	73.37
Singapore	159	2.46	75.83
Slovak Republic	193	2.99	78.82
Spain	192	2.97	81.80
Sweden	186	2.88	84.68
United States	122	1.89	86.57
England (United Kingdom)	154	2.39	88.95
Flanders (Belgium)	168	2.6	91.55
Dhabi (United Arab Emirates)	166	2.57	94.13
Alberta (Canada)	182	2.82	96.95
Romania	197	3.05	100
Total	*6,455*	*100*	*100*

Taken together, the findings reinforce the distributed perspective taken by Spillane, Camburn, & Pareja (2007) in which leadership is stretched over leaders, followers, and the situation. The various leadership functions included in this study define many roles and responsibilities and possible participants. Further, situations are somewhat taken into account by controlling for country. Previous studies used different outcome variables and have different results with respect to who should be involved and for what tasks. The results of this study offer sufficient promise that certain kinds of distributed leadership investments make important contributions to organizational cohesion and individual satisfaction and commitment.

Appendix: Participating Countries

In all, thirty-four countries and economies participated in the second round of TALIS in 2013. Except for countries, there are subnational entities that participated in TALIS including Alberta in Canada, the Flemish Community in Belgium, the nation of England and the emirate of Abud Dhabi. Throughout the document the province of Alberta, in Canada, is referred to as Alberta (Canada), the Flemish Community of Belgium is referred to as Flanders (Belgium), the nation of England is referred to as England (United Kingdom) and the emirate of Abu Dhabi is referred to as Abu Dhabi (United Emirates). This study included 32 countries that have public data.

REFERENCES

Angelle, P. S. (2010). An organizational perspective of distributed leadership: A portrait of a middle school. *RMLE Online 33*(5), 1.

Bennett, N., Wise, C., Woods, P., & Harvey, J. (2003). *Distributed leadership.* Oxford: National College for School Leadership.

Bogler, R., & Somech, A. (2004). Influence of teacher empowerment on teachers' organizational commitment, professional commitment and organizational citizenship behavior in schools. *Teaching and teacher education 20*(3), 277–289.

Bolden, R. (2011). Distributed leadership in organizations: A review of theory and research. *International Journal of Management Reviews 13*(3), 251–69. doi:10.1111/j.1468-2370.2011.00306.x.

Boudreaux, W. (2011). *Distributed leadership and high-stakes testing: Examining the relationship between distributed leadership and LEAP scores.* (Ph.D.), Southeastern Louisiana

University, ProQuest, UMI Dissertations Publishing.

Bowen, N. K., & Guo, S. (2012). *Structural equation modeling*. New York: Oxford University Press.

Bryk, A. S., Sebring, P. B., Allensworth, E., Luppescu, S., & Easton, J. Q. (2010). *Organizing schools for improvement: Lessons from Chicago.* Chicago: University of Chicago Press.

Chang, I. H. (2011). A study of the relationships between distributed leadership, teacher academic optimism and student achievement in Taiwanese elementary schools. *School Leadership and Management 31*(5), 491–515. doi:10.1080/13632434.2011.614945

Chudgar, A., & Luschei, T. F. (2009). National income, income inequality, and the importance of schools: A hierarchical cross-national comparison. *American Educational Research Journal 46*(3), 626–658.

Chudgar, A., Luschei, T. F., & Zhou, Y. (2013). Science and mathematics achievement and the importance of classroom composition: Multicountry analysis using TIMSS 2007. *American Journal of Education 119*(2), 295–316. doi:10.1086/668764

Cohen, J., McCabe, L., Michelli, N. M., & Pickeral, T. (2009). School climate: Research, policy, practice, and teacher education. *Teachers College Record 111*(1), 180–213.

Davis, M. W. (2009). *Distributed leadership and school performance.* (Ph.D.), The George Washington University, ProQuest, UMI Dissertations Publishing.

Dewan, S., & Kraemer, K. L. (2000). Information technology and productivity: evidence from country-level data. *Management Science 46*(4), 548–562.

Den Hartog, D. N., House, R. J., Hanges, P. J., Ruiz-Quintanilla, S. A., & Dorfman, P. W. (1999). Culture specific and cross-culturally generalizable implicit leadership theories: Are attributes of charismatic/transformational leadership universally endorsed? *Leadership Quarterly 10*(2), 219–56.

Desai, P., Karahalios, V., Persuad, S., & Reker, K. (2014). Social-emotional learning. *Communique 43*(1), 14–16.

Edwards, G. (2011). Concepts of community: A framework for contextualizing distributed leadership. *International Journal of Management Reviews 13*(3), 301–12. doi:10.1111/j.1468-2370.2011.00309.x.

Elmore, R. F. (2000). *Building a new structure for school leadership.* Washington, DC: Albert Shanker Institute.

Firestone, W. A., & Martinez, C. M. (2007). Districts, teacher leaders, and distributed leadership: Changing instructional practice. *Leadership and Policy in Schools 6*(1), 3–35. doi:10.1080/15700760601091234.

Firestone, W. A., & Pennell, J. R. (1993). Teacher commitment, working conditions, and differential incentive policies. *Review of Educational Research 63*(4), 489–525.

doi:10.2307/1170498.

Fitzsimons, D., James, K. T., & Denyer, D. (2011). Alternative approaches for studying shared and distributed leadership. *International Journal of Management Reviews 13*(3), 313–28. doi: 10.1111/j.1468-2370.2011.00312.x.

Fusarelli, L. D., Kowalski, T. J., & Petersen, G. J. (2011). Distributive leadership, civic engagement, and deliberative democracy as vehicles for school improvement. *Leadership and Policy in Schools 10*(1), 43–62. doi:10.1080/15700760903342392.

Garson, G. D. (2013). *Hierarchical linear modeling: Guide and applications.* Thousand Oaks, CA: Sage.

Goddard, Y. L., Goddard, R. D., & Tschannen-Moran, M. (2007). A theoretical and empirical investigation of teacher collaboration for school improvement and student achievement in public elementary schools. *Teachers college record* 109(4), 877–896.

Gordon, Z. V. (2005). *The effect of distributed leadership on student achievement.* (Ph.D.), Central Connecticut State University, ProQuest, UMI Dissertations Publishing.

Gronn, P. (2002). Distributed leadership as a unit of analysis. *Leadership Quarterly 13*(4), 423–51. doi:10.1016/S1048-9843(02)00120-0.

Gronn, P. (2008). The future of distributed leadership. *Journal of Educational Administration 46*(2), 141–58. doi:10.1108/09578230810863235.

Gronn, P. (2011). Hybrid configurations of leadership. In A. Bryman, D. Collinson, K. Grint, B. Jackson, & M. Uhl-Bien (eds.), *The Sage handbook of leadership*. London: Sage.

Hallinger, P., & Murphy, J. (1985). Assessing the instructional management behavior of principals. *Elementary School Journal 86*(2), 217–47.

Hargreaves, A., & Fink, D. (2006). *Sustainable leadership.* San Francisco: Jossey-Bass.

Hargreaves, A., & Shirley, D. L. (2012). *The global fourth way: The quest for educational excellence.* Thousand Oaks, CA: Corwin.

Harris, A. (2003). Teacher leadership as distributed leadership: Heresy, fantasy or possibility? *School Leadership and Management 23*(3), 313–24. doi:10.1080/1363243032000112801.

Harris, A. (2006). Opening up the "black box" of leadership practice: Taking a distributed leadership perspective. *International Studies in Educational Administration 34*(2), 37–45.

Harris, A. (2009). Distributed leadership: What we know. In A. Harris (ed.), *Distributed leadership: Different perspectives*. Milton Keynes: Springer.

Harris, A., & Gronn, P. (2008). The future of distributed leadership. *Journal of Educational Administration 46*(2), 141–58. doi:10.1108/09578230810863235.

Harris, A., Spillane, J. P., Camburn, E. M., Pustejovsky, J., Stitziel Pareja, A., & Lewis, G. (2008). Taking a distributed perspective. *Journal of Educational Administration 46*(2), 189–213. doi:10.1108/09578230810863262.

Hartley, D. (2010). Paradigms: How far does research in distributed leadership 'stretch"? *Educational Management Administration and Leadership 38*(3), 271–85. doi:10.1177/17411432100380010301.

Heck, R., & Hallinger, P. (2009). Assessing the contribution of distributed leadership to school improvement and growth in math achievement. *American Educational Research Journal 46*(3), 659–89. doi:10.3102/0002831209340042.

Heikka, J., Waniganayake, M., & Hujala, E. (2013). Contextualizing distributed leadership within early childhood education: Current understandings, research evidence and future challenges. *Educational Management Administration and Leadership 41*(1), 30–44. doi:10.1177/1741143212462700.

Hu, L.-T., & Bentler, P. (1999). Cutoff criteria for fit indexes in covariance structure analysis: Conventional criteria versus new alternatives. *Structural Equation Modeling 6*(1), 1–55. doi:10.1080/10705519909540118.

Hulpia, H., Devos, G., Rosseel, Y., & Vlerick, P. (2012). Dimensions of distributed leadership and the impact on teachers' organizational commitment: A study in secondary education. *Journal of Applied Social Psychology 42*(7), 1745–84. doi:10.1111/j.1559-1816.2012.00917.x.

Kline, R. B. (2011). *Principles and practice of structural equation modeling*. New York: Guilford Press.

Langeheine, R., & Rost, J. (2013). *Latent trait and latent class models.* N.p.: Springer Science & Business Media.

Lashway, L. (2006). Distributed leadership. In S. C. P. K. P. Smith (ed.), *School leadership: Handbook for excellence in student learning*. Thousand Oaks, CA: Corwin.

Leithwood, K. A., & Mascall, B. (2008). Collective leadership effects on student achievement. *Educational Administration Quarterly 44*(4), 529–61. doi:10.1177/0013161x08321221.

Leithwood, K. A., Mascall, B., & Strauss, T. (2009). *Distributed leadership according to the evidence*. New York: Routledge.

Leithwood, K. A., Mascall, B., Strauss, T., Sacks, R., Memon, N., & Yashkina, A. (2007). Distributing leadership to make schools smarter: Taking the ego out of the system. *Leadership and Policy in Schools 6*(1), 37–67. doi:10.1080/15700760601091267.

Leithwood, K. A., & Seashore-Louis, K. (2012). *Linking leadership to student learning.* San Francisco: Jossey Bass.

Marks, H. M., & Printy, S. M. (2003). Principal leadership and school performance: An integration of transformational and instructional leadership. *Educational Administration Quarterly 39*(3), 370–97. doi:10.1177/0013161X03253412.

Mascall, B., Leithwood, K. A., Straus, T., & Sacks, R. (2008). The relationship between distributed leadership and teachers' academic optimism. *Journal of Educational*

Administration 46(2), 214–28. doi:10.1108/09578230810863271.

Organisation for Economic Co-operation and Development (OECD). (2014). TALIS 2013 technical report. Retrieved from http://www.oecd.org/edu/school/TALIS-technical-report-2013.pdf.

Pont, B., Nusche, D., & Moorman, H. (2008). *Improving school leadership.* Vol. 1. Paris: OECD.

Price, H. E. (2012). Principal-teacher interactions: How affective relationships shape principal and teacher attitudes. *Educational Administration Quarterly 48*(1), 39–85. doi:10.1177/0013161X11417126.

Printy, S. M. (2008). Leadership for teacher learning: A community of practice perspective. *Educational Administration Quarterly 44*(2), 187–226. doi:10.1177/0013161X07312958.

Printy, S. M. (2010). Principals' influence on instructional quality: Insights from US schools. *School Leadership and Management 30*(2), 111–26. doi:10.1080/13632431003688005.

Randeree, K., & Ghaffar Chaudhry, A. (2012). Leadership: Style, satisfaction and commitment. *Engineering, Construction and Architectural Management 19*(1), 61–85. doi:10.1108/09699981211192571.

Raudenbush, S. W., & Bryk, A. S. (2002). *Hierarchical linear models: Applications and data analysis methods.* 2nd ed. Thousand Oaks, CA: Sage.

Rosenholtz, S. J. (1989). Workplace conditions that affect teacher quality and commitment: Implications for teacher induction programs. *The Elementary School Journal* 89(4), 421–439.

Rosseel, Y., Devos, G., & Hulpia, H. (2009). The relationship between the perception of distributed leadership in secondary schools and teachers' and teacher leaders' job satisfaction and organizational commitment. *School Effectiveness and School Improvement 20*(3), 291–317. doi:10.1080/09243450902909840.

Sleegers, P., Nguni, S., & Denessen, E. (2006). Transformational and transactional leadership effects on teachers' job satisfaction, organizational commitment, and organizational citizenship behavior in primary schools: The Tanzanian case. *School Effectiveness and School Improvement 17*(2), 145–77. doi:10.1080/09243450600565746.

Spector, P. E. (1997). *Job satisfaction: Application, assessment, cause, and consequences.* Thousand Oaks, CA: Sage.

Spillane, J. P. (2005). Distributed leadership. *Educational Forum 69*(2), 143–50. doi:10.1080/00131720508984678.

Spillane, J. P. (2006). *Distributed leadership.* San Francisco: Jossey-Bass.

Spillane, J. P., & Diamond, J. B. (2007). *Distributed leadership in practice.* New York: Teachers College, Columbia University.

Spillane, J. P., Camburn, E. M., & Stitziel Pareja, A. (2007). Taking a distributed perspective to the school principal's workday. *Leadership and policy in schools* 6(1), 103–125.

Spillane, J. P., Halverson, R., & Diamond, J. B. (2004). Towards a theory of leadership practice: A distributed perspective. *Journal of Curriculum Studies 36*(1), 3–34.

Thorpe, R., Gold, J., & Lawler, J. (2011). Locating distributed leadership. *International Journal of Management Reviews 13*(3), 239–50. doi:10.1111/j.1468-2370.2011.00303.x.

Tian, M., Risku, M., & Collin, K. (2015). A meta-analysis of distributed leadership from 2002 to 2013: Theory development, empirical evidence and future research focus. *Educational Management Administration and Leadership 44*(1), 146–64. doi:10.1177/1741143214558576.

Tschannen-Moran, M., & Barr, M. (2004). Fostering student learning: The relationship of collective teacher efficacy and student achievement. *Leadership and Policy in Schools 3*(3), 189–209. doi:10.1080/15700760490503706.

Wahab, J. A., Fuad, C. F. M., Ismail, H., & Majid, S. (2014). Headmasters' transformational leadership and their relationship with teachers' job satisfaction and teachers' commitments. *International Education Studies 7*(13), 40–48. doi:10.5539/ies.v7n13p40.

Weick, K. E. (1976). Educational organizations as loosely coupled systems. *Administrative Science Quarterly 21*(1), 1–19.

Zhou, Y. (2014). The relationship between school organizational characteristics and reliance on out-of-field teachers in mathematics and science: Cross-national evidence from TALIS 2008. *Asia-Pacific Education Researcher 23*(3), 483–97. doi:10.1007/s40299-013-0123-8.

Mexican Dance Group

Breaking Barriers One Tap at a Time

Tatiana Cevallos

I resolutely believe that respect for diversity is a fundamental pillar in the eradication of racism, xenophobia, and intolerance.

—Rigoberta Menchú

It [is] important to stand up for your rights, and regardless of who you are and where you come from, to hold your heads up high with dignity and respect.

—Hilda Solis

With a growing number of Hispanic students in schools (Díaz-Rico & Weed, 2014; Oregon Department of Education, 2012), many educators wonder how to make the school community more accessible to Hispanic parents (González, Moll, & Amanti, 2005; Gorski & Pothini, 2014; Valdés, 1996; Wink, 2005). The dance group described in this chapter demonstrates a natural way in which one teacher has accomplished Hispanic parental accessibility and, in doing so, positively impacted her school community. Rosa Floyd, the director of Nellie Muir's Dance Group, has been teaching in Spanish-English bilingual classrooms for more than nineteen years. She came from Mexico as an adult and learned English, becoming an instructional assistant and subsequently a teacher. She has chosen to work with Hispanic students and regards her work as a bridge between Mexican parents and schools. Bilingual and bicultural, Rosa understands the Mexican community as well as the Anglo-dominated school culture. For several years, she has effectively facilitated cross-cultural relationships between parents and teachers through the use of traditional dance groups. The months of practice preparing for the Cinco de Mayo presentations provide a catalyst for change as the teachers and parents address the invisible barriers that have kept Hispanic parents separated from the school community. Rosa's efforts have led to a more welcoming and respectful school environment that embraces Mexican parents and reinforces students' sense of cultural identity and heritage pride.

Establishing the dance group emerged from Rosa's desire to preserve a cultural tradition. But in so doing she also created a teaching tool for both parents and teachers that helps penetrate cultural barriers. In Rosa's words (translated by author):

> My purpose with the dance was not only cultural but also didactic for both sides. I wanted teachers to learn from students' culture, that they respect their students' culture and show children that *they* [teachers] are proud of their [students'] culture. . . . Also, teachers are showing respect to parents. That is the idea for the dance, not only dancing. And that is why our group is formed by teachers and parents.

For Rosa, it is crucial to include parents in schooling. She brings parents to school through the dance group, providing them with an authentic opportunity to interact with teachers. This created a nonthreatening environment where Mexican parents do not feel alienated (González, Moll, & Amanti, 2005; Gorski & Pothini, 2014; Valdés, 1996; Wink, 2005). According to Rosa,

> The other reason that I want to involve the parents is because I want them to work at the same level as the teachers. A lot of our parents are afraid, or are ashamed and do not know how to integrate [with the school].

By embracing a cultural tradition—traditional Mexican dances—Rosa purposefully changes the dynamics of parent-teacher interactions and extends culturally responsive practices beyond confines of the classroom (Gorski & Pothini, 2014; Wink, 2005).

FIGURE 1. Third and Fifth Grade Dance Group

Context

The story of Rosa Floyd and the dance group comes from a series of phenomenological interviews (Seidman, 2006) from a larger study of bilingual reading specialists. This section provides an overview of the school community and dual-language program in which Rosa teaches. In this chapter, I have chosen to use the term "Hispanic" to refer to the Spanish-speaking Woodburn community comprised mainly of Mexican parents and students of first, second, and third generations who live in this agricultural region of Oregon. "Hispanic" is a cognate to the Spanish word *hispano* that Rosa uses when describing the school community, parents, and students with whom she works. I also use the term "Mexican" when referring to this population and related cultural elements, such as the dance or other customs parents have brought from their country of origin. At the time of the study, all the Hispanic students and their parents were from Mexico.

The Local Community

Rosa is a teacher at a bilingual school in a community that has a significant population of families from Mexico or of Mexican descent. The Hispanic community is a mix of Mexican families that have been established in the area for several generations, coupled with new immigrants who are attracted to the location because of family ties, cultural and language networks, and work opportunities. The community is in the heart of Oregon's Willamette Valley, where the local public institutions are under the direction of Anglo mainstream personnel. In this sense, the community reflects the larger state, where Anglo mainstream members hold economic, social, and political power. Interactions between Anglo and Hispanic members of this community are mainly limited to commerce and work-related relationships. While parents see one another at school, they rarely develop strong friendships, and their interactions may be limited to polite greetings. The Anglo community in Woodburn includes an older and retired population, families who have lived in the area for a long time, and newer families who have found affordable homes along the I-5 corridor and work in the Portland metro area. The Hispanic community, formed predominantly by Mexican immigrants, typically works in the agricultural and service sectors. Hispanic parents tend to have lower rates of completion of high school than Anglo parents. In some cases, Hispanic parents may not have attended school beyond sixth grade in Mexico. Thus, while the Hispanic and Anglo populations inhabit the same geographical area, they have not established strong intercultural or interracial relationships and friendships. The cultural division evident in the community is due to a combination of language barriers, the geographically segregated neighborhoods in which the groups live, and prevailing cultural differences.

The School and School District

At the time of this study, 80 percent of the students in this district qualified for free and reduced lunch, 60 percent of the students entered school as English learners, and 20 percent came from a migrant background. The school district is highly diverse: 78 percent of students are Spanish dominant, 11 percent are English dominant, and 11 percent are of Russian heritage (Collier & Thomas, 2014). Moreover, the school district offers bilingual education from preschool to grade 12 in Spanish/English and Russian/English.

In the past decade, the school district moved from offering a late-exit transitional bilingual program at the elementary level to a dual-language (DL) program P–12. The former program served only Spanish-speaking students and is aimed at teaching children strong English skills to be successful in school once they transition to middle school—where instruction took place only in English. The current dual-language program, in contrast, serves both Spanish-speaking and English-speaking children and promotes bilingualism and biliteracy.

Rosa teaches kindergarten in the Spanish-English dual program at Nellie Muir Elementary. Her kindergarten classroom is composed of Mexican Spanish-speaking children and Anglo English-speakers. Both groups learn content in English and Spanish and study side-by-side. The school follows an 80/20 model for language instruction: 80 percent of content instruction in kindergarten is delivered in Spanish and 20 percent of instruction in English. Students learned to first read in Spanish. At each grade level, the percentage of English instruction increases. By fifth grade, students spent 50 percent of their day learning in Spanish and 50 percent of their day learning in English. In addition to promoting bilingualism and biliteracy, one of the goals for the dual-language program is to promote the integration of the Spanish-speaking and English-speaking student groups (Freeman, Freeman, & Mercuri, 2005). Whereas a late-exit bilingual program is frequently regarded as a remedial approach designed to help English learners overcome the English barrier at school, a dual-language program model values minority students' native language as an asset and offers the potential for Spanish-speakers to assume a positive attitude toward their language and culture. Ultimately the goal is for students to feel validated within their school (Freeman, Freeman, & Mercuri, 2005; Lindholm-Leary, 2004).

Dual-Language Programs

There has been an explosion of dual-language programs across the nation in the past few years (Collier & Thomas, 2014; Harris, 2015; Lindholm-Leary, 2012). These programs are the most effective in reducing the opportunity gap, educating linguistically and culturally diverse students whose first language is not English. Additionally, they provide the opportunity for native-English speakers to acquire another language from an early age (Collier & Thomas, 2014; Lindholm-Leary, 2004, 2012). Dual-language programs bring students from different ethnic, language, and cultural groups together to learn content in two languages. Students tend to remain together as a cohort for the entirety of their school experience, as in some cases these programs are only a strand within a school.

Seminal work by Valdés (1997) at the initiation of dual-language programs in schools involved inviting administrators, teachers, and other stakeholders to examine opportunities to use the dual-language initiatives as social change agents. She identified critical economic, social, and cultural factors that render Hispanic families at an academic disadvantage in school and that ultimately hinder social mobility within the United States. This critical analysis has led Valdés to question the lasting potential for isolated school programs, at a micro level, to change the dynamics of the larger society and its inequities. Most specifically, she has speculated about the true potential dual-language programs have for relationships and friendships among Anglo and Hispanic students to develop outside the school walls. Valdés remains critical, yet hopeful, that educators will take an active role in facilitating equal relationships among students that would place minority Spanish-speaking children in a status comparable to that of their majority English-speaking classmates (Macedo, Dendrinos, & Gounari, 2003). Although Rosa's dance group project remains at a micro-scale, it is a testament to the power individuals have to promote positive intergroup interactions. Efforts such as Rosa's have lasting effects inside and outside of school among the Hispanic parents, Anglo parents, and Anglo teachers involved in the dance group.

Rosa Floyd

I have known Rosa for seventeen years and have always admired the way she connects with students and parents to create a positive learning environment. Even years after her kindergarten students have left her class, they and their parents remain in contact with her. She is often invited to celebrate *quinceañeras* (a traditional and formal celebration in Hispanic culture for fifteen-year-old girls transitioning into adulthood), high school graduations, and other important family events. Rosa sees herself as "their teacher for life." And she certainly is, as her Hispanic and Anglo students enter formal education through her kindergarten class.

Indeed, Rosa has a gift for putting students at ease during the transition from home to school, prioritizing the well-being of the child and enlisting parents as crucial supporters in this process. Everyone who has met Rosa knows of her smile, kindness, enthusiasm, energy, positive attitude, and commitment. Everything about the way she carries herself and how she interacts with students and adults is welcoming, respectful, and affirming. She is the kind of teacher people remember and admire.

Dancer and Teacher

Rosa was born and raised in Guadalajara, Mexico. She obtained her undergraduate degree in architecture and continued with graduate studies in Spanish language and literature in Spain. She then worked at the Universidad de Guadalajara in the audiovisual department, designing instructional materials for high school students for a national education program. She also developed programs for mathematics and provided professional development to teachers on how to use those materials and programs. Rosa learned to dance at the age of six and has been dancing ever since. During her university years she was part of two professional dance groups, for the Universidad de Guadalajara and for Guadalajara's City Hall. She continued to be involved in professional dance groups once she moved to Oregon and has balanced her teaching career with being a dancer.

When Rosa first moved to the United States, she worked as an instructional assistant at a migrant summer school and then at a high school. Besides the school counselor and Spanish teacher, she was the only staff person who spoke Spanish at a high school with 25 percent Hispanic students. As a result, Rosa became a liaison between the school and Spanish-speaking families. She also supported high schoolers who needed help to earn credits toward graduation. This work motivated her to learn English faster. Seeing the needs of Mexican students at the high school enacted a career change in Rosa's life that brought her to pursue a teaching license.

Rosa taught at an immersion Spanish program at a private school in Oregon for six years before she was recruited by the Title I school district where she currently teaches. She obtained her teaching license through a graduate teaching program at a public university and has been teaching in bilingual classrooms for the past fourteen years. In all the schools in which she had taught, Rosa has started and directed traditional Mexican dance groups and has encouraged parents and teachers to participate. This initiative has always been well received by school administrators, teachers, parents, students, and the community.

Cultural Bridge

Rosa takes advantage of being a cultural insider in Hispanic culture, having grown up in Mexico, yet she also understands the culture of mainstream American schools. She uses this knowledge to navigate and establish relationships within and outside the school. In the process, Rosa functions as a cultural bridge between Hispanic parents and Anglo teachers.

Her effectiveness as teacher and cultural bridge comes from a deep commitment to equity and to what she calls *mi gente* (my people). In fact, she specifically refers to herself as a bridge for communication between parents and the school: "I feel like a bridge between parents and school. I feel that is my work here." As a kindergarten teacher, the work she does with Hispanic parents is an investment that will eventually translate into greater parental involvement and student success. She strives to provide Hispanic parents with critical information about school culture and practices. She informs parents about their responsibilities as well as their rights. Rosa acknowledges power differentials that can result from cultural differences. Hispanic parents who come from small rural towns frequently regard the priest and schoolteacher as the community authorities. They often do not feel comfortable asking questions or even coming to school. Understanding this, Rosa attempts to prepare Mexican parents to communicate freely and confidently, despite their limited English proficiency. This is important because such parental engagement can be central for student success. "And if they want their children to be successful, they (parents) need to know how to communicate. They need to know how to dialogue and how to come and ask and what they can do to help." Subsequently, when parents begin to understand the importance of communication (especially regarding cultural differences) while their students are in kindergarten, her efforts pave the road for future interactions with teachers and school staff.

Indeed, working to improve communication and an understanding of U.S. school culture is one of the first deliberate steps Rosa takes with Hispanic parents. She is aware that school personnel and Hispanic families frequently make assumptions about each other and about their roles in students' education (Faber, 2015; Valdés, 1996). As a result, Rosa explicitly addresses cultural differences with parents:

> Sometimes there are problems communicating with parents, because of culture, right? . . . Hispanic parents don't understand the culture; sometimes they say, "The teacher is too cold." . . . But part of it is to understand that American culture has its

FIGURE 2. Rosa Kindergarten Dance Group

ways and our culture has another way. But if we don't tell them, they are not going to know how to work with teachers.

Hispanic parents sometimes perceive Anglo teachers and the school environment as cold and intimidating. For instance, Rosa recalled an instance when Hispanic parents believed that Anglo teachers were not welcoming when they showed up to a classroom unannounced and the teachers requested they make an appointment with the office to talk about volunteering. The cultural norm of valuing a teacher's time and setting up prior appointments to talk to her was perceived as aloof and uninviting. The resulting interaction may have harmed parents' future attempts to volunteer at school. In contrast, parents find Rosa's classroom as always open. When parents drop in for a few minutes and offer their help, she quickly finds activities for them to do, even if it only means sharpening pencils. The task she assigns on the spot is not as important as the validation and gratitude she conveys to parents for their help. Rosa is convinced that cultural misunderstandings can easily be avoided if rules, procedures, and classroom norms are explicitly yet sensitively explained to parents at the beginning of the school year. She, in fact, begins the communication process at the beginning of their child's education.

Culturally Responsive Activist

A teacher's ability to speak Spanish is not enough when communicating with Hispanic parents. It is also important and necessary to be culturally sensitive, to understand how Hispanic families view school, and to examine and question ones' own biases against values and beliefs that are different from mainstream culture (Gorski & Pothini, 2014; Valdés, 1996). Valdés (1996) conducted an ethnographic study with ten Mexican families who lived in the borderlands of Texas. She examined how middle-class Anglo-European mainstream dispositions toward school and parental involvement are different from those of Mexican parents. Valdés contends that Mexican parents frequently operate with the traditional values they have carried from their upbringing in small towns in Mexico. Among those traditional values is that children learn to be responsible, respectful, and productive members who contribute to the family unit. Further, parents consider "school learning as the province of teachers" (Valdés, 1996, p. 180). Thus, children learn that academic learning is the domain of teachers.

While Mexican parents believe education is important, their understanding of the role of parental involvement can sharply differ from what teachers in U.S. schools expect. Mexican families may not always observe school routines such as monitoring homework time, reading to children, or helping students acquire materials for school projects requested by teachers. This is because many Mexican immigrant parents face daunting time and economic restrictions preventing them from accomplishing many academic activities with their children. In some cases, parents may not be fully literate or are not proficient in English. These and other limitations may perpetuate the misconception and unexamined bias that "Hispanic parents are neither committed to nor involved in their children's education" (Valdés, 1996, p. 33). Nevertheless, Valdés identified multiple ways in which families in her study were involved in the education of their children. She invites educators and other stakeholders to focus on the strengths Mexican immigrants have and avoid deficit views of them.

Rosa desires to change the deficit view that some Anglo teachers hold about the lack of school involvement among Hispanic parents. She emphasizes that Hispanic parents want to come to school but they also desire to do so in ways they can feel successful: "Parents want to participate but in things that they can do, or that they know how to do, or in those where they can feel successful." Rosa's efforts as cultural bridge and her active role in changing parent-teacher dynamics with the dance group aimed to make the school environment feel more friendly, approachable, and welcoming to Hispanic parents.

Rosa's experiences, along with scholarly work by such scholars as Valdés, have great professional and personal resonance with me. In my own work with preservice teachers, I have encountered some of the misconceptions and biases about Hispanic parental involvement that Valdés (1996) challenges. The negative perceptions that Hispanic families are uninvolved and lack commitment to their children's education is something I have heard in subtle as well as explicit comments. I should add that these were not always intentionally malicious comments. However, naive or not, as Rosa recognizes, these perceptions need to be addressed by teacher educators. Preservice and in-service teachers may equate mere parental presence in school with parental involvement (Gorski & Pothini, 2014). However, barriers that keep parents from coming to school are often unexamined. Parents do not necessarily feel comfortable coming to school if to them this institution seems foreign, intimidating, unapproachable, and, ultimately, uninviting (Faber, 2015; González, Moll, & Amanti, 2005; Gorski & Pothini, 2014; Valdés, 1996; Wink, 2005).

Furthermore, schools may not be operating with culturally relevant information pertaining to Hispanic parental involvement when planning for school activities. For instance, Rosa explained that another cultural difference experienced by Mexican parents at her school was the end-of-kindergarten celebration. In Mexico, this was a big school event celebrated and planned in conjunction with parents. Students wore regalia and there was a formal graduation ceremony with diplomas, music, speeches, and food. This was the students' first transition and it was well celebrated; children danced the waltz during the graduation ceremony. In contrast, the kindergarten graduation in the United States occurred on a smaller scale and parents did not co-plan the event. This lack of knowledge of a cultural tradition was grounds for unfortunate and unnecessary misunderstanding. Mexican parents who were not invited to take part in the planning process of the kindergarten graduation celebration in the United States felt excluded from the school. The exclusion reinforced the perception of being a cultural outsider. It is easy to see how culturally responsive teachers, when made aware of such a small yet important cultural difference, could easily revise their practice and invite parents to take part in the planning and organization of kindergarten graduations. This would require teachers not only to acknowledge a difference in tradition and respond in a culturally appropriate way, but also to view parents as partners and equals (Wink, 2005).

The Dance Groups

Rosa has participated in dance groups since her youth. This cultural expression is an integral part of both her personal and professional life. She values students' cultural roots and recognizes the need within Mexican communities to enjoy and preserve different forms of art and artistic traditions. Rosa incorporates art as a tool for learning, creative expression, and cultural exploration. She also teaches students, parents, and teachers to dance *danzas tradicionales* (traditional dances).

Rosa uses this cultural tradition as a deliberate device not only to bring parents to school but to challenge cultural barriers. In her view, Mexican parents identify with this cultural expression because they grew up listening to Mexican music and seeing dances performed in their native country. They get excited about their children continuing to experience and value a cherished cultural expression. They are grateful to have traditional dances showcased in the school and presented to the larger community. Moreover, they feel this was an activity in which they can participate. All the while, Rosa carefully encourages Hispanic parents to communicate with teachers and integrate into the school community.

There are three main venues in which Rosa teaches traditional dance. The first group is her kindergarten class. The second group is Hispanic and Anglo students in third through fifth grades. The third group is a collection of Hispanic parents and Anglo teachers.

Kindergarten Dance Group

Rosa incorporates dance into her teaching as a tool to connect with students as well as to expand on students' appreciation of this art form. For instance, over the course of several morning meetings, she teaches her kindergarteners the steps of a dance named *los viejitos*. She does this daily, adding a few steps at a time to what students perceive as physical movement routines, until the whole dance choreography is complete. Both her Hispanic and her Anglo students learn to dance in a natural, nonstressful, and fun way. Once the choreography is ready and students approach the Cinco de Mayo celebration, Rosa shares with them pictures of previous classes that danced in the school assembly. Students come to realize they have been learning traditional dances and respond with emotions ranging from excitement to shyness. As the assembly date approaches, Rosa adds performance elements and prepares her five-year-old students to dance in front of a full school audience that includes family and community members. She helps them to overcome stage fright and works hard to ensure they will be successful and proud of their performance.

Third- to Fifth-Grade Student Dance Group

This group is formed by Hispanic and Anglo students who meet after school to learn traditional Mexican dances. Some of the students are former kindergarten students in Rosa's class, while other students are new to the group. There is no cost for students to participate in the dance lessons, but in order to be admitted, they need to be at grade level in reading (so as not to miss instructional time when performing in the community). This dance group also creates serendipitous opportunities for Hispanic and Anglo parents to interact as they wait for the dance lessons to end or when they need to coordinate transportation to and from the community places where students perform.

Parent and Teacher Traditional Mexican Dance Group

Hispanic parents and Anglo teachers come together to learn and perform traditional Mexican dances for the school assembly and other community presentations. The group learns the dances' steps, their meaning, and the geographical region where each dance originated. The dances in fact originate from different regions in Mexico—Veracruz, Tamauilpas, Oaxaca, and Jalisco.

By all estimations this is an extremely important group in achieving intercultural communication and interaction. And it involves a significant number of adults. For instance, in 2013 eleven parents and fourteen teachers formed the group. Some of the parents had had their students in Rosa's kindergarten class at some point, and over the years these parents invited other parents who were interested in the dance group and enjoyed showcasing their culture. On occasion, parents and teachers have had to meet and rehearse in small groups. It is important to note that these smaller groups require that Hispanic parents and Anglo teachers negotiate, frequently in their second language, and teach each other the dance steps and moves.

Mexican Dance Group as Catalyst for Cultural Understanding

All three of the dance groups Rosa forms are important and contribute to cultural understanding. However, among all of her efforts, the parent-teacher Mexican dance group especially has resulted in lasting and meaningful effects for equity and collegiality in the community. Rosa's deliberate efforts to use this group to create a welcoming and respectful school community for Mexican parents have paid off. Several factors contribute to this project's success. First, the dance group promotes interracial and intercultural interactions among parents and teachers. Second, the months of practice spent together preparing for the Cinco de Mayo dance assembly allow parents and teachers to break barriers, overcome boundaries, and simply get to know each other. Third, Rosa's efforts have led to a more welcoming and respectful school environment where Mexican parents participate with increasing frequency.

More importantly, the parent-teacher dance group, as a culturally relevant practice, impacted all involved for complex psychological and sociological reasons (Gay, 2000; González, Moll, & Amanti, 2005; Gorski & Pothini, 2014; Ladson-Billings, 2009; Milner, 2013; Valdés, 1996; Wink, 2005). Anglo teachers, Hispanic parents, and Mexican students all benefited in unique ways simply as a result of a culturally competent teacher's wise use of dance.

Anglo Teachers

For Anglo teachers, the exposure to Mexican traditions and experiences through the dance group is enormously beneficial. Anglo teachers discover and learn Mexican traditions and cultural elements about their students' heritage. This exposure and experience holds great potential to support culturally relevant practices. Teachers learn not only dance steps, but also more about individual students through interactions with their parents. The insights they gain into their students' lives and culture enhance their understanding of Hispanic culture and work to support student learning. Also, teachers have an opportunity to communicate in unstructured and informal interactions in Spanish with parents who are native speakers of Spanish. Unlike structured and formal parent-teacher conferences, the social and linguistic exchanges the group dance provides allow teachers to learn and practice communication styles that are perceived by Hispanic parents as warm. Rosa prepares teachers for these exchanges. She instructs them, "We have to try to listen to parents because we have to give them space. This is a different setting, so we have to make it more warm-hearted."

For Anglo teachers who work with culturally and linguistically diverse students, it is not enough to read about other ethnic groups and internalize cultural and linguistic concepts and attempt to apply them to instruction. Gay (2002) has identified critical aspects of linguistic structures and communication styles among various ethnic communities. According to Gay, culturally responsive teachers must understand these structures and styles and respond appropriately during their instruction. These include complex components such as cultural nuances, discourse characteristics, vocabulary usage, intonation, gestures, and role relationships between speakers and listeners. Gay writes, "Cultural markers and nuances embedded in the communicative behaviors of highly ethnically affiliated Latino, Native, Asian, and African Americans are difficult to recognize, understand, accept, and respond to without corresponding cultural knowledge of these groups" (p. 111). Exposure to and interaction with Hispanics, where cultural elements and communication patterns are experienced firsthand, far surpass textbook knowledge. Rosa's dance group creates a space for Hispanic parents and Anglo teachers to experience these patterns of communication, to negotiate meaning, and to clarify concepts. Simply put, it allows both groups to experience cross-cultural communication that is respectful, affirming, and informative.

Rosa also notes that Anglo teachers experience an increased understanding of Hispanic culture and develop more flexibility in the ways they interact with parents. She refers to this as a practice of "opening their doors little by little." For instance, when parents now come to school without a previously arranged appointment and offer their time to volunteer at school, teachers in the dance group are more open and ready to work with them on the spot. Their response is now, "Come to my class, I have work to do."

The dance group helps parents and teachers to know each other and it creates trust. Moreover, teachers feel more comfortable navigating Hispanic culture and have more tools to interact with parents in different settings. Participation in the dance group also provides an opportunity for teachers to reevaluate their assumptions about parental involvement in school and results in greater recognition of the assets Hispanic parents bring to school (González, Moll, & Amanti, 2005; McIntyre, Rosebery, & González, 2001). They see parents committed to their children success. They say, "I am going to work with parents, and it is different. It is no longer sit down here, I am the teacher. Is understanding that we need to work together."

Hispanic Parents

For Hispanic parents, participation in the dance group opens doors to the school culture and community. Rosa recognizes that Mexican families were marginalized from school, in part due to language barriers, but also because of a lack of understanding and familiarity with the school culture (Valdés, 1996). The dance group invites parents to be involved in an experience where they can be successful, and one that is culturally appropriate for them. The space created for parents and teachers to come together during rehearsals changes the interaction among these groups. Rosa uses the dance group as an equalizer in the relationships between Hispanic parents and Anglo teachers, thus reducing power differentials. Moreover, she does this intentionally:

> The dance [group] started to bring parents and teachers at the same level. Last year we had eleven mothers dancing with fourteen teachers. It is something powerful because the children see it, your mom is dancing with the teachers, and parents can do things together. No one is higher than anybody, we all have to learn. I have as much to learn from them as they can learn from us.

Equalizing the relationship between the parents and teachers is likely the most powerful way the dance group reduces cultural barriers. Rosa is aware of the status of English as the language of power (Macedo et al., 2003) and aware that many Hispanic families view school teachers as authority figures (Valdés, 1996). By bringing parents and teachers together, she provides an opportunity for both groups to get to know each other and to develop relationships where both parties are equals (Everett & Onu, 2013; Pettigrew & Tropp, 2006). Teachers and parents must learn to dance together, and neither is seen as an expert: "You have to reach an equal level where both groups feel comfortable." This simple yet profound social device helps parents become more comfortable at school. According to Rosa, parents gain trust, realize they can participate in school, are more willing to use English, and improve their self-esteem.

Furthermore, after taking part in the dance group, Hispanic parents feel more at ease coming to school and approaching teachers on their own. In past years, Hispanic parents would come to see Rosa (a kindergarten teacher) and ask her about the requirements of upper-grade classrooms because they did not feel comfortable talking to the Anglo teachers. In contrast, after participating in the dance group and establishing relationships with teachers, parents now say, "OK, I have been with the teacher, I know how she is and if I need anything, I can go talk to her."

In addition, Hispanic parents who have participated in the dance group come to school more often and generally display greater involvement in other school

FIGURE 3. Parents and Teachers Dance Group

activities with Anglo parents. The various dance groups enable Hispanics and Anglos to collaborate in different ways to carry through performances, which ultimately results in positive interactions in school between the two groups. Even their perception of Anglo parents tends to change. According to Rosa, Hispanic parents make comments like, "I thought that mom was a snob, but she is really nice."

Mexican Students

Rosa's main intended beneficiaries for the dance groups are students. In tandem, parents and teachers embrace Mexican traditions, and thereby help to reinforce cultural identity among Hispanic students. Seeing their Mexican culture and traditions celebrated at school provides students with an additional sense of appreciation for their culture beyond what parents alone communicate at home. In fact, Rosa relates that students often show a renewed interest in their own traditions and heritage once they see their teachers embrace them. She emphasizes how the dance group and presentations convey to students the importance of their culture: "It is so important that parents and teachers are learning [the dances]."

Hispanic students also feel great pride in seeing their parents dancing with their teachers. "Children feel proud to see the mothers and teachers dancing together. They say 'Oh, my mom danced with teacher Johnson!'"

For Hispanic students who live in an Anglo-dominated society, observing their culture valued and celebrated, in combination with watching their parents interact at the same level with teachers, boosts their cultural identity and self-esteem in powerful ways. Indeed, research demonstrates that providing Hispanic students with instruction that values their language and culture helps reduce feelings of alienation and serves to increase school persistence (Lindholm-Leary, 2004; McIntyre, Rosebery, & González, 2001; Wink, 2005). This is certainly not an insignificant issue given the lower than average high school graduation rates among Hispanic students in both the state of Oregon and the nation (Díaz-Rico & Weed, 2014; National Center for Education Statistics, 2015; Oregon Department of Education, 2012).

Seeds for Change

Parent and teacher relationships are often limited to the ones created by school. Traditionally, parents are invited to participate in school events, attend conferences, and volunteer at school. School events are often organized by school staff, and parents tend to be educated or informed on how to best support their children at home. According to Wink (2005), school-family relationships and activities are normally framed within a transmission model. In this model, teachers and schools own the knowledge; parents attend meetings and learn from teachers. Wink posited that a transformational approach to parent involvement would view families, students, and teachers all as owners of knowledge. Everyone would learn together. Clearly the relationships developed between parents, students, and teachers involved in the dance groups fall under what Wink would consider transformational interactions.

To some, the Cinco de Mayo Dance Assembly may be seen as a stereotypical way to celebrate Hispanic culture one day of the year. However, the dance groups have more profound effects: Most notable in this regard is the parent-teacher traditional Mexican dance group. It has proven to be a powerful tool to reduce cultural obstacles for Hispanic parents and create greater cultural understanding among Anglo teachers. The dance group produces a natural and collegial environment where parents and teachers can come together and get to know each other personally. With the possible exception of sports, it is not often that schools provide opportunities for diverse racial or ethnic groups, people with different socioeconomic statuses, and those of differing educational levels to come together, spend time doing a common activity, and be treated as genuine social equals. Rosa has found a powerful way to provide such an uncommon opportunity. One may think that Hispanic parents and Anglo teachers connected by a bilingual school frequently interact with each other. Unfortunately, these interactions are limited in nature and time. They are usually confined to a few events with set agendas that focus on academic and behavioral reports on how children are doing in school. Some of the interactions parents and teachers have are limited to the drop-off or pickup times that may only allow for pleasant greetings or quick check-ins. Even the interactions during teacher-parent conferences are tightly structured and focus on academics. Teachers meeting parents during conferences have little time to expand their conversations outside of what must be covered about student progress. Parents and teachers may share rudimentary information about the children, but one wonders when they have time to talk about themselves and get to know each other as individual people. How does each group become more culturally knowledgeable and competent about the other group unless they spend time together?

Rosa has pondered all these questions. Her initiative has affected the hearts and attitudes of those involved in the dance groups. She has planted critically important seeds for intergroup contact where the "acquaintance potential" (Pettigrew, 1998) can bring about change on how Hispanic and Anglo people relate to each other inside and outside of school. Although some of the interracial interactions may be temporary and merely limited to the time the dance groups are in session, some other interactions have long-lasting effects. During my time with Rosa, she was greatly moved when sharing how Hispanic and Anglo parents interact outside of school after participating in the dance group. She remembered an Anglo mother who came to her once and asked her how to say in Spanish, in preparation for a birthday party for her daughter, "You may stay if you would like. You are welcome to come in." The mother wanted to invite the Hispanic parents to stay at her home when they came to drop off their children. Neither set of parents spoke the other's language. They had to rely on their children as translators. Yet, as a direct result of the dance group, after two years of having contact with the Hispanic parents, the Anglo mother opened her home to them, overcoming language and racial barriers.

FIGURE 4. Parents and Teachers Dance Group II

Rosa's efforts to bring Hispanic and Anglo groups together will continue to produce cumulative, effective changes in the community. As we spoke together, she assessed the effects of the dance groups. Referring to interracial contact among parents she related,

> [American parents] have tried to coexist with them [Hispanic parents], and language would not be a barrier. . . . They have found ways to communicate . . . This tells you that something good is happening and that is creating a relationship regardless of language or place of origin. And they are valuing something and working for the children. After all, this is the community where they live and the people that live here. And this is where their children will be involved until they become adults. This is their community.

The dance groups are not controlled experiments designed to bring interracial groups together to reduce prejudice (Pettigrew & Tropp, 2006). They are real-world efforts and exemplify the impact educators can have in their local communities. Rosa's work is an inspiring story about the benefits that result when a teacher is committed to enhancing cultural understanding and respect. Rosa successfully brings Hispanic and Anglo groups closer together. She does so not in theory, not in concept, but in reality. Her wise use of dance as a teaching tool and culturally responsive practice has made the school community more welcoming to all parents.

REFERENCES

Collier, V. P., & Thomas, V. P. (2014). *Creating dual language schools for a transformed world: administrators speak.* Albuquerque, NM: Fuente Press.

Díaz-Rico, L. T., & Weed, K. Z. (2014). *The cross-cultural, language, and academic development handbook: A complete K–12 reference guide.* 5th ed. Boston: Allyn & Bacon.

Everett, J. A., & Onu, D. (2013). Intergroup contact theory: Past, present, and future. *Inquisitive Mind 2*(17). Retrieved from http://www.in-mind.org/article/intergroup-contact-theory-past-present-and-future.

Faber, N. (2015). Connecting with students and families through home visits. *American Educator 39*(3), 24–27.

Freeman, Y., Freeman, D., & Mercuri, S. (2005). *Dual language essentials for teachers and administrators.* Portsmouth, NH: Heinemann.

Gay, G. (2000). *Culturally responsive teaching: Theory, research, and practice.* New York: Teachers College Press.

Gay, G. (2002). Preparing for culturally responsive teaching. *Journal of Teacher Education, 53*(2), 106–116.

González, N., Moll, L., & Amanti, C. (2005). *Funds of knowledge: Theorizing practices in households, communities, and classrooms.* Mahwah, NJ: Lawrence Erlbaum Associates.

Gorski, P. C., & Pothini, S. G. (2014). *Case studies on diversity and social justice education.* New York: Routledge.

Harris, E. A. (2015, October 8). Dual-language programs are on the rise, even for native English speakers. *New York Times.* Retrieved from http://www.nytimes.com/2015/10/09/nyregion/dual-language-programs-are-on-the-rise-even-for-native-english-speakers.html?_r=1.

Ladson-Billings, G. (2009). *The dreamkeepers: Successful teachers of African American children.* 2nd ed. San Francisco: Jossey-Bass.

Lindholm-Leary, K. (2004). The rich promise of two-way immersion. *Educational Leadership 62*(4), 56–59.

Lindholm-Leary, K. (2012). Success and challenges in dual language education. *Theory into*

Practice 51(4), 256–62.

Macedo, D., Dendrinos, B., & Gounari, P. (2003). *The hegemony of English*. Boulder, CO: Paradigm.

McIntyre, E., Rosebery, A., & González, N. (2001). *Classroom diversity: Connecting curriculum to students' lives*. Portsmouth, NH: Heinemann.

Milner, H. R. (2013). *Start where you are, but don't stay there: Understanding diversity, opportunity gaps, and teaching in today's classrooms*. Cambridge, MA: Harvard Education Press.

National Center for Education Statistics (2015). *Public high school 4-year adjusted cohort graduation rate (ACGR), by race/ethnicity and selected demographics for the United States, the 50 states, and the District of Columbia: School year 2012–13*. Retrieved from http://nces.ed.gov/ccd/tables/ACGR_RE_and_characteristics_2012–13.asp.

Oregon Department of Education. (2012). *Statewide report card: An annual report to the legislature on Oregon public schools 2010–2011*. Retrieved from http://www.ode.state.or.us/data/annreportcard/rptcard2012.pdf.

Pettigrew, T. F. (1998). Intergroup contact theory. *Annual Review of Psychology 49*, 65–85.

Pettigrew, T. F., & Tropp, L. R. (2006). A meta-analytic test of intergroup contact theory. *Journal of Personality and Social Psychology 90*(5), 751–83.

Seidman, I. (2006). *Interviewing as qualitative research: A guide for researchers in education and social sciences*. 3rd ed. New York: Teachers College Press.

Valdés, G. (1996). *Con respeto: Bridging the distances between culturally diverse families and schools. An ethnographic portrait*. New York: Teachers College Press.

Valdés, G. (1997). Dual-language immersion programs: A cautionary note concerning the education of language-minority students. *Harvard Educational Review 67*(3), 391–429.

Wink, J. (2005). *Critical pedagogy: Notes from the real world*. 3rd ed. Boston: Pearson.

The Future of Education

Nouveau "Plus Ça Change . . ."

Brian J. Boggs

> Honest and earnest criticism from those whose interests are most nearly touched,—criticism of writers by readers, of government by those governed, of leaders by those led,—this is the soul of democracy and the safeguard of modern society.
>
> —W. E. B. DuBois

One of the many impactful papers that I have read by David Cohen is entitled "Teaching Practice: Plus Ça Change . . ." (1988). While it is a great paper on the history of teaching practices, the paper is not what I want to discuss, but rather the title. Specifically, the last part of the title, "Plus Ça Change," which is part of a larger French phrase, "Plus ça change, plus c'est la même chose." The phrase means the more things change, the more they stay the same, which is one of the best ways to describe education now and in the future—or as I am calling it, the "nouveau plus ca change . . ." This epigram led to an interesting thought exercise, which has become the basis for this chapter: trying to answer the question, What will education look like in fifteen years?

I think the answer to this question lies right before us. As we progress into the future, current trends seem to lend themselves to a crescendo of major conflicts in education as the pendulum of control and reform swings to and fro. Looking through a critical policy lens (Boggs, 2014), I examine several key areas, including local versus state control and choice versus traditional public schools, which may lead to an educational civil war of sorts as we approach a time when, as a society, we are more uncertain than ever of the purposes we want education to serve.

Critical Policy Lens: Theoretical Framework

To fully capture the political element and undertake a political analysis of the changes in education likely to occur in the future, it is necessary to examine them through a common lens. For this purpose, I propose to couple critical theory with an analytical view of policy and political actions, thereby creating a critical policy theoretical framework (Boggs, 2014; Boggs & Dunbar, 2015).

Critical theory "seeks to decloak the seemingly ... neutral, and color-blind ways ... of constructing and administering ... appraisals ... of law, administrative policy, electoral politics ... political discourse [and education]" (Denzin & Lincoln, 2000, p. 159). A major element of this concept "is that ideologies work to distort reality," and require looking at these "distorting ideologies and the associate structures, mechanisms, and processes that help to keep them in place" (Glesne, 2011, p. 9). This critical approach "enacts an ethnic epistemology, arguing that ways of knowing and being are shaped by the individual's standpoint, or position in the world" (Denzin & Lincoln, 2000, p. 159). In other words, it acknowledges that we cannot divorce ourselves from ourselves to remove bias and become completely objective. If beauty lies in the eyes of the beholder, reality lies in the minds of the experiencer and is different from person to person.

However, critical theory is more than just realizing that absolute objectivity does not exist; it is also about being able to "disrupt and challenge the status quo" (Kincheloe & McLaren, 2000, p. 279) and realizing that the West, despite its outwardly democratic ways, is not free of problems that marginalize, dehumanize, and de-democratize citizens (Strauss, 1964). The world is not as simple as blaming or crediting fate for the turn of events. Instead, critical theory "rejects economic determinism and focuses on the media, culture, language, power, desire, critical enlightenment, and critical emancipation" to examine why the world exists as it does (Denzin & Lincoln, 2000, p. 160). It makes us look at the "tacit rules that regulate what can and cannot be said, who can speak with the blessings of authority and who must listen, whose social constructions are valid and whose are erroneous and unimportant" (Kincheloe, J., & McLaren, P., quoted in Glesne, 2011, p. 10). Critical theorists see "research as a political act because it not only relies on values systems, but challenges value systems" (Glesne, 2011, p. 10).

Critical theory makes us ask how we look at experiences, especially those of race. As Dunbar et al. stated, in the context of the Western world, "Being 'white' is the unreflected-upon standard from which all other racial identities vary" (2001, p. 280).[1] In other words, White is normalized and is the backdrop to which all other races and cultures are juxtaposed. This normalized White has affected all levels of society, including the interpretation and formation of policy, especially for minority and urban populations. Is life simply being reproduced by the powerful, privileged dominant culture?

As Hesse-Biber argued, "A critical paradigm centers on examining issues of power, control, and ideology that are said to dominate one's understanding of the social world (e.g., how power dynamics within a social system serve to generate a given set of meanings [dominant ideologies] about social reality and lived experiences)" (2010, p. 455). Kincheloe and McLaren (2000) argued that "power is a basic constituent of human existence that works to shape the oppressive and productive nature of the human tradition" (p. 283). This focus on examining issues of power is the main reason for employing critical theory in this chapter. Focusing on issues of power and politics in the policymaking process is paramount.

In traditional rational models used to examine policy, several elements are left out, mainly because the political process (while rule bound) is not rational in regard to people's actions, and the recent federal and state push for educational accountability has changed the actors and policy instruments involved in the policy cycle. It is important to discuss who has been invited to the table, but it is also important to note whose voices are not being heard, as well as issues of power and political influence. The policy literature alludes to this (Cohen, 1982; Cusick & Borman, 2002; Henig, 2013; Kingdon, 1997; Shipps, 2011; Boggs & Dunbar, 2015), but several studies still rely on rational models or complex abstract models without engaging the role of the seemingly powerful and elite. This is why it is necessary to couple policy-level analyses with critical theory, especially issues of power.

So, what does critical theory especially add to the rational policy perspective? To answer this question, we must look at the concrete application of critical theory to traditional policy cycles. This can be done by applying critical theory through what Kincheloe and McLaren referred to as a "power matrix" (2000). Specially, they discussed this in terms of a hegemonic field, which "with its bounded sociopsychological horizons, garners consent to an inequitable power matrix—a set of social relations that are legitimated by their depiction as natural and inevitable" (Kincheloe & McLaren, 2000, p. 283). We can examine this matrix by using critical theory to look at political acts, tactical rules, and praxis that occur in the policy cycle and are not accounted for in a rational model (Glesne, 2011). Table 1 isolates how these three concepts from critical theory were applied in this chapter.

These specific critical theory elements help to untangle the issues of power from the policy cycle and illustrate who came to shape policy and how. By looking at political acts, tactical rules, and praxis, we come to see how dependent any policy is on actor-centered interactions and power.

Discussion and Analysis

When thinking about how education will change and develop over the next fifteen years, it is important to think about how the system is set up. If we go back to the previously proposed critical policy framework (Boggs, 2014; Boggs & Dunbar, 2015), this is an examination of not only the tactical rules, but also the players who carry out political acts. Many different players[2] and many different interest groups want some of the resources that are available to schools. However, resources such as money and school time (time for something to happen in education) are limited, and there are not enough for everyone to get what they want. This creates an economic and psychological environment of scarcity, shifting the supply demand curve and resulting in increased competition for these resources. Schools can be thought of as an arena where various groups are battling for a piece of the educational system (Cusick, 1992). This comprises the system, which is made up of bureaucracy (formal rules) and the various compromises among actors. What we see, then, is the outward manifestation of the system. All of these interest groups are part of the organization and, at some point, reach an informal (sometimes formal) compromise over available resources (Cusick, 1992).

While the system is under pressure to change rapidly and many reform initiatives attempt to do this (e.g., the Every Student Succeeds Act), little change will happen over the long haul. In part, this is because the same players that are competing for resources in the school environment also have stakes in the political governance system. So, if there is a system of bureaucracy for the school system, there is also one for government in general because education in America exists as

TABLE 1. Critical Theory Power Matrix: Application of Critical Theory to the Policy Cycle Perspective

CRITICAL THEORY ASPECT	DESCRIPTION
Political acts	"Focus on issues of power and domination and . . . advocate understanding" (Glesne, 2011, p. 10)
Tactical rules	"What can and cannot be said, who can speak with the blessing of authority and who must listen, whose social constructions are valid and whose are erroneous and unimportant" (J. Kincheloe and P. McLaren, 2000, quoted in Glesne, 2011, p. 10)
Praxis	"A relationship between thought and action, between theory and practice. Praxis refers to more than putting theory into action; it also involves continual reflection on and inquiry into experience and the meaning of concepts used in everyday interactions" (Glesne, 2011, p. 283) such as to "incorporate dialogue and critical reflection . . . to reveal unexamined assumptions" (10)

a subsection of government. The arena gets bigger and has more players, but these players are not going to let go of their piece of the pie. Even if various legislative bodies change the rules of the system (e.g., tenure laws), they too are part of the bureaucracy. This is why all three dimensions of the framework must be examined in addition to actual policies to understand the impact and meaning to education.

However, the various people involved in the bureaucracy can switch roles. So the teachers who may lose tenure also are the voters who get to decide if the legislators continue in their positions. The legislature also engages with these various special interest groups for support during elections. If we think of education as one bureaucracy, we can think of government as another, and it becomes concentric circles of a projected system within a system with various players who can switch roles. This system intermingles the components of the critical policy framework. All this leads me to believe there will be very little change in the bureaucracy due to the complexity of interactions, which may, in fact, inhibit the system from changing. However, this does not mean that the rules of engagement (the way we interact with the bureaucracy)—the tactical rules—will not change.

This battle between the formal system and the organization can be a problem; however, it is not a problem that education and people concerned with education are keen on fixing. Instead of looking at the resources spent on bureaucratic compromises, we focus on the failure of the classroom. It is a problem when we think that reforming education in the classroom will fix other problems, such as bureaucracy. This line of thinking will lead to flipping back and forth between classroom curriculum and interventions without success because we are not addressing the problem. We also do not wait for results, accurately make comparisons, examine our metrics used, or make decisions based on data—our decisions are often political in nature. As soon as we implement one reform, we expect results instantaneously, which will not happen.

There is always another special interest group with a reform idea waiting in the wings to compete for resources, and if the group gets its way, there will be another change in direction. All of this leads to relativism, the idea that education is subjective, subject to the perception of another group or individual, being swept along with each new educational reform wind that blows without any certainty. We may not think so, but, according to Chubb and Moe (1991), interest group ideas and reforms promulgated are directly related. Schools that have more school and district personnel overall and bureaucratic governance restrictions have lower classroom achievement. We will fail at achieving change because we are not addressing the bureaucracy, where everything must start and end. In trying to forward reform and change, we forget that the system functions exactly the way it was designed to—to maintain itself. As Cohen (1982) argues, the system inhibits good reform with the same zeal that it inhibits bad reform because these are relative and value-laden concepts. People disagree on the degree of change, the direction, or the goal, and this ultimately creates resistance. This causes change to be slow, if it occurs at all. As a result, the system functions as the people that are in it want it to.

Another question to consider is, "Will the goal of education change in the next fifteen years?" Well, this is a complicated question because I am not sure that there is a goal—or if there is, whether we collectively agree on it. Straus would argue that we have "become uncertain of its purpose" and, therefore, lack direction (1964, p. 3). If we need direction, what should it be? This is as true now as when it was when these words were initially published in 1964.

It is appropriate to remember Schumpeter (1947) and his belief that there is not any common (or collective) good.[3] This is why there are various competitors in the educational arena all pulling in different directions (Cusick, 1992) and why a critical policy framework will assist in analyzing these policy issues. However, I think there is a common concept that various groups are backing under the auspices that it will create a common good—equality[4] (Schumpeter, 1947; Strauss, 1964). We are still running on the goal of equality posed by President Johnson in the War on Poverty, and this will continue to be the mantra of education into the future. So how do we achieve equality?—because we have not done it so far.

One might argue there need to be rules to achieve equality and centralized control. This then would fold into formalism and procedures, which creates bureaucracy, which we already have. Straus (1964) would also argue that equality can only be achieved through a "universal state," which means major control and increased formalism with the goal of uniformity across the country. If the current forced centralization is not working and decentralization is not favorable to the goal, then the only way left for the government to proceed in the future is to push for strong increases in centralization and formalism. This will lead to an increase in bureaucracy as additional resources will be allocated to departments of education (both the federal departments and the state departments) to manage this larger educational superstructure.

I am not sure that it can be achieved, but I am sure such a high-modernist approach to centralization will be tried (Scott, 1999). This will also definitely lead to major power struggles and power solidification as America's educational system becomes more centralized and more federally controlled. This is where the educational civil war takes place. It will be local control versus state control, and here I use the term "state" to represent government oversight, both federal and by individual state. This does not mean that state governments are going to agree with the federal bureaucracy, and in point of fact, the representative legislative bodies often do not agree, but ultimately it is only the local educational agency performs the act of schooling. Despite these differences, individual state education agencies are becoming simply an arm of the federal government.

There are two main reasons for this. The first is that almost all state education departments are heavily subsidized by federal money. This does not give the federal government legal authority over the education in each state—that is still a right reserved for each state under the U.S. Constitution—however, without indirect money from federal programs,[5] many of these state education agencies would lose what limited capacity they have. Therefore, they carry out federal mandates to keep funding allocations. For example, federals funds given to operate the Michigan Department of Education over the last sixteen years have ranged between 70 percent and 94 percent of the department's total operating budget (Senate Fiscal Agency 2016). This makes it nearly impossible for the organization to function without federal funds. Second, a state working with the federal government just gives the latter an excuse to get heavily involved in local education. The state gains the ability to blame a higher level of bureaucracy—the federal government—for the requirements that the state education agencies are pushing on the local education agencies.

This process will not be quick, but rather slow and deliberate, and will go mostly unnoticed—and more than likely, the power and authority will coalesce at the individual state educational agency level. As time marches on, the citizenry will not realize that they have lost local control until it is too late. Part of this will be because, as Cohen (1982) points out, the federal and state governments will have given local districts more work to keep them busy and make them feel part of the process; all the while the state and federal governments will be absorbing local control. He continues, "Local school organizations have thus grown more complex and fragmented as they responded to various state and federal interventions, and to a more demanding political environment" (Cohen, 1982, p. 493). After local control is eroded, then the battle will begin to try and regain what was lost. The problem will be that the system will have become so formalized that it will be inaccessible to most people, and it will be hard to regain what was lost. It reminds me of the old adage that you do not know what you have until it is gone.

The federal government will continue to attempt to implement a nationwide system, which will consist of modernist approaches. The states are on board not just because the federal government is funding them, but also because they will receive much of the control that is stolen from the local systems. According to Cohen, "Characteristically, when the federal government assumes a new function, it takes only part of it, leaving substantial discretion and authority in the state hands" (1982, p. 478). The current theory is that everyone must be on the college prep course, and while everyone will be better for knowing the material, not everyone is going to go to college. The universal assembly line approach to educational reform that high modernism is prone to will not fit everyone, and in some cases will cause great disharmony. For example, the students of rural Vanderbilt, Michigan, and the students of urban Flint, Michigan, are part of a completely different economic and social systems, both distinct from each other as well as from the state. Their values and life realities are different. So, a highly centralized approach will negate all of the local cultural values. The problem with a universal system is that it is filled with rigidity that ignores *mētis*, Scott's term for knowledge gained through practical experience (Scott, 1999, p. 6). Without the presences of local knowledge and being able to adopt policy to the environment, major reform cannot succeed.

High modernism hopes to have the local adapt to the universal and pushes for conformity to the policy, further solidifying the centralization of education and educational policy.

There will also be a civil war over our approach to reform, especially with the issue of choice.[6] I think over the next fifteen years (having had choice then for about thirty-five years), we will realize that choice was not the solution. As Chubb and Moe (1991) point out, the problem is with the system and its governance. Choice did not fix the system, it created an alternate system. Competition is not a solution to the problem, but rather a quick fix to a messy structural problem that is too political to change. Choice might have worked in Michigan if the economy had not fallen apart. Now there are too few resources available and too many people competing for them (charter schools are a duplication of services being offered).[7]

Instead of public schools getting those resources, there are more schools to support. It is almost the inverse of the consolidation of schools in the 1960s that created the district-wide high school systems that we currently have in Michigan today. In the end, the money will be spread too thin, and public schools will have been hurt too badly to recover and will cause many of them to fail or, at the very least, to be irreparably harmed. There will also not be enough interest or resources for sustained charter schools because many of them do not provide all of the services that public schools provide, like busing, which is an important part of the bureaucracy because it provides for those who cannot or will not transport their children. So charter schools will not be able to reach their full potential or provide all of the services that public schools have, and the current research has mixed results on their successes compared to traditional public schools.

Formalism actually helps public schools in this regard because they have set and servable boundaries, whereas charters do not. So, in the end, instead of competing with each other, they will "eat away" at each other, causing the entire system to have diminished results. However, I think that choice between districts will continue without regulation because it is viewed as being a "free market" approach within the traditional system. When schools compete, the only people that lose are those who back the failing school and those who have to pay for the free market interplay between public entities that would not otherwise be in competition with each other. Choice and charter schools added more players to the arena, but did not change the rules of the arena (Cusick and Borman, 2002)—schooling still operates very much as it did fifty years ago, and many argue that charter schools have not become the bastion of innovation they were promised to be.

Concluding Thoughts

The present trends of centralization and choice are likely to continue; however, they will be subtle in their approach. Before we know it, the system will have become more centralized and formal, and, therefore, fraught with more bureaucracy. However, there is hope. Perhaps this change will be cyclical. Diane Ravitch (2011) points out in *Death and Life of the Great American School System* that New York went through something very similar.

In the nineteenth century, the education system was decentralized, which implies it was centralized before. Then, in 1890, there was yet another demand for centralization and this pendulum went back and forth until in the 1960s, when there was another call for decentralization (Ravitch, 2011). If history is any indicator of things to come, there will be an interesting shift in education yet again. All of this will no doubt play out in local school board meetings, state and federal legislative bodies, state and federal departments of education, classrooms, colleges of education, and many social interactions of various special interest groups. All of these groups are in the arena, and part of the compromise from their interactions with each other is the educational system that will result. However, Bourdieu (1996) would probably also tell us to be mindful of people's motivations in reforming education—especially since education has taken the new role for maintaining the old aristocracy, which is why it is essential to have a framework for analyzing these shifts. In the end, the new change will be like the old change, and the more things change, the more they stay the same.

NOTES

1. Dunbar's perspective derives from a U.S. analysis; however, it is applicable to non-Western cultures by substituting for "white" the dominant or ruling-class culture and ideology.
2. The use of "players" is intentional here instead of "stakeholders" mainly because not all political players have true direct stakes in the outcomes.
3. David Labaree (1997) builds on this concept in his examination of the paradoxical purposes and conflicts of education, including education as a public and private good, and the idea of education creating social mobility. Hochschild and Scovronick (2004) also add a perspective that education has three goods—collective, group, and individual.
4. Equality here is defined in relation to the formalism and rule creation discussed by

Schumpeter (1947) and Strauss (1964).

5. Indirect rates are funds retained for administrating a program or service. In this case, most state education agencies are allowed to charge an indirect rate to manage and run federal programs in their local states. These funds often go to fund those employees.
6. Choice here is denoted as a market-based educational reform effort (Hess, 2010).
7. Charter schools in this chapter's context are public school academies—not private schools. In the state of Michigan, school funding cannot be used for private schools by law.

REFERENCES

Boggs, B. (2014). The dark side of education: State level policymaking in the age of accountability. Ph.D. diss., Michigan State University.

Boggs, B. J., & Dunbar, C. (2015). An interpretive history of urban education and leadership in age of perceived racial invisibility. In M. Khalifa, N. Witherspoon Arnold, A. F. Osanloo, & C. M. Grant (eds.), *Handbook of Urban Educational Leadership*. Lanham, MD: Rowman and Littlefield.

Bourdieu, P. (1996). *The State Nobility: Elite Schools in the Field* of Power. Trans. Lauretta C. Clough. Stanford, CA: Stanford University Press.

Chubb, J. E., & Moe, T. M. (1991). *Politics, markets and America's schools*. Washington, DC: Brookings Institution.

Cohen, D. K. (1982). Policy and organization: The impact of state and federal educational policy on school governance. *Harvard Educational Review 52*(4), 474–99.

Cohen, D. K. (1983). Teaching practice: Plus ça change . . . In P. Jackson (ed.), *Contributions to educational change: Perspectives on research in practice issues*. Berkeley, CA: McCutchan.

Cusick, P. A. (1992). *The educational system: Its nature and logic*. McGraw-Hill College.

Cusick, P. A., & Borman, J. (2002). Reform of and by the system: A case study of a state's effort at curricular and systemic reform. *Teachers College Record 104*(4), 765–86.

Denzin, N. K., & Lincoln, Y. S. (2000). *Handbook of qualitative research*. Thousand Oaks, CA: Sage.

Dunbar, Christopher Jr., Dalia Rodriguez, & Laurence Parker. (2001). Race, subjectivity, and the interview process. In Jaber F. Gubrium and James A. Holstein (eds.) *Handbook of interview research: Context and method*. Thousand Oaks, California: Sage Publications.

Glesne, C. (2011). *Becoming qualitative researchers: An introduction*. 4th ed. Boston: Pearson Education.

Hess, F. M. (2010). Does school choice "work"? *National Affairs 5*(1), 35–53.

Hesse-Biber, S. (2010). Qualitative approaches to mixed methods practice. *Qualitative Inquiry 16*(6), 455–68.

Henig, J. R. (2013). *The end of exceptionalism in American education: The changing politics of school reform*. Cambridge, MA: Harvard Education Press.

Hochschild, J. L., & Scovronick, N. (2004). *The American dream and the public schools.* New York: Oxford University Press.

Kingdon, J. (1997). *Agendas, alternatives, and public policies*. 2nd ed. Hammersmith, UK: HarperCollins.

Kincheloe, J., and McLaren, P. (2000). Rethinking critical theory and qualitative research. In N. Denzin & Y. Lincoln (eds.), *Handbook of qualitative research*. 2nd ed. Thousand Oaks, CA: Sage.

Labaree, D. F. (1997). Public goods, private goods: The American struggle over educational goals. *American Educational Research Journal 34*(1), 39–81.

Ravitch, D. (2011). *The death and life of the great American school system: How testing and choice are undermining education.* New York: Basic Books.

Schumpeter, J. (1947). *Capitalism, socialism, & democracy.* New York: Harper & Brothers.

Scott, J. (1999). *Seeing like a state: How certain schemes to improve the human condition have failed.* New Haven: Yale University Press.

Senate Fiscal Agency (2016). State-Wide Budget. Retrieved from: http://www.senate.michigan.gov/sfa/StatewideBudget/StatewideBudget.html.

Shipps, D. (2011). The politics of educational reform: Idea champions and policy windows. In D. E. Mitchell, R. L. Crowson, and D. Shipps (eds.), *Shaping education policy: Power and process*. New York: Routledge.

Strauss, L. (1964). *The City and Man*. Chicago: University of Chicago Press.

Contributors

Shetay N. Ashford, Ph.D., is an Assistant Professor at Texas State University. She has thirteen years of industry experience as a global training program manager, technical trainer, and IT consultant for Fortune 50 and 500 companies in the high-tech, management consulting, and pharmaceuticals / life sciences industries, which informs her research agenda. Her research focuses on broadening the participation of women of color and African Americans in the STEM/Computing (e.g., computer science, management information systems, and information technology) workforce through the exploration of their experiences; development of school, industry, and community partnerships; and culturally responsive program design, development, and evaluation. As a certified evaluator, Shetay is committed to assist community-based organizations, school districts, governments, and social enterprises with developing effective, culturally responsive programs. Shetay is also the founder and CEO of the Technology 4 Life Institute, a culturally relevant, educational technology intervention that educates youth and adults about twenty-first-century technology, career clusters and critical employability and career readiness skills needed to thrive in today's global economy.

Brian J. Boggs, Ph.D., serves as Outreach and Development Specialist in the Office of K–12 Outreach in the College of Education at Michigan State University. His area of expertise is policy development and analysis in the areas of school reform, and he holds a dual-major Ph.D. in educational policy and administration from MSU. In addition, Brian holds a special certification in urban education from MSU and is a graduate of the Michigan Educational Policy Fellowship Program (2012–13). Brian has served as a high school English teacher and central office administrator. With a bachelor's degree in English and history and his master's degree in English language and literature, he has taught college rhetoric and critical writing courses at the University of Michigan, Flint, in addition to doctoral courses in educational policy and school administration. He has written extensively on the subject of organizational and instructional complexity. His research interests include organizational theory, policymaking, sociology of education, experimental design, school improvement, and the history and politics of U.S. education. Brian has studied urban school education in UK and has had held local public office for over thirteen years, where he focuses on issue of community engagement.

Tatiana Cevallos, Ed.D., is in the Master of Arts Teaching Department in the College of Education at George Fox University. Prior to working at George Fox, she was an elementary teacher and later a bilingual coordinator at Lincoln Elementary School in Woodburn, Oregon. She also taught Spanish at Portland Community College and at Chemeketa Community College. Her research interests are second-language acquisition, bilingual education, biliteracy development, multicultural education, program evaluation, and staff development. She has taught internationally at the Catholic University and at L'Alliance Française in Quito, Ecuador.

Deborah Gabriel, Ph.D., is a senior lecturer at Bournemouth University in the Faculty of Media and Communication. Her research interests are focused around online political communication, political discourse, raced and gendered constructions and representations in media and popular culture, equality, inclusion and liberation in educational practice, and the dynamics of race, ethnicity, and culture in higher education. Key areas of expertise are in race equality and in delivering programs of curriculum diversification and inclusive teaching practice through social justice pedagogy within her own institution and as a consultant for other universities. Deborah is vice chair of the Race Equality Charter Committee at Bournemouth University and the founder and director of Black British Academics, an independent network aimed at tackling racial inequality in UK higher education.

Barbara Guzzetti, Ph.D. is a Professor at Arizona State University in the New College of Interdisciplinary Arts and Sciences, Humanities Arts and Cultural Studies, Department of English. She is also an Affiliated Faculty member in the Mary Lou Fulton Teachers College, Educational Leadership and Innovation, and an Affiliated Faculty member in the School for Social Transformation, Women's and Gender Studies. Her research and teaching focus on new media, particularly participatory or do-it-yourself (DIY) media, and youth culture and gender issues in new media.

William A. Howe, Ed.D., has been an educator for more than thirty-five years in the United States and Canada and has made seven trips to China, one to South Africa, and one to Cuba to study multicultural education. In 2007 he made his first trip to Israel to study the Holocaust. He has given more than four hundred workshops, lectures, and keynotes on diversity, multicultural education, and organizational development. He is a regular presenter at state and national conferences and has appeared on both radio and television on diversity issues. Over the years, he has trained more than fifteen thousand educators. Dr. Howe has coauthored (with P. L. Lisi) a textbook on multicultural education, *Becoming a Multicultural Educator: Developing Awareness, Gaining Skills, and Taking Action* This book, now in its second printing, won the 2013 Philip C. Chinn Book Award from the National Association for Multicultural Education. He is also a coauthor of *Multicultural Education: From Ethnic Studies to NCLB to Common Core—a PK–12 Perspective in Multicultural Education. A Renewed Paradigm of Transformation and Call to Actio*n (2015).

Natalie S. King, Ph.D., is a graduate of the University of Florida and an Assistant Professor at Georgia State University in the Department of Middle and Secondary Education. As a former high school science teacher, Natalie is passionate about using a community partnership approach to provide high-quality STEM learning experiences to children of color, particularly those who live in high poverty areas. In 2012, Natalie founded a community-based informal STEM program, Fostering Opportunities and Cultivating Upstanding Students (FOCUS). FOCUS provides comprehensive curricula for K–12 students that embrace their cultural and lived experiences. Natalie merges her service and scholarship, and directly engages in communities to prepare students to become critically conscious and scientifically literate citizens in a global society. Natalie's research agenda focuses on K–12 science education with an emphasis on middle grades science experiences; advancing Black girls in STEM careers; community-based informal STEM programs; and the role of curriculum in fostering equity in science teaching and learning.

Mellinee Lesley, Ph.D. is a Professor in the Language, Diversity and Literacy Studies program and the Associate Dean of Graduate Education and Research for the College of Education at Texas Tech University. She has previously worked as a classroom teacher in Texas and served as the Director for Developmental Reading at Eastern New Mexico University. Dr. Lesley has earned several teaching awards at the secondary and university level and is a fellow of the National Writing Project and past interim director for the New Mexico High Plains Writing Project.

Yan Liu, Ph.D., is an Assistant Professor in the Department of Educational Leadership, Policy and Instructional Technology at Central Connecticut State University. Her research interest is primarily school leadership and its impact on teaching and learning. She is particularly interested in the research of distributed leadership that involves broad stakeholders with diverse needs and expertise in school decision-making in order to improve school effectiveness and increase school social justice.

Tiffany M. Nyachae is a Ph.D. candidate at the University at Buffalo, the State University of New York in the Reading Education program with a Curriculum, Instruction, and the Science of Learning extension. She has experience as an instructional coach through the Buffalo Partnerships Project: A Common Core Collaborative at the university. Tiffany is currently serving as Education Chair and board member for the Buffalo Urban League Young Professionals, Co-chair for the Literacy Research Association's Doctoral Student Innovative Community Group, Graduate Student Junior Representative for the American Educational Research Association's Division B, and Assistant Co-chair for the American Educational Studies Association's Graduate Student Group. Tiffany has worked for six years as a middle school social studies teacher and one year as a language arts teacher in an urban school operating under the Teachers College Reading and Writing Project. During her tenure at this school, she helped to create Sisters of Promise, a character development program for girls in fifth through eighth grades through Buffalo Promise Neighborhood and served as codirector of the after-school program for one year while organizing other projects, events, and activities. Her current research interests include how supporting the ideological becoming and enactment of in-service urban teachers committed to social justice influences the perceptions of students of color on the education they are receiving. Tiffany is published in a special issue of the *Gender and Education* journal on the contributions of Black women scholars to curriculum studies. Tiffany received her M.S. in education through the literacy specialist program at Buffalo State College and her B.A. in early childhood, elementary, and middle school education with a social studies concentration from Canisius College.

Christie M. Poitra holds a doctorate in educational policy from Michigan State University. She received her master of arts degree in American Indian studies from UCLA, and her bachelor of arts degree in legal studies from UC Berkeley. Prior to graduate study, Dr. Poitra was an elementary school teacher on the Navajo Nation in New Mexico. Dr. Poitra's research interests include the political processes of American Indian tribal governments, American Indian P–20 educational issues, and American Indian educational policy.

Susan Printy, Ph.D., is an Associate Professor of K–12 educational administration at Michigan State University. Her research interests center on the idea that schools improve when they are learning organizations. Her research has had a particular focus on the leadership shared by principals and teachers and the use of data in promoting school improvement. Her current work examines the professional impact of social learning that occurs within teachers' professional learning communities. The recent emphasis on teacher evaluation motivates her explorations of the ways in which processes used for evaluation, such as observation in classrooms, can be also used to build organizational learning capacity. With the advent of the Doctor of Educational Leadership program, Dr. Printy is increasingly invested in understanding the value of coherent educational systems and the role district leaders play.

Theodore S. Ransaw, Ph.D., is a Research Specialist for Residential Arts and Humanities and Affiliate Faculty of African American and African Studies at Michigan State University. He has been an instructor in both K–12 and higher education. His research areas include masculinity, fatherhood, gendered literacy, and educational outcomes. He is the author of *The Art of Being Cool: The Pursuit of Black Masculinity* and has publications in the *Journal of Black Masculinity* and *Spectrum: The Journal of Black Males*.

Felix Peter Umeana is a Ph.D. candidate at Michigan State University in the College of Education, Department of K–12 Educational Administration. His research interests are in comparative and international education; urban education; educational policy; gender and environmental studies; globalization; African studies; history; civilizations, philosophy, and ethical theories; as well as French language.

Jessica Alyce Wilson is a Ph.D. candidate in the Department of Teaching and Learning: Mathematics Education at the University of South Florida (USF). She has a bachelor of science and a master of science in mathematics from Tennessee State University. Jessica began her journey as a mathematics educator, teaching developmental mathematics courses and college-level mathematics courses at Tennessee State University, Nashville State Community College, and ITT Technical Institute of Nashville and most recently at USF. Jessica has also taught teacher preparation courses in mathematics at USF. Additionally, she has spent time substitute teaching for K–12 schools and has taught mathematics in multiple summer academy programs serving middle and high school students. In Jessica's most recent position, she served as a program director and developer for a robotics outreach program at USF developed for underrepresented middle school and undergraduate students. Jessica developed a culturally relevant curriculum for the program that builds upon students' technical and life skills. Jessica currently serves on the American Society for Engineering Education Diversity Committee as the Student Division Delegate-Elect. Jessica's research interest includes factors contributing to high mathematics achievement, racially and gender-diverse student learners in mathematics, social justice in mathematics education, Black women in undergraduate-level mathematics and engineering programs, and mentorship in STEM education.

Index